Margaret C. Moran
W. Frances Holder

# AP* SUCCESS

# English Language & Composition

**PETERSON'S**

**THOMSON LEARNING** ™

Australia • Canada • Mexico • Singapore • Spain • United Kingdom • United States

**About Peterson's**

Founded in 1966, Peterson's, a division of Thomson Learning, is the nation's largest and most respected provider of lifelong learning resources, both in print and online. The Education Supersite$^{SM}$ at www.petersons.com—the Internet's most heavily traveled education resource—has searchable databases and interactive tools for contacting U.S.-accredited institutions and programs. In addition, Peterson's delivers unmatched financial aid resources and test-preparation tools. Peterson's serves more than 100 million education consumers annually.

Peterson's is a division of Thomson Learning, one of the world's largest providers of lifelong learning. Thomson Learning serves the needs of individuals, learning institutions, and corporations with products and services for both traditional and distributed learning. Headquartered in Stamford, Connecticut, with offices worldwide, Thomson Learning is a division of The Thomson Corporation (www.thomson.com), one of the world's leading e-information and solutions companies in the business, professional, and education marketplaces. For more information, visit www.thomsonlearning.com.

Special thanks to Heidi Sheehan

For more information, contact Peterson's, 2000 Lenox Drive, Lawrenceville, NJ 08648; 800-338-3282; or find us on the World Wide Web at: www.petersons.com/about

ISBN 0-7689-0727-6

Printed in the United States of America

10  9  8  7  6  5  4  3  2  1     03  02  01

# ACKNOWLEDGMENTS

Text from the Preface of *Modern American Poetry*, 5th Revised Edition by Louis Untermeyer. Copyright 1919, 1921, 1925, 1930, 1936 by Harcourt, Brace & Co, Inc. Reprinted by permission of Professional Publishing Service.

Text excerpt from "Politics and the English Language" from *Shooting an Elephant and Other Essays* by George Orwell. Copyright 1946 by Sonia Brownell Orwell and renewed 1974 by Sonia Orwell. Reprinted by permission of harcourt, Inc. and A. M. Heath & Company, Ltd.

"Addressing the Graduating Class" from *Essays, Speeches & Public Letters by William Faulkner* ed. by James B. Meriweather. Copyright 1951 by William Faulkner. Reprinted by permission of Random House, Inc. and Chatto & Windus, Ltd.

# CONTENTS

Quick Reference Guide . . . . . . . . . . . . . . . . . . . . . . . . . . . . . .   vii

Table of Literary Works. . . . . . . . . . . . . . . . . . . . . . . . . . . . . .   ix

**Red Alert**
   10 Strategies for Acing the Test . . . . . . . . . . . . . . . . . . .   1
   10 Facts About the AP English Language and
      Composition Test . . . . . . . . . . . . . . . . . . . . . . . . . . . . .   3
   Scoring High on the AP English Language and
      Composition Test . . . . . . . . . . . . . . . . . . . . . . . . . . . . .   6
   Practice Plan for Studying for the AP English
      Language and Composition Test. . . . . . . . . . . . . . .   10
   The Panic Plan . . . . . . . . . . . . . . . . . . . . . . . . . . . . . . . . .   15
   Suggested Reading . . . . . . . . . . . . . . . . . . . . . . . . . . . . . .   17
   Why Take the Diagnostic Test?. . . . . . . . . . . . . . . . . . .   21

**Diagnostic Test** . . . . . . . . . . . . . . . . . . . . . . . . . . . . . . . .   **23**
           Section I. . . . . . . . . . . . . . . . . . . . . . . . . . . . . . . . .   24
           Section II . . . . . . . . . . . . . . . . . . . . . . . . . . . . . . . .   38
           Answers and Explanations. . . . . . . . . . . . . . . . . . .   43

**Chapter 1**   **About Answering Multiple-Choice
               Questions. . . . . . . . . . . . . . . . . . . . . . . . . .   63**
           Practice Set 1 . . . . . . . . . . . . . . . . . . . . . . . . . . . . . .   84
           Practice Set 2 . . . . . . . . . . . . . . . . . . . . . . . . . . . . . .   90
           Practice Set 3 . . . . . . . . . . . . . . . . . . . . . . . . . . . . . .   96
           Practice Set 4 . . . . . . . . . . . . . . . . . . . . . . . . . . . . . .   101

**Chapter 2**   **About Writing the Essays . . . . . . . . . . . .   107**
           Practice Set 1 . . . . . . . . . . . . . . . . . . . . . . . . . . . . . .   132
           Practice Set 2 . . . . . . . . . . . . . . . . . . . . . . . . . . . . . .   135
           Practice Set 3 . . . . . . . . . . . . . . . . . . . . . . . . . . . . . .   138

**Chapter 3   A Quick Review: Parts of Speech, Grammar, Mechanics, and Usage Tips............. 143**

Grammar for the Multiple-Choice Questions ........ 143
Some Practical Advice on Writing Your Essays ...... 147
Sentence Structure............................ 147
Mechanics and Punctuation .................... 152
Diction..................................... 157
98 Common Usage Problems .................... 163

**Chapter 4   A Quick Review of Literary and Rhetorical Terms...................... 173**

**Practice Test 1................................. 181**

Section I ................................... 182
Section II................................... 197
Explanation of Answers........................ 202

**Practice Test 2................................. 221**

Section I ................................... 222
Section II................................... 236
Explanation of Answers........................ 241

**Practice Test 3................................. 259**

Section I ................................... 260
Section II................................... 273
Explanation of Answers........................ 277

**Sample Answer Sheets......................... 293**

# QUICK REFERENCE GUIDE

|  | PAGE |
|---|---|
| Analyzing Literature (checklist) . . . . . . . . . . . . . . . . . . . . . . . | 112 |
| A Quick Review of Literary and Rhetorical Terms . . . . . . . . . | 173 |
| A Quick Review: Parts of Speech, Grammar, Mechanics, and Usage Tips (a helpful grammar guide for writing your essays) . . . . . . . . . . . . . . . . . . . . . . . . . . . . . . . . . . . . . . . . . | 143 |
| Basic Information About the Multiple-Choice Section . . . . . . . | 64 |
| Basic Information About the Essay Section . . . . . . . . . . . . . . . | 108 |
| Educated Guessing for Multiple-Choice Questions . . . . . . . . . | 73 |
| Effective Strategies for Reading Selections . . . . . . . . . . . . . . . | 66 |
| The Essay: A Quick Review . . . . . . . . . . . . . . . . . . . . . . . . . . . | 114 |
| Essay Types . . . . . . . . . . . . . . . . . . . . . . . . . . . . . . . . . . . . . . . | 120 |
| Guidelines for Exposition . . . . . . . . . . . . . . . . . . . . . . . . . . . . | 120 |
| Guidelines for Persuasion . . . . . . . . . . . . . . . . . . . . . . . . . . . . | 122 |
| Logic: Questions for Valid Reasoning . . . . . . . . . . . . . . . . . . . | 125 |
| Multiple-Choice Question Types . . . . . . . . . . . . . . . . . . . . . . . | 67 |
| Starting an Idea Bank for Your Essays . . . . . . . . . . . . . . . . . . | 162 |
| Strategies for Acing the Essays . . . . . . . . . . . . . . . . . . . . . . . . | 109 |
| Strategies for Acing the Multiple-Choice Section . . . . . . . . . . | 69 |

## 6 IMPORTANT STRATEGIES

1. If it's a main idea or theme question, look for the answer that is the most general and can be supported by evidence in the selection.

2. All elements in an answer must be correct for the answer to be correct.

3. Don't rely on your memory go back to the passage.

4. For vocabulary questions, substitute the definitions in the sentence. Always read a line or two above and a line or two below the reference to check the context.

5. With *not/except* questions, ask yourself if an answer choice is true about the selection. If it is, cross it out and keep checking answers.

6. If you aren't sure about an answer but know something about the question, eliminate what you know is wrong and make an educated guess.

# TABLE OF LITERARY WORKS

The following list represents all the works discussed in this book.

**DIAGNOSITC TEST**

Mary Wollstonecraft, from *A Vindication of the Rights of Women* . . . . . . . . . . . . . . . . . . . . . . . . . . . . . . . . . . . . . . . .  24

Walt Whitman, from "Preface" to the 1855 Edition of *Leaves of Grass* . . . . . . . . . . . . . . . . . . . . . . . . . . . . . . . . . .  28

George Orwell, from *Politics and the English Language* . . .  31

Mark Twain, from *Roughing It* . . . . . . . . . . . . . . . . . . . . . .  35

William Faulkner, "Address to the Graduating Class, University High School, Oxford, Mississippi" . . . . . . . . .  38

Andrew Carnegie, from *Wealth* . . . . . . . . . . . . . . . . . . . . .  40

Abigail Adams, "Letter to Her Daughter from the New White House" . . . . . . . . . . . . . . . . . . . . . . . . . . . . . . . . . . .  41

**CHAPTER 1**

Hector St. John de Crèvecoeur, from the third essay of *Letters from an American Farmer* . . . . . . . . . . . . . . . . .  74

From the Iroquois Confederacy's "The Law of the Great Peace" . . . . . . . . . . . . . . . . . . . . . . . . . . . . . . . . . . . . . . . . . .  84

Elizabeth Cady Stanton, from the "Declaration of Rights and Sentiments" . . . . . . . . . . . . . . . . . . . . . . . . . . . . . . . . . .  90

*New York Herald*, "Assassination of President Lincoln" . . . . .  96

L.H. Heller, from "Extinct Animals" in *Americana*, 1908 . . . .  101

**CHAPTER 2**

Ralph Waldo Emerson, from *Self-Reliance*, . . . . . . . . . . . . . .  127

James Boswell, from "Feelings" in *The Life of Samuel Johnson* . . . . . . . . . . . . . . . . . . . . . . . . . . . . . . . . . . . . . . . .  132

Mark Twain, "Advice to Little Girls" . . . . . . . . . . . . . . . . . . .  135

## PRACTICE TEST 1

Louis Untermeyer, from the "Preface" of *Modern American Poetry, a Critical Anthology* . . . . . . . . . . . . . . . . . . . . . .   182

Benjamin Franklin, from "Dialogue Between Gout and Mr. Franklin" . . . . . . . . . . . . . . . . . . . . . . . . . . . . . .   186

Adam Smith, from *The Wealth of Nations* . . . . . . . . . . . . .   191

Emil Brugsch Bey, from "Finding the Pharaoh," in *Century Magazine* . . . . . . . . . . . . . . . . . . . . . . . . . . . . . .   194

Mary Shelley, from *Introduction to Frankenstein* . . . . . . . .   197

Ralph Waldo Emerson, from "The American Scholar" . . . . . .   199

Samuel Johnson, from *Preface to Shakespeare* . . . . . . . . . . .   200

## PRACTICE TEST 2

Elizabeth I, "Speech to Her Last Parliament" . . . . . . . . . . . . .   222

Richard Steele, "Dueling" . . . . . . . . . . . . . . . . . . . . . . . . .   225

Alexander Johnston, from "The American Game of Football," in *Century Magazine* . . . . . . . . . . . . . . . . . .   229

Frederick Douglass, from *My Bondage and My Freedom* . . .   233

Henry David Thoreau, from *Civil Disobedience* . . . . . . . . . .   236

Elizabeth Keckley, "The Death of President Lincoln" . . . . . . .   238

Woodrow Wilson, "Appeal for Neutrality" . . . . . . . . . . . . . .   240

## PRACTICE TEST 3

Thomas Paine, from *The Crisis*. . . . . . . . . . . . . . . . . . . . . .   260

Mary Chesnut, from *Mary Chesnut's War* . . . . . . . . . . . . . .   264

Chief Joseph, "I will fight no more forever" . . . . . . . . . . . . .   267

Samuel Johnson, "Letter to Lord Chesterfield". . . . . . . . . . . .   269

Abraham Lincoln, "First Inaugural Address" . . . . . . . . . . . . .   273

Frances A. Kimble, from *Record of a Girlhood*. . . . . . . . . . . .   274

## 10 STRATEGIES FOR ACING THE TEST

### PREPARING FOR THE TEST

1. Read the *AP Course Description for English* available from the College Board, and *10 Facts About the AP English Language and Composition Test*, on pages 1 and 2 in this book.

2. Choose your Practice Plan from page 10 in this book.

3. Choose a place and time to study every day, and stick to your routine and your plan.

4. Even though they are time-consuming, complete the *Diagnostic* and *Practice Tests* in this book. They will give you just what they promise: practice—practice in reading and following the directions, practice in pacing yourself, practice in understanding and answering multiple-choice questions, and practice in writing timed essays.

5. Complete all your assignments for your regular AP English class. Ask questions in class, talk about what you read and write, and enjoy what you are doing. The test is supposed to measure your development as an educated and thinking reader.

### THE NIGHT BEFORE THE TEST

6. Assemble what you will need for the test: your admission materials, four number 2 pencils, two pens, a watch (without an alarm), and a healthy snack for the break. Put these items in a place where you will not forget them in the morning.

7. Don't cram. Relax. Go to a movie, visit a friend—but not one who is taking the test with you. Get a good night's sleep.

# THE DAY OF THE TEST

8. Wear comfortable clothes. If you have a lucky color or a lucky piece of clothing or jewelry, wear it—as long as you won't distract anyone else. Take along a lucky charm if you have one.

9. If you do not usually eat a big breakfast, this is not the morning to change your routine, but it is probably a good idea to eat something nutritious if you can.

10. If you feel yourself getting anxious, concentrate on taking a couple of deep breaths. Remember, you don't have to answer all the questions, you can use EDUCATED GUESSES, and you don't have to write three "9" essays.

# 10 FACTS ABOUT THE AP ENGLISH LANGUAGE AND COMPOSITION TEST

1. **THE ADVANCED PLACEMENT PROGRAM OFFERS HIGH SCHOOL STUDENTS AN OPPORTUNITY TO RECEIVE COLLEGE CREDIT FOR COURSES THEY TAKE IN HIGH SCHOOL.**

   The AP program is a collaborative effort of secondary schools, colleges and universities, and the College Board through which students who are enrolled in AP or honors courses in any one or more of nineteen subject areas may receive credit or advanced placement for college-level work completed in high school. While the College Board makes recommendations about course content, it does not prescribe content. As a result, the annual testing program ensures a degree of comparability among courses in the same subject.

2. **MORE THAN 2,900 COLLEGES AND UNIVERSITIES PARTICIPATE IN THE AP PROGRAM.**

   Neither the College Board nor your high school awards AP credit. You need to find out from the colleges to which you are planning to apply whether they grant credit and/or use AP scores for placement. It is IMPORTANT that you obtain each school's policy IN WRITING so that when you actually choose one college and register, you will have proof of what you were told.

3. **THE AP ENGLISH LANGUAGE AND COMPOSITION TEST MEASURES YOUR ABILITY TO ANALYZE THE RHETORIC OF PROSE PASSAGES AND TO WRITE ESSAYS IN VARIOUS RHETORICAL MODES.**

   According to the College Board's course description, an AP course in language and composition will enable students to develop and refine their writing styles by writing extensively. The course will also provide extensive opportunities for students to read a variety of rhetorical modes to analyze how writers' choices affect style. The AP test then assesses how well students have learned to analyze the composition of prose passages and how well they have developed their own writing styles from the models they have read.

## 4. THE AP ENGLISH LANGUAGE AND COMPOSITION TEST HAS TWO PARTS: MULTIPLE CHOICE AND ESSAYS.

**Study Strategy**

*See Chapter 1 for multiple-choice questions.*

*See Chapters 4 to 7 for strategies for writing essays.*

Section I: Multiple Choice has 50–60 questions divided among five to six prose passages. This section counts for 45 percent of your total score, and you have 60 minutes to complete it.

In Section II, you have three essays to write. The questions usually consist of one that requires a rhetorical analysis of a passage, one that calls for a stylistic and rhetorical analysis, and one that requires an argument in response to a passage or to an assigned topic. The essays count for 55 percent of your total score, approximately 18 percentage points for each essay. You have 40 minutes to write each essay (120 minutes total).

## 5. THE PROSE PASSAGES ARE TAKEN FROM A VARIETY OF SUBJECT AREAS.

**Study Strategy**

*See "Suggested Reading," p. 16.*

According to the information from the College Board, you might find selections on the AP exam written by autobiographers, biographers, diarists, historians, critics, essayists, journalists, political writers, and science and nature writers. The styles will vary as the subject matter varies. There is no way you can read every possible piece of literature that might appear, but you can hone your skills of rhetorical and stylistic analysis and work on refining your own writing style.

## 6. THERE IS NO REQUIRED LENGTH FOR YOUR ESSAYS.

It is the quality, not the quantity, that counts. Realistically, a one-paragraph essay is not going to garner you a high mark because you cannot develop a well-reasoned analysis or argument and present it effectively in one paragraph. An essay of five paragraphs is a good goal. By following this model, you can set out your ideas with an interesting introduction, develop a reasoned body, and provide a solid ending.

## 7. YOU WILL GET A COMPOSITE SCORE FOR YOUR TEST.

**Test-Taking Strategy**

*See "Scoring High on the AP English Language and Composition Test," p. 6.*

The College Board reports a single score from 1 to 5 for the two-part test, with 5 being the highest. By understanding how you can balance the number of correct answers in the multiple-choice section and the essay score you need in order to receive at least a "3," you can relieve some of your anxiety about passing the test.

## 8. EDUCATED GUESSING CAN HELP.

No points are deducted for questions that go unanswered on the multiple-choice section, and don't expect to have time to answer them all. A quarter of a point is deducted for each wrong answer. The College Board suggests guessing IF you know something about a question and can eliminate a couple of the answer choices. Call it "educated guessing."

## 9. THE TEST IS GIVEN IN MID-MAY.

Most likely, the test will be given at your school, so you do not have to worry about finding a strange school building in a strange city. You will be in familiar surroundings—that should reduce your anxiety a bit. If the test is given in another school, be sure to take identification with you.

Plan your route to the other school and acutally take the trip once before test day—drive or take public transportation, whichever way you will go on test day—to be sure you won't get lost the morning of the test. Add extra time because you may be going during the morning rush hour.

## 10. STUDYING FOR THE TEST CAN MAKE A DIFFERENCE.

**Study Strategy**

*Stop first at p. 10 and read "Practice Plan for Studying for the AP English Language Test."*

The first step is to familiarize yourself with the format and directions for both parts of the test. Then you will not waste time on the day of the test trying to understand what you are supposed to do. The second step is to put those analytical skills you have been learning to work, dissecting and understanding the kinds of questions you will be asked; the third step is to practice "writing-on-demand" for the essays.

# SCORING HIGH ON THE AP ENGLISH LANGUAGE AND COMPOSITION TEST

Around early July, you and the colleges you designate will receive a score from 1 to 5, with 5 being the highest, for your AP English Language and Composition Test, and your high school will receive its report a little later. The multiple-choice section is graded by machine, and your essays are graded during a marathon reading session by high school and college teachers.

A different reader grades each of your essays. None of the readers know who you are (that's why you fill in identification information on your pink Section II booklet and then seal it) or how the others scored your other essays. Each reader is familiar with the work discussed in the essay question she or he is reading. The grading is done on a holistic system; that is, the overall essay is scored, not just the development of your ideas, your spelling, or your punctuation. For each essay, the College Board works out grading criteria for the readers to use, much as your teacher uses a rubric to evaluate your writing.

## WHAT THE COMPOSITE SCORE MEANS

The College Board refers to the composite score as "weighted" because a factor of about 1.3 (the exact number varies from year to year) for the multiple-choice questions and a factor of 3.0556 for the essay questions are used to determine a raw score for each section. That is, the actual score you get on the multiple-choice questions—say 35—is multiplied by about 1.3 (1.2273 for 55 questions in a recent year). The actual score that you get on the essay test—say 21—is multiplied by 3.0556. Those two numbers, your raw scores, are then added and the resulting score—somewhere between 0 and 150 (107, based on the above example)—is then equated to a number from 5 to 1.

A score of 107 would have been good enough to get you a "4" for the test in a recent year. But 5 more points—112—would have gotten you a "5." The range in a recent year was 112 to 150 for a "5."

*Peterson's AP Success:*
*English Language & Composition*

# WHAT DOES ALL THIS MEAN TO YOU?

**Study Strategy**

*See Chapter 1 for help in raising your score.*

You can leave blank or answer incorrectly some combination of 20 questions on a 55-question multiple-choice section, get a 7 for each of your three essays, and still get a "5." It is not as easy as it may seem, or the majority of students would not fall into the "3" range, although a 3 may be good enough to get you college credit or advanced placement. A score of 4 certainly will.

Take a look at the charts below. It takes work, but raising your score may not be that impossible. Sometimes, the difference between a 3 and a 4 or a 4 and a 5 is only a couple of points.

| POSSIBLE SCORE DISTRIBUTION FOR A 55-QUESTION MULTIPLE-CHOICE SECTION | | | | | |
|---|---|---|---|---|---|
| SCORE = 5 | | SCORE = 4 | | SCORE = 3 | |
| MC | Essays (3) | MC | Essays (3) | MC | Essays (3) |
| 25 | 25 (8.33 ) | 25 | 21 (7) | 25 | 14 (4.66) |
| 30 | 23 (7.66) | 30 | 19 (6.33) | 30 | 12 (4) |
| 35 | 21 (7) | 35 | 17 (5.66) | 35 | 10 (3.33) |
| 40 | 19 (6.33) | 40 | 15 (5) | 40 | 8 (2.66) |
| 45 | 17 (5.66) | 45 | 13 (4.33) | 45 | 6 (2) |

The highest score you can receive on an essay is a 9, so the highest total essay score is 27. It is possible to get a variety of scores on your essays—7, 5, and 5, for example. The chances are that you will not get a wide range of individual essay scores like 6, 2, and 5. Even if you did, you could still get at least a 3 and possibly a 4, depending on how many correct answers you have in the multiple-choice section weighed against how many wrong answers you have.

| AP Grade | AP Qualifier | Composite Scores | Probability of Receiving Credit |
|---|---|---|---|
| 5 | Extremely Well Qualified | 112–150 | Yes |
| 4 | Well Qualified | 95–111 | Yes |
| 3 | Qualified | 76–94 | Probably |
| 2 | Possibly Qualified | 48–75 | Rarely |
| 1 | No Recommendation | 0–47 | No |

According to the College Board, about 62 percent of the 60,000 students who took the test in a recent year received a 3 or better. The cut-off point for passing grades may change from year to year, but it remains around this range. This chart shows the actual conversion scale in a recent year. What it means is that you neither have to answer all the questions, nor do you have to answer them all correctly, nor write three "9" essays to receive your AP credit.

## SOME THINGS TO REMEMBER

**Red Alert!**

*These facts are straight from the College Board.*

1. The 50 to 60 multiple-choice section is worth 45 percent of your total score.

2. Students who perform acceptably on the essays can receive a 3 if they answer correctly 50 to 60 percent of the multiple-choice questions.

3. There is no deduction for unanswered questions.

4. There is a quarter-point deduction for wrong answers.

5. The three essays together account for 55 percent of your total score, with each essay being counted equally, that is, each essay accounts for 18.33 percentage points.

# WHY ARE WE TELLING YOU THESE FACTS?

Because you can use them to your advantage.

1. It is important to spend time practicing the kinds of questions that you will find in the multiple-choice section, because 45 percent of your score comes from that section. You do not have to put all your emphasis on the essay questions.

**Test-Taking Strategy**

*The* Diagnostic *and* Practice Tests *will help you pace yourself in the exam.*

2–3. You can leave some questions unanswered and still do well. Even though you will be practicing pacing yourself as you use this book, you may not be able to complete all 50-odd questions on the day of the test. If you come across a really incomprehensible passage, you can skip it and come back to it later and still feel that you are not doomed to a low score.

**Test-Taking Strategy**

*See Chapter 1 for strategies on education guessing.*

4. There is a guessing penalty. If you do not know anything about the question or the choices, do not take a chance. However, IF you know something about the question and can eliminate one or more of the answer choices, then it is probably worth your while to choose one of the other answers. You would need to answer four questions incorrectly to lose one point, but answering even one question correctly would gain you another point. Rather than calling it guessing, call it EDUCATED GUESSING. Even the College Board suggests this strategy.

5. Although all three essays count for the same number of points, you need to pace yourself so that you spend approximately the same amount of time planning and writing each essay. You are not expected to write perfect essays. As the College Board teacher's guide to the AP English Language and Composition course states: ". . . faculty consultants are reminded that the student essays must be recognized as first drafts written under the constraints of time . . . and intellectual and emotional pressure, and that the essays should be rewarded for what they do well."

# PRACTICE PLAN FOR STUDYING FOR THE AP ENGLISH LANGUAGE AND COMPOSITION TEST

The following plan is worked out for nine weeks. The best study plan is one that continues through a full semester. Then you have time to think about ideas and to talk with your teacher and other students about what you are learning, and you will not feel rushed. Staying relaxed about the test is important. A full-semester study plan also means that you can apply what you are learning here to class work—your essay writing—and apply your class work—everything that you are studying and reading—to test preparation. The plan is worked out so that you should spend about three hours on each lesson.

## Week 1

**First:** Take the *Diagnostic Test*, pp. 23–42, and complete the self-scoring process. List the areas that you had difficulty with such as timing, question types, and writing on demand, etc.

**Then:** Reread pp. 1–5 about the basic facts of the test and its scoring.

## Week 2

**Lesson 1**
- Read *Top 10 Strategies for Acing the Test*, pp. 1–2.
- Reread *Scoring High on the AP Language and Composition Test* on pp. 6–9 to remind yourself that at least a "3" is achievable.
- Read Chapter 1, *About the Multiple-Choice Questions*, pp. 63–106.
- Practice by completing *Practice Set 1*.
- Correct the activities with the answer key and Answers and Explanations for the set.
- Note areas that need improvement.

**Lesson 2**
- Read "Grammar for the Multiple-Choice Questions" in Chapter 3, pp. 143–146, and Chapter 4, "A Quick Review of Literary and Rhetorical Terms," pp. 172–179.
- Practice answering multiple-choice questions by completing *Practice Sets 2* and *3* in Chapter 1.
- Correct the activities with the answer key and Answers and Explanations for the set.
- Note those areas where you have improved and those areas that still need work.

*Peterson's AP Success:*
*English Language & Composition*

# Week 3

**Lesson 1**
- Review Chapter 1, *About Answering Multiple-Choice Questions*, pp. 63–106; Chapter 3 for grammar, pp. 143–146; and Chapter 4 for literary and rhetorical terms, pp. 173–179.

- Practice answering multiple-choice questions by completing *Practice Set 4* in Chapter 1.

- Correct the activities with the answer key and Answers and Explanations for the set.

- Note those areas where you have improved and those areas that still need work.

**Lesson 2**
- Read Chapter 2, *About Writing the Essays*, pp. 107–141.

- Write *Essay Practice Set 1*. Time yourself to see how well-developed and complete an essay you can plan and write in 40 minutes.

- Complete the self-evaluation and ask a responsible friend, an AP classmate, or teacher, or classmate to evaluate your essay.

- With your and your evaluator's comments in mind, revise your essay.

# Week 4

**Lesson 1**
- Reread Chapter 2, pp. 107–141, as needed. Write *Essay Practice Set 2* in 40 minutes.

- Complete the self-evaluation and ask a responsible friend, an AP classmate, or teacher, or classmate to evaluate your essay.

- With your and your evaluator's comments in mind, revise your essay.

**Lesson 2**
- Reread Chapter 2, pp. 107–141, as needed. Write *Essay Practice Set 3* in 40 minutes.

- Complete the self-evaluation and ask a responsible friend, an AP classmate, or teacher, or classmate to evaluate your essay.

- With your and your evaluator's comments in mind, revise your essay.

# Week 5

**Lesson 1**
- Review the list you made after you took the *Diagnostic Test* to see what you need to review about the multiple-choice section.

- With these areas in mind, reread Chapter 1, *About Answering Multiple-Choice Questions*.

- Review the Practice Sets in the chapter and the Answers and Explanations. Pay particular attention to the strategies for answering the questions.

- Determine if there are areas that you are still unsure of.

**Lesson 2**
- Review the list you made after you took the *Diagnostic Test* to see what you need to review about the essay section of the AP exam.

- Reread Chapter 2, pp. 107–141.

- Revise the first two essays on the *Diagnostic Test*.

- Use the Self-Evaluation Rubric to assess how much you have improved since you originally wrote the two essays.

- Note any areas that you think you still need to need improve.

- Revise the remaining essay if necessary.

# Week 6

**Lesson 1**
- Take Practice Test 1.

- Score your answers against the Quick-Score Answers and evaluate your essay against the rubric.

- Ask a responsible friend, an AP classmate, or a teacher to evaluate your essay on the scoring guide.

- Read the Answers and Explanations for all the multiple-choice questions including the ones you answered correctly.

- Compare your scores on *Practice Test 1* to the scores on the *Diagnostic Test*. Where did you improve? What do you still need to work on?

**Lesson 2**
- Choose a selection that is used for one of the essay questions in the *Diagnostic Test* and analyze it as though you were going to create your own multiple-choice test. Be sure to ask yourself about the mode of the piece, any literary devices that are employed, and the theme of the piece.

- Choose one of the selections in the *Diagnostic Test* that is used as the basis for multiple-choice questions and turn it into a practice essay activity. Develop a question and then answer it in an essay.

# Week 7

**Lesson 1**
- Take *Practice Test 2*.
- Score your answers against the Quick-Score Answers and evaluate your essay against the rubric.
- Ask a responsible friend, an AP classmate, or a teacher to evaluate your essay on the scoring guide.
- Read the explanations for all the multiple-choice questions including the ones you answered correctly.
- Compare your scores on *Practice Test 2* to the scores on the *Diagnostic Test*. Where did you improve? What do you still need to work on?

**Lesson 2**
- Choose a selection that is used for one of the essay questions in the *Diagnostic Test* and analyze it as though you were going to create your own multiple-choice test. Be sure to ask yourself about the mode of the piece, any literary devices that are employed, and the theme of the piece.
- Choose one of the selections in the *Diagnostic Test* that is used as the basis for multiple-choice questions and turn it into a practice essay activity. Develop a question and then answer it in an essay.

# Week 8

**Lesson 1**
- Take *Practice Test 2*.
- Score your answers against the Quick-Score Answers and evaluate your essay against the rubric.
- Ask a responsible friend, an AP classmate, or a teacher to evaluate your essay on the scoring guide.
- Read the Answers and Explanations for all the multiple-choice questions including the ones you answered correctly.
- Compare your scores on *Practice Test 2* to the scores on the *Diagnostic Test*. Where did you improve? What do you still need to work on?

**Lesson 2**
- Choose a selection that is used for one of the essay questions in the *Diagnostic Test* and analyze it as though you were going to create your own multiple-choice test. Be sure to ask yourself about the mode of the piece, any literary devices that are employed, and the theme of the piece.
- Choose one of the selections in the *Diagnostic Test* that is used as the basis for multiple-choice questions and turn it into a practice essay activity. Develop a question and then answer it in an essay.

# Week 9

**Lesson 1**
- Read and analyze articles in magazines such as *The New Yorker* and selections in anthologies to practice your skills.
- Review Chapters 1 and 2.
- Review Chapters 3 and 4.

**Lesson 2**
- Randomly choose selections from Section I of the *Diagnostic Test* and the *Practices Tests* and review the Answers and Explanations to remind yourself of the strategies you can use to unlock the answers.
- Reread *Scoring High on the AP English Language and Composition Test*, pp. 6-9, and *10 Strategies for Acing the Test*, pp. 1-5.
- Assemble all materials you will need on test day: pens, pencils, a watch, and your registration information.

# THE PANIC PLAN

Eighteen weeks, nine weeks, how about two weeks? If you are the kind of person who puts everything off until the last possible minute, here is a two-week Panic Plan. Its objectives are to make you familiar with the test format and directions, to help you get as many right answers as possible, and to write the best essays you can.

**Week 1**
- Read *10 Strategies for Acing the Test*, p. 1-5, and *Scoring High on the AP English Language and Composition Test*, pp. 6-9.

- Take the *Diagnostic Test*. Read the directions carefully and use a timer for each section.

- Complete the self-scoring process. You can learn a lot about the types of questions in the multiple-choice section by working through the answers.

- Read Chapters 1 and 2 and complete the *Practice Sets*.

**Multiple Choice**
- Answer the multiple-choice section on *Practice Test 1*.

- Complete the self-scoring process, and see where you may still be having problems with question types.

- Read all the answer explanations including those you identified correctly.

- Answer the multiple-choice section on *Practice Test 2*, concentrating on the question types that are still tricky.

- Complete the self-scoring process.

- Read all the answer explanations including those you identified correctly.

**Essays**
- Complete the essay section on *Practice Test 1*.

- Score your essays using the rubric.

- Score your essays against the rubric, noting areas for improvement.

- Ask a responsible friend, an AP classmate, or a teacher to evaluate your essays against the scoring guide as well. Compare your scores to those on the *Diagnostic Test*.

- Complete the essay section on *Practice Test 2*, concentrating on the areas of weakness.

- Score your essays against the rubric, noting areas for improvement.

- Again, ask a responsible friend, an AP classmate, or a teacher to evaluate your essay on the scoring guide. Compare it with the score on the *Diagnostic Test*.

# Week 2

- Reread *10 Strategies for Acing the Test*, pp. 1–5, *Scoring High on the AP English Language and Composition Test*, pp. 6–9, and Chapters 1, 2, 3, and 4.

- Assemble all materials you will need on test day: pens, pencils, a watch, and your registration material.

**Multiple Choice**
- Answer the multiple-choice questions in *Practice Tests 3* and *4*.

- Complete the self-scoring process.

- Reread Chapter 1, 3, and/or 4 if you are still unsure of any of the strategies or information about answering multiple-choice questions.

**Essays**
- Write the essay from *Practice Tests 3* and *4*, working on strengthening your areas of weakness.

- Score the essays against the rubric.

- Ask a responsible friend, an AP classmate, or a teacher to evaluate your essays. Choose one essay to revise.

# SUGGESTED READING

The following list of autobiographers, diarists, biographers, writers of history, critics, essayists, journalists, political writers, and science and nature writers draws heavily from the selection of writers that the College Board suggests students read during an AP English language and composition course. The works have been chosen from a variety of sources to provide a representative list. There are also suggestions for books on composition and critical analysis. Reading essays in magazines like *The New Yorker* and the *New Republic* and columnists on the Op-Ed page of *The New York Times* will introduce you to writers like Cynthia Ozick, Gary Wills, William Safire, and Maureen Dowd. In studying for the test, use this list as well as writers you are introduced to do in class to practice developing essay responses. If you are looking for models of analysis, check pages 00–00 for a list of all works discussed and analyzed in this book.

## AUTOBIOGRAPHERS AND DIARISTS

Angelou, Maya, *I Know Why the Caged Bird Sings, The Heart of a Woman*

De Quincey, Thomas, *Autobiographic Sketches*

Douglass, Frederick, *Narrative of the Life of Frederick Douglass, an American Slave*

Franklin, Benjamin, *Autobiography*

Hellman, Lillian, *An Unfinished Woman, Scoundrel Time*

Hurston, Nora Zeale, *Dust Tracks on the Road*

Keller, Helen, *The Story of My Life, Helen Keller's Journal*

Kingston, Maxine Hong, "No Name Woman"

Lawrence, T.E., *The Seven Pillars of Wisdom*

Malcolm X, *Autobiography of Malcolm X*

Newman, John Henry, *Apologia pro vita sua*

Pepys, Samuel, *Diary of Samuel Pepys*

Welty, Eudora, *One Writer's Beginnings*

Wright, Richard, *Black Boy*

## BIOGRAPHERS AND HISTORIANS

Boswell, James, *The Life of Samuel Johnson*

Carlyle, Thomas, *On Heroes, Hero Worship and the Heroic in History*

Catton, Bruce, *Mr. Lincoln's Army, A Stillness at Appomattox*

Churchill, Winston, *My Early Life*

DeLoria, Vine, Jr., *Custer Died for Your Sins*

Edel, Leon, 5-volume biography of Henry James, *James Joyce: The Last Journey*

Ellmann, Richard, *James Joyce*

Franklin, John Hope, *From Slavery to Freedom, Race and History*
Fraser, Antonia, *The Weaker Vessel*
Gibbon, Edward, *The History of the Decline and Fall of the Roman Empire*
Lerner, Gerda, *The Majority Finds Its Past, The Creation of Feminist Consciousness*
Macaulay, Thomas, "Milton," *History of England*
Morison, Samuel Eliot, *Admiral of the Ocean Sea, John Paul Jones*
Parkman, Francis, *Oregon Trail*
Schlesinger, Arthur M., *The Age of Jackson, A Thousand Days*
Takaki, Ronald, *A Different Mirror*
Trevelyan, George, *American Revolution*
Tuchman, Barbara, *The Guns of August, Practicing History* (collection)

## CRITICS

Arnold, Matthew, *Essays in Criticism, Culture and Anarchy*
Clark, Kenneth, *Civilization*
Emerson, Ralph Waldo, "Self-Reliance," "The Over Soul"
Hazlitt, William, *Sketches and Essays*
Hooks, Bell, *Teaching to Transgress*
Johnson, Samuel, *The Rambler, The Idler*
Pater, Walter, *The Renaissance, Appreciations*
Ruskin, John, *Modern Painters, The Stones of Venice*
Santayana, George, *The Sense of Beauty*
Sontag, Susan, *Against Interpretation*
Wilson, Edmund, *Axel's Castle*

## ESSAYISTS

Addison, Joseph, *The Tatler, The Spectator*
Angelou, Maya, *Wouldn't Take Nothing for My Journey Now*
Baldwin, James, *Notes of a Native Son*
Chesterton, G.K., *Tremendous Trifles*
Didion, Joan, "Miami: The Cuban Presence," "The Liquid City"
Lamb, Charles, *Essays of Elia*
Mairs, Nancy, "On Being a Scientific Booby"
Márquez, Gabriel García, "Eye of a Blue Day"
Montaigne, *Essays*
Naipaul, V.S., *The Return of Eva Peron with Killings in Trinidad*
Orwell, George, *Shooting Elephants and Other Essays*
Selzer, Richard, *Mortal Lessons: Notes on the Art of Surgery*, "The Masked Marvel's Last Toehold"
Steele, Richard, *The Tatler, The Spectator*
Thoreau, Henry David, *On Walden Pond*, "Resistance to a Civil Government"

Walker, Alice, "In Search of Our Mothers' Gardens," "Beauty: When the Other Dancer is the Self"
White, E.B., "The Ring of Time"
Woolf, Virginia, *A Room of One's Own,* "Old Mrs. Grey"

## JOURNALISTS

Baker, Russell, *Growing Up*
Drew, Elizabeth, *Washington Journal*
Fitzgerald, Frances, *America Revised*
Mencken, H.L., *Prejudices,* "The Feminine Mind"
Steffens, Lincoln, *The Shame of the Cities*
Wolfe, Tom, *The Right Stuff*

## POLITICAL WRITERS

Arendt, Hannah, *The Origins of Totalitarianism*
de Beauvoir, Simone, *The Second Sex*
Buckley, William F., *Up from Liberalism*
Crévecoeur, Hector St. John de, *Letters from an American Farmer*
Du Bois, W. E. B., *Souls of Black Folks*
Fuller, Margaret, *Woman in the Nineteenth Century*
Galbraith, John Kenneth, *The Affluent Society*
Gilman, Charlotte Perkins, *Women and Economics*
Hobbes, Thomas, *The Leviathan*
Jefferson, Thomas, "The Declaration of Independence"
Kennan, George, *Memoirs*
King, Martin Luther, Jr., "Letters from a Birmingham Jail"
Locke, John, *Second Treatise of Civil Government*
Machiavelli, Niccolò, *The Prince*
Mill, John Stuart, *On Liberty*
Milton, John, *Areopagitica*
More, Thomas, *Utopia*
Paine, Thomas, *Common Sense, The Crisis*
Swift, Jonathan, "A Modest Proposal"
de Tocqueville, Alexis, *Democracy in America*
Wollstonecraft, Mary, *Vindication of the Rights of Women*

## SCIENCE AND NATURE WRITERS

Abbey, Edward, *The Monkey Wrench Gang*
Bronowski, Jacob, *The Descent of Man*
Carson, Rachel, *Silent Spring*
Dillard, Annie, *Teaching a Stone to Talk*
Eiseley, Loren, "The Brown Wasps"
McPhee, John, *Annals of the Former World*
Sagan, Carl, *The Dragons of Eden, Cosmos*

## WORKS ON COMPOSITION AND ANALYSIS

Axelrod, Rise B. and Cooper, Charles, *The St. Martin's Guide to Writing*

Barzun, Jacques, *Simple an Direct: A Rhetoric for Writers*

Berthoff, Ann E., *The Making of Meaning: Metaphors, Models, and Maxims for Writing Teachers*

Cooley, Thomas, *The Norton Sampler: Short Essays for Composition*

Corbett, Edward J., *Classical Rhetoric for the Modern Student*

Costello, Krin Bergstrom, *Gendered Voices: Readings from the American Experience*

Cox, Don Richard and Giddnes, Elizabeth, *Crafting Prose*

DiYanni, Robert and Hoy II, Pat C., *The Scribner Handbook for Writers*

Elbow, Peter, *Writing with Power*

Gibson, Walker, *Persona: A Style Study for Readers and Writers*

Hall, Donald, ed., *The Contemporary Essay*

Lanham, Richard, *Analyzing Prose; The Electronic Word: Democracy, Technology, and the Arts; Revising Prose*

Murray, Donald, *The Craft of Revision*

Strunk, W., Jr., and White, E. B., *The Elements of Style*

Zinsser, William K., *On Writing Well: An Informal Guide to Writing Nonfiction*

Warriner, John E., *English Composition and Grammar, Complete Course*

# WHY TAKE THE DIAGNOSTIC TEST?

What do you know about the format and questions on an AP English Language and Composition Test? If you knew all you needed to know, you would probably not be reading this book. Taking a practice test is one way to learn about the test and what it will be like to take it on the real test day. It is a long test, and you will need to pace yourself in answering the multiple-choice questions and in planning and writing your essays. Taking the test will help you learn how much time to spend on each item.

Practice may not make perfect, but practice will improve your score. The more you learn about your strengths and weaknesses in test-taking abilities and in literary skills, and the more you work on strengthening them, the better your score will be.

How should you take this test? Just as though it were the real test, so that means setting aside 3 hours of uninterrupted quiet time to take the test, plus the time to score your answers.

- Make a photocopy of an answer sheet at the back of this book.

- Assemble four number 2 pencils and two pens along with enough paper on which to make notes and write your three essays.

- Get a timer or a stopwatch to time each section of the test.

- Follow the directions for each section of the test—the multiple-choice section and each of the three essays. Set your timer for the allotted time for each section.

- When you have finished the complete test, check how many questions you were able to answer on the multiple-choice test and how far you got in completing the essays. This information will help you in pacing yourself for the other practice tests and for the real test.

- Then check the multiple-choice questions against *Quick-Score Answers,* p. 43.

- Read the explanation for each answer, even if your answer was correct. You might learn something that will help you on the real test.

- Review each of your essays against the rubric. Score each essay. Be honest in your evaluation. Knowing your weaknesses is the only way to turn them into strengths.

- Turn to the Practice Plan and design your study plan from now until test day.

# Diagnostic Test

## AP ENGLISH LANGUAGE AND COMPOSITION

On the front page of your test booklet, you will find some information about the test. Because you have studied this book, none of it should be new to you, and much of it is similar to other standardized tests you have taken.

The page will tell you that the following exam will take 3 hours—1 hour for the multiple-choice section and 2 hours for the three essays—and that there are two booklets for this exam, one for the multiple-choice section and one for the essays.

The page will also say that SECTION I

- is 1 hour.

- has 50 questions (or some number from 50 to 60).

- counts for 45 percent of your total grade.

Then you will find a sentence in capital letters telling you not to open your exam booklet until the monitor tells you to open it.

Other instructions will tell you to be careful to fill in only ovals 1 through 50 (or whatever the number is) in Section I on your separate answer sheet. Fill in each oval completely. If you erase an answer, erase it completely. You will not receive any credit for work done in the test booklet, but you may use it for making notes.

You will also find a paragraph about the guessing penalty—a deduction of one-quarter point for every wrong answer—but also words of advice about guessing if you know something about the question and can eliminate several of the answers.

The final paragraph will remind you to work effectively and to pace yourself. You are told that not everyone will be able to answer all the questions. The page suggests that you skip questions that are difficult and come back to them if you have time—just what we have been telling you.

| SECTION I | TIME—60 MINUTES |
|---|---|

> **Directions:** This section consists of selections of literature and questions on their content, style, and form. After you have read each passage, select the response that best answers the question and mark the corresponding space on the answer sheet.

**Questions 1 through 11** refer to the following selection. Read the passage carefully, and then choose the answers to the questions.

## FROM *A VINDICATION OF THE RIGHTS OF WOMEN*

Line
It is difficult for us purblind mortals to say to what height human discoveries and improvements may arrive when the gloom of despotism subsides, which makes us stumble at every step; but, when mortality shall be settled on a more solid basis, then, without being
5 gifted with a prophetic spirit, I will venture to predict that woman will be either the friend or slave of man. We shall not, as at present, doubt whether she is a moral agent, or the link which unites man with brutes. But, should it then appear, that like the brutes they were principally created for the use of man, he will let them patiently bite
10 the bridle, and not mock them with empty praise; or, should their rationality be proved, he will not impede their improvement merely to gratify his sensual appetites. He will not, with all the graces of rhetoric, advise them to submit implicitly their understanding to the guidance of man. He will not, when he treats of the education of
15 women, assert that they ought never to have the free use of reason, nor would he recommend cunning and dissimulation to beings who are acquiring, in like manner as himself, the virtues of humanity.

Surely there can be but one rule of right, if morality has an eternal foundation, and whoever sacrifices virtue, strictly so called, to
20 present convenience, or whose *duty* it is to act in such a manner, lives only for the passing day, and cannot be an accountable creature.

The poet then should have dropped his sneer when he says

If weak women go astray,
The stars are more in fault then they.

25 For that they are bound by the adamantine chain of destiny is most certain, if it be proved that they are never to exercise their own reason, never to be independent, never to rise above opinion, or to feel the dignity of a rational will that only bows to God, and often forgets that the universe contains any being but itself and the model

30 of perfection to which its ardent gaze is turned, to adore attributes
that, softened into virtues, may be imitated in kind, though the
degree overwhelms the enraptured mind.

If, I say, for I would not impress by declamation when Reason
offers her sober light, if they be really capable of acting like rational
35 creatures, let them not be treated like slaves; or, like brutes who are
dependent on the reason of man, when they associate with him; but
cultivate their minds, give them the salutary, sublime curb of principle, and let them attain conscious dignity by feeling themselves only
dependent on God. Teach them, in common with man, to submit to
40 necessity, instead of giving, to render them more pleasing a sex to
mortals.

Further, should experience prove that they cannot attain the
same degree of strength of mind, perseverance, and fortitude, let
their virtues be the same in kind, though they may vainly struggle for
45 the same degree; and the superiority of man will be equally clear, if
not clearer; and truth, as it is a simple principle, which admits of no
modification, would be common to both. Nay. The order of society as
it is at present regulated would not be inverted, for woman would
then only have the rank that reason assigned her, and arts could not
50 be practised to bring the balance even. Much less to turn it.

These may be termed Utopian dreams. Thanks to that Being who
impressed them on my soul, and gave me sufficient strength of mind
to dare to exert my own reason, till, becoming dependent only on
him for support of my virtue, I view, with indignation, the mistaken
55 notions that enslave my sex.

I love man as my fellow; but his sceptre, real, or usurped,
extends not to me, unless the reason of an individual demands my
homage; and even then the submission is to reason, and not to man.
In fact, the conduct of an accountable being must be regulated by the
60 operations of its own reason; or on what foundations rests the throne
of God?

It appears to me necessary to dwell on these obvious truths,
because females have been insulated, as it were; and, while they have
been stripped of the virtues that should clothe humanity, they have
65 been decked with artificial graces that enable them to exercise a
short-lived tyranny. Love, in their bosoms, taking place of every
nobler passion, their sole ambition is to be fair, to raise emotion
instead of inspiring respect; and this ignoble desire, like the servility
in absolute monarchies, destroys all strength of character. Liberty is
70 the mother of virtue, and if women be, by their very constitution,
slaves, and not allowed to breathe the sharp invigorating air of
freedom, they must ever languish like exotics, and be reckoned
beautiful flaws in nature.

—Mary Wollstonecraft

1. This selection conveys which of the following sentiments?

    (A) God created women for men's pleasure.
    (B) The future for women is bright.
    (C) A fervent sense of the unjust status of women.
    (D) The helpful nature of women.
    (E) A plea for understanding between the sexes.

2. Wollstonecraft argues that

    (A) men are inferior to women intellectually
    (B) women are the stronger gender emotionally
    (C) women are more independent than men are
    (D) women should have the same education as men
    (E) women provide more stability to a society than men

3. The writer would agree with which of the following statements?

    (A) Women need to develop their intuitive powers.
    (B) Women are obligated to develop their rational powers to the fullest extent.
    (C) Women need to follow the lead of men and be more demonstrative.
    (D) Women must break their chains and enter the business and political arenas.
    (E) Women cannot change their status without the help of men.

4. What is the meaning of "adamantine" (line 25)?

    (A) Extensive
    (B) Elastic
    (C) Unyielding
    (D) Self-imposed
    (E) Fragile

5. Which of the following is true about the tone of this selection?

    (A) Argumentative and overwrought
    (B) Appealing to reason, convincing
    (C) Subtly persuasive
    (D) Desultory and emotional
    (E) Optimistic and uplifting

6. According to Wollstonecraft, what qualities did the society of her time value in women?

    (A) To be attractive and cause men to admire them.
    (B) To inspire respect and consideration.
    (C) To love liberty and freedom.
    (D) To be servile and deceitful.
    (E) To fight for female suffrage.

7. In the first line of the last paragraph, "Utopian dreams" is an example of an

    (A) Allegory
    (B) Allusion
    (C) Aphorism
    (D) Conundrum
    (E) Synecdoche

8. In the sentence, "Liberty is the mother of virtue, and if women be, by their very constitution, slaves, and not allowed to breathe the sharp invigorating air of freedom, they must ever languish like exotics, and be reckoned beautiful flaws in nature," there are examples of which of the following literary devices?

    (A) Personification and conundrum
    (B) Simile and allusion
    (C) Alliteration and onomatopoeia
    (D) Hyperbole and metaphor
    (E) Metaphor and simile

**9.** In the first sentence, what does the author mean by the word "purblind"?

(A) A hiding place for hunters
(B) Direction
(C) Chauvinistic
(D) Enlightened
(E) Lacking in vision and understanding

**10.** With which of the following statements would Wollstonecraft agree?

(A) The rationality of women need not be a concern to men as long as they pay compliments to women.
(B) When women are deprived of opportunities, all of society is diminished.
(C) Women are superior in intellect to men.
(D) By their nature, women are more virtuous then men.
(E) Women live in their imaginations, where they create a perfect world for themselves.

**11.** The rhetoric in the following sentence from the first paragraph contains all of the following elements EXCEPT

He will not, when he treats of the education of women, assert that they ought never to have the free use of reason, nor would he recommend cunning and dissimulation to beings who are acquiring, in like manner as himself, the virtues of humanity.

I. subordination and an infinitive
II. a participial phrase and subjunctive mood
III. a transitive verb and progressive tense
IV. an appositive and an alliteration

(A) I only
(B) I and II
(C) III only
(D) IV only
(E) II and IV

**Questions 12 through 24** refer to the following selection. Read the passage carefully, and then choose the answers to the questions.

# FROM THE PREFACE TO THE 1855 EDITION OF *LEAVES OF GRASS*

Line America does not repel the past or what it has produced under its
forms or amid other politics or the idea of castes or the old religions
. . . accepts the lesson with calmness . . . is not so impatient as has
been supposed that the slough still sticks to opinions and manners
5 and literature while the life which served its requirements has passed
into the new life of the new forms . . . perceives that the corpse is
slowly borne from the eating and sleeping rooms of the house . . .
perceives that it waits a little while in the door . . . that it was fittest
for its days . . . that its action has descended to the stalwart and
10 well-shaped heir who approaches . . . and that he shall be fittest for
his days.
  The Americans of all nations at any time upon the earth have
probably the fullest poetical nature. The United States themselves are
essentially the greatest poem. In the history of the earth hitherto the
15 largest and most stirring appear tame and orderly to their ampler
largeness and stir. Here at last is something in the doings of man that
corresponds with the broadcast doings of the day and night. Here is
not merely a nation but a teeming nation of nations. Here is action
untied from strings necessarily blind to particulars and details
20 magnificently moving in vast masses. Here is the hospitality which
forever indicates heroes . . . Here are the roughs and beards and
space and ruggedness and nonchalance that the soul loves. Here the
performance disdaining the trivial unapproached in the tremendous
audacity of its crowds and groupings and the push of its perspective
25 spreads with crampless and flowing breadth and showers its prolific
and splendid extravagance. One sees it must indeed own the riches
of the summer and winter, and need never bankrupt while corn
grows from the ground or orchards drop apples or the bays contain
fish or men beget children upon women. . . .

              —Walt Whitman

12. Which of the following is the best statement of the theme of this passage?

    (A) A portrait of the beauty of the United States.
    (B) A forecast of the future of poetry in the United States.
    (C) A merging of new and old literary styles.
    (D) A discussion of the resources and poetry of the United States.
    (E) A poetic definition of the United States.

13. In line 6, to what does the word "corpse" refer?

    (A) Old forms of poetry
    (B) The past
    (C) Slough
    (D) Older opinions and manners
    (E) Current politics

14. How does Whitman suggest that the past and the present are linked?

    I. The past nourishes and educates the present.
    II. In the present, the past is viewed differently.
    III. The present is merely a mirror image of the past.
    IV. The present can be seen only in the context of the past.

    (A) I only
    (B) II only
    (C) III only
    (D) IV only
    (E) I, II, and IV

15. Which of the following statements does not reflect Whitman's ideas about the United States?

    (A) It is larger than most other countries.
    (B) The population is more literate than that of other nations.
    (C) The people of the United States have built a unique nation.
    (D) It is a country of vast riches in people and nature.
    (E) It is a country in transition.

16. When Whitman wrote "perceives that the corpse is slowly borne from the eating and sleeping rooms of the house," (lines 6-7) he used what type of literary device?

    (A) Personification
    (B) Meter
    (C) Oxymoron
    (D) Conceit
    (E) Metaphor

17. Which is the best interpretation of Whitman's statement "the United States themselves are essentially the greatest poem" in lines 13-14?

    (A) The greatest volume of good poetry is from the United States.
    (B) The nation's vibrancy, beauty, and diversity are poetic.
    (C) The people of the nation are very poetic.
    (D) The United States is the leader in finding new forms of poetry.
    (E) Literature in the United States has poetry at its root.

**18.** The sentence "Here are the roughs and beards and space and ruggedness and nonchalance that the soul loves" (lines 21–22) is intended as

(A) a challenge presented to humanity
(B) symbolic of emotional highs and lows
(C) a metaphor for the American land-scape; physical and cultural
(D) a contrast between something easy and something difficult
(E) a reference to style and dress at the time of writing

**19.** Which of the following descriptions would best characterize the United States, according to Whitman?

(A) Rigid
(B) Malleable
(C) Anti-intellectual
(D) Exuberant
(E) Enshrining the past

**20.** What does Whitman mean when he comments that the United States "is not merely a nation but a teeming nation of nations" (lines 17–18)?

(A) New Americans have tremendously increased the population.
(B) The nation's resources can support a large population.
(C) People come to the United States to make their fortunes.
(D) Native Americans represent a nation within a nation.
(E) The United States is a culturally diverse nation.

**21.** In the second paragraph, Whitman uses the word "here" to begin numerous sentences. What effect does he create?

(A) A ponderous feeling
(B) A sense of predictability
(C) Formality
(D) Exuberance
(E) A musical, poetic feeling

**22.** The following sentence contains which of the elements listed?

Here the performance disdaining the trivial unapproached in the tremendous audacity of its crowds and groupings and the push of its perspective spreads with crampless and flowing breadth and showers its prolific and splendid extravagance.

(A) A gerund phrase
(B) A participial phrase
(C) An infinitive phrase
(D) All of the above
(E) None of the above

**23.** The compound verb in the sentence beginning, "Here the performance" (lines 22–23) is

(A) push and spreads
(B) unapproached and showers
(C) unapproached and disdaining
(D) spreads and showers
(E) crowds and showers

**24.** What is Whitman saying in the sentence "Here at last is something in the doings of man that corresponds with the broadcast doings of the day and night" (lines 16–17)?

(A) The people of the United States follow a pattern like day becomes night.
(B) The nation's actions are unpredict-able.
(C) The influence of the United States spreads as widely as day and night.
(D) A person meets challenges on a day-to-day basis.
(E) People have found a place in the United States where their actions are compatible with nature.

**Questions 25 through 38** refer to the following selection. Read the passage carefully, and then choose the answers to the questions. In *Politics and the English Language,* George Orwell expresses a concern for the English language and the manipulation of language in the modern world.

# FROM *POLITICS AND THE ENGLISH LANGUAGE*

Line   Most people who bother with the matter at all would admit that the
English language is in a bad way, but it is generally assumed that we
cannot by conscious action do anything about it. Our civilization is
decadent and our language—so the argument runs—must inevitably
5      share in the general collapse. It follows that any struggle against the
abuse of language is a sentimental archaism, like preferring candles to
electric light or hansom cabs to aeroplanes. Underneath this lies the
half-conscious belief that language is a natural growth and not an
instrument which we shape for our own purposes. . . .
10         . . . The defense of the English language implies more than this,
and perhaps it is best to start by saying what it does not imply.
           To begin with it has nothing to do with archaism, with salvaging
of obsolete words and turns of speech, or with the setting up of a
"standard English" which must never be departed from. On the
15     contrary, it is especially concerned with the scrapping of every word
or idiom which has out worn its usefulness. It has nothing to do with
correct grammar and syntax, which are of no importance so long as
one makes one's meaning clear, or with the avoidance of American-
isms, or with having what is called a "good prose style." On the other
20     hand it is not concerned with fake simplicity and the attempt to
make written English colloquial. Nor does it even imply in every case
preferring the Saxon word to the Latin one, though it does imply
using the fewest and the shortest words that will cover one's
meaning. What is above all needed is to let the meaning choose the
25     word, and not the other way about. In prose, the worst thing one can
do with words is to surrender to them. When you think of a concrete
object, you think wordless, and then, if you want to describe the
thing you have been visualizing you probably hunt about till you find
the exact words that seem to fit it. When you think of something
30     abstract you are more inclined to use words from the start, and
unless you make a conscious effort to prevent it, the existing dialect
will come rushing in and do the job for you, at the expense of
blurring or even changing your meaning. Probably it is better to put
off using words as long as possible and get one's meaning as clear as
35     one can through pictures or sensations. Afterwards one can choose—
not simply *accept*—the phrases that will best cover the meaning, and
then switch round and decide what impression one's words are likely

to make on another person. This last effort of the mind cuts out all stale or mixed images, all prefabricated phrases, needless repetitions,
40 and humbug and vagueness generally. But one can often be in doubt about the effect of a word or a phrase, and one needs rules that one can rely on when instinct fails. I think the following rules will cover most cases:

45    (i) Never use a metaphor, simile, or other figure of speech which you are used to seeing in print.
   (ii) Never use a long word where a short one will do.
   (iii) If it is possible to cut a word out, always cut it out.
   (iv) Never use the passive where you can use the active.
   (v) Never use a foreign phrase, a scientific word, or a jargon
50       word if you can think of an everyday English equivalent.
   (vi) Break any of these rules sooner than say anything outright barbarous.

These rules sound elementary, and so they are, but they demand a deep change in attitude in anyone who has grown used to writing in
55 the style now fashionable. One could keep all of them and still write bad English, but one could not write the kind of stuff that I quoted in those five specimens at the beginning of this article.

I have not here been considering the literary use of language, but merely language as an instrument of expressing and not for
60 concealing or preventing thought. . . . One can at least change one's own habits, and from time to time one can even, if one jeers loudly enough, send some worn-out and useless phrase—some *jackboot, Achilles' heel, hotbed, melting pot, acid test, veritable inferno* or other lump of verbal refuse—into the dustbin where it belongs.

—George Orwell

**25.** The chief topic of this selection is

   (A)  poor use of English

   (B)  diction

   (C)  chauvinistic disregard for foreign words and phrases

   (D)  grammar and mechanics

   (E)  scientific language and jargon

**26.** This passage is primarily concerned with

   (A)  the meanings of words

   (B)  the rules of syntax and structure in the English language

   (C)  the use of colloquialisms in the English language

   (D)  some rules to be used for better writing

   (E)  integration of scientific and foreign words into the English language

**27.** Which of the following best expresses one of the author's goals?

   (A)  To expand the use of the English language.

   (B)  To introduce new grammar rules.

   (C)  To teach creative writing.

   (D)  To find new means of expression.

   (E)  To simplify word use and sentence structure.

**28.** The author advocates which of the following actions?

   (A)  Using simplicity to make English colloquial.

   (B)  The use of detailed, descriptive phrasing.

   (C)  Simple, direct word selection.

   (D)  The use of common idioms.

   (E)  The occasional use of foreign phrases to add interest.

**29.** The general tone of this passage is

   (A)  subtly humorous

   (B)  serious and persuasive

   (C)  ironic

   (D)  satirical

   (E)  dramatic and portentous

**30.** George Orwell would agree with which of the following statements?

   (A)  You can break the rules whenever you want.

   (B)  You should never break the rules.

   (C)  You can break the rules if the writing makes better sense.

   (D)  You can break the rules early in a document if you are consistent.

   (E)  Rules are useful conventions.

**31.** In the second paragraph, the author identifies what situation under which rules are necessary?

   (A)  When vagueness is required.

   (B)  When one's sense of what is good fails.

   (C)  When there are no guidelines.

   (D)  Whenever one is writing informally.

   (E)  Rules are never required.

**32.** What does the author think will happen if his rules are followed?

   (A)  Anything written will be good.

   (B)  Writing will be easier to read.

   (C)  More people will read.

   (D)  Writing will be as good as possible.

   (E)  More people will write.

**33.** What is the best paraphrase for the following sentence: "What is above all needed is to let the meaning choose the word, and not the other way about" (lines 24–25)?

  (A) Definitions of words should change depending on context.
  (B) A writer's meaning should determine word choice.
  (C) Words should always have the same meaning no matter how they are used.
  (D) A universal English system should be used.
  (E) The shortest and fewest words should be used.

**34.** According to Orwell's rules, why would he object to the following sentence: "The rich treasury of our language might go down the drain"?

  (A) Never use a metaphor, simile, or other figure of speech that you are used to seeing in print.
  (B) Never use a long word where a short one will do.
  (C) If it is possible to cut a word out, always cut it out.
  (D) Never use the passive where you can use the active.
  (E) Never use a foreign phrase, a scientific word, or a jargon word if you can think of an everyday English equivalent.

**35.** In the third paragraph, Orwell first uses the pronoun "one" and then switches to the pronoun "you." What is the effect of that change?

  (A) By so doing, he spotlights poor syntax.
  (B) By using "you," he relates more directly to the reader.
  (C) He is following his own advice; to simplify.
  (D) He is using an everyday English equivalent.
  (E) He is using standard English.

**36.** This sentence from the second paragraph, "In prose, the worst thing one can do with words is to surrender to them," (lines 25–26) contains which of the following?

  (A) Simile
  (B) Metaphor
  (C) Personification
  (D) Onomatopoeia
  (E) Alliteration

**37.** Which of the following is the best explanation of the author's rationale for saying that grammar and syntax are not important?

  (A) Grammar and syntax rules are too strict.
  (B) Grammar and syntax are never a major problem.
  (C) Grammar and syntax are not so important, as long as the meaning is clear.
  (D) Grammar and syntax rules are too lax.
  (E) Grammar and syntax are not universally understood.

**38.** What is the meaning of "colloquial" in line 21?

  (A) Fresh, colorful
  (B) Conversational, informal
  (C) Regional, provincial
  (D) Intriguing, fascinating
  (E) Understandable, comprehensible

**Questions 39 through 55** refer to the following selection. Read the passage carefully, and then choose the answers to the questions.

## FROM *ROUGHING IT*

Line  It was always very cold on that lake shore* in the night, but we had plenty of blankets and were warm enough. We never moved a muscle all night, but waked at early dawn in the original positions, and got up at once, thoroughly refreshed, free from soreness, and

5  brim full of friskiness. There is no end of wholesome medicine in such an experience. That morning we could have whipped ten such people as we were the day before—sick ones at any rate. But the world is slow, and people will go to "water cures" and "movement cures" and to foreign lands for health. Three months of camp life on

10  Lake Tahoe would restore an Egyptian mummy to his pristine vigor, and give him an appetite like an alligator. I do not mean the oldest and driest mummies, of course, but the fresher ones. The air up there in the clouds is very pure and fine, bracing and delicious. And why shouldn't it be?—it is the same the angels breathe. I think that hardly

15  any amount of fatigue can be gathered together that a man cannot sleep off in one night on the sand by its side. Not under a roof, but under the sky; it seldom or never rains there in the summertime. I know a man who went there to die. But he made a failure of it. He was a skeleton when he came, and could barely stand. He had no

20  appetite, and did nothing but read tracts and reflect on the future. Three months later he was sleeping out of doors regularly, eating all he could hold, three times a day, and chasing game over the mountains three thousand feet high for recreation. And he was a skeleton no longer, but weighed part of a ton. This is no fancy sketch, but the

25  truth. His disease was consumption. I confidently commend his experience to other skeletons.

—Mark Twain

---
* Lake Tahoe on the California-Nevada border

39. What is the tone of the passage?

    (A) Witty
    (B) Serious, scientific
    (C) Insightful
    (D) Argumentative
    (E) Questioning, curious

40. Which of the following is the best statement of the theme of this passage?

    (A) Lake Tahoe is beautiful.
    (B) Going to Lake Tahoe can be helpful.
    (C) The air and water quality of Lake Tahoe are outstanding.
    (D) Lake Tahoe and its environs have recuperative powers.
    (E) It is important to keep Lake Tahoe pristine.

41. This selection can be classified as a(n)

    (A) Expository essay
    (B) Dramatic dialogue
    (C) Exaggerated anecdote
    (D) Modern myth
    (E) Persuasive essay

42. The writer's purpose in this selection is

    (A) to amuse and entertain his audience
    (B) to inform the audience about Lake Tahoe
    (C) to teach about the environment
    (D) to advocate a national park system through interesting readers in natural wonders
    (E) to subtly suggest a healthy lifestyle

43. What is the setting of this selection?

    (A) The Appalachian mountains in the mid-1800s.
    (B) The West in the late twentieth century.
    (C) The high deserts of the Southwest in the late 1700s.
    (D) The mountains of the West in the mid-1800s.
    (E) The Finger Lakes region of New York at the turn of the century.

44. Which of the following is the best characterization of Mark Twain's diction?

    (A) He uses a great deal of folksy language.
    (B) Twain's diction is erudite.
    (C) His style is very sophisticated.
    (D) He is somewhat careless and irresponsible in his word choices.
    (E) The passage is structured and static.

45. This passage from *Roughing It* could be considered an example of

    (A) romanticism
    (B) realism
    (C) naturalism
    (D) classicism
    (E) regionalism

46. When Twain writes, "But the world is slow," in lines 7–8, he is saying that

    (A) people lack energy
    (B) it takes time to communicate
    (C) people take time to learn
    (D) it takes a long time to get to a new place
    (E) there is little that is new

47. The reference to the Egyptian mummies in line 10 emphasizes

    (A) the dryness of the region
    (B) the age of the lake
    (C) the rehabilitative powers of the region
    (D) the spiritual aspects of the area
    (E) the beauty of the region

*Peterson's AP Success:*
*English Language & Composition*

48. When Twain writes "I think that hardly any amount of fatigue can be gathered together that a man cannot sleep off in one night on the sand by its side," (lines 14–16) he is saying that the speaker thinks

(A) people never get enough sleep
(B) many people sleep too much
(C) sand forms a relaxing bed
(D) anyone can get fully rested at Lake Tahoe
(E) the sands at Lake Tahoe have medicinal qualities

49. The words "bracing" and "delicious" (line 13) suggest that the air is

(A) cold and tasteful
(B) supportive and tasty
(C) invigorating and enjoyable
(D) refreshing and supportive
(E) invigorating and refreshing

50. Based on this passage, what conclusion can be drawn about Twain's feelings for the locale?

   I.   He enjoys the environment of Lake Tahoe.
  II.   He finds the mountain region invigorating.
 III.   He feels it lacks the depth of the East.

(A) I only
(B) II only
(C) III only
(D) I and II
(E) I, II, and III

51. When Twain states, the air is what "angels breathe," (line 14) he is alluding to what aspect of the environment?

(A) The altitude
(B) The cold
(C) The moisture
(D) The heavenly scent from the pines
(E) The perfection of the biosphere

52. Which of the following does not apply to Twain's style in this selection?

(A) He uses specific details to create a sense of realism.
(B) He captures the local color.
(C) The speaker seems to be an ordinary person, the common man.
(D) The language has the flavor and rhythms of common speech.
(E) It imitates Shakespearean sentence structure.

53. How would you characterize the phrase "fancy sketch" (line 24)?

(A) An elaborate drawing
(B) A short, nonfiction anecdote
(C) A medical tract discussing cures
(D) A short skit or humorous act
(E) A tall tale, a humorous account

54. All of the following rhetorical features are evident in this passage EXCEPT

(A) personal anecdote
(B) figures of speech
(C) tall tale
(D) colloquialism
(E) simple sentence

 **END OF SECTION I**

## SECTION II                    TIME—2 HOURS

**Question 1**
Suggested time—40 minutes.

> **Directions:** Read the passage below carefully. Write a well-organized essay that evaluates the elements of rhetoric and style found in the passage. Explain how the writer uses these elements to communicate with his audience and to achieve his purpose.

"Address to the Graduating Class"
University High School
Oxford, Mississippi, May 28, 1951

Years ago, before any of you were born, a wise Frenchman said, "If youth knew; if age could." We all know what he meant: that when you are young, you have the power to do anything, but you don't know what to do. Then, when you have got old and experience and observation have taught you answers, you are tired, frightened; you don't care, you want to be left alone as long as you yourself are safe; you no longer have the capacity or the will to grieve over any wrongs but your own.

So you young men and women in this room tonight, and in thousands of other rooms like this one about the earth today, have the power to change the world, rid it forever of war and injustice and suffering, provided you know how, know what to do. And so according to the old Frenchman, since you can't know what to do because you are young, then anyone standing here with a head full of white hair, should be able to tell you.

But maybe this one is not as old and wise as his white hairs pretend or claim. Because he can't give you a glib answer or pattern either. But he can tell you this, because he believes this. What threatens us today is fear. Not the atom bomb, nor even fear of it, because if the bomb fell on Oxford tonight, all it could do would be to kill us, which is nothing, since in doing that, it will have robbed itself of its only power over us: which is fear of it, the being afraid of it. Our danger is not that. Our danger is the forces in the world today which are trying to use man's fear to rob him of his individuality, his soul, trying to reduce him to an unthinking mass by fear and bribery—giving him free food which he has not earned, easy and value-less money which he has not worked for; the economies or ideologies or political systems, communist or socialist or democratic, whatever they wish to call themselves, the tyrants and the politicians, American or European or Asiatic, whatever they call themselves, who would reduce man to one obedient mass for their own aggrandizement and power, or because they themselves are baffled and afraid, afraid of, or incapable of, believing in man's capacity for courage and endurance and sacrifice.

That is what we must resist, if we are to change the world for man's peace and security. It is not men in the mass who can and will save Man. It is Man himself, created in the image of God so that he shall have the power and the will to choose right from wrong, and so be able to save himself because he is worth saving;—Man, the individual, men and women, who will refuse always to be tricked or frightened or bribed into surrendering, not just the right but the duty too, to choose between justice and injustice, courage and cowardice, sacrifice and greed, pity and self;—who will believe always not only in the right of man to be free of injustice and rapacity and deception, but the duty and responsibility of man to see that justice and truth and pity and compassion are done.

So, never be afraid. Never be afraid to raise your voice for honesty and truth and compassion, against injustice and lying and greed. If you, not just you in this room tonight, but in all the thousands of other rooms like this one about the world today and tomorrow and next week, will do this, not as a class or classes, but as individuals, men and women, you will change the earth; in one generation all the Napoleons and Hitlers and Caesars and Mussolinis and Stalins and all the other tyrants who want power and aggrandizement, and the simple politicians and time-servers who themselves are merely baffled or ignorant or afraid, who have used, or are using, or hope to use, man's fear and greed for man's enslavement, will have vanished from the face of it.

—William Faulkner

**Question 2**

Suggested time—40 minutes.

> **Directions:** Read this passage about the accumulation and distribution of wealth carefully. Write a well-organized, persuasive essay that defends, challenges, or qualifies the assertions made by the author. Use evidence from your observations, experience, or reading to develop your position. Bear in mind the structure of an argument, the types of arguments, and the premises.

There remains, then, only one mode of using great fortunes; but in this we have the true antidote for the temporary unequal distribution of wealth, the reconciliation of the rich and the poor—a reign of harmony—another ideal, differing, indeed, from that of the Communist in requiring only the further evolution of existing conditions, not the total overthrow of our civilization. It is founded upon the present most intense individualism, and the race is prepared to put it in practice by degrees whenever it pleases. Under its sway we shall have an ideal state, in which the surplus wealth of the few will become, in the best sense, the property of the many, because administered for the common good; and this wealth, passing through the hands of the few, can be made a much more potent force for the elevation of our race than if it had been distributed in small sums to the people themselves. Even the poorest can be made to see this, and to agree that great sums gathered by some of their fellow citizens and spent for public purposes, from which the masses reap the principal benefit, are more valuable to them than if scattered among them through the course of many years in trifling amounts.

—Andrew Carnegie, "Wealth," 1889

## Question 3

Suggested time—40 minutes.

**Directions:** This passage is from a letter written by Abigail Adams to her daughter in November of 1800. Read the letter carefully. Write a well-organized essay discussing how the author uses language to create impressions of the new White House. Explain how her selection of words and details conveys her attitude toward living in the new capital. Be sure to include elements such as diction, tone, style, and narrative pace.

Washington, 21 November, 1800

My Dear Child:

. . . woods are all you sees from Baltimore until you reach the *city*,* which is only so in name. Here and there is a small cot, without a glass window, interspersed amongst the forests, through which you travel miles without seeing any human being. In the city there are buildings enough, if they were compact and finished, to accommodate Congress and those attached to it; but as they are, as scattered as they are, I see no great comfort for them. The river, which runs up to Alexandria, is in full view of my window, and I *see* the vessels as they pass and repass. The house is upon a grand and superb scale, requiring about thirty servants to attend and keep the apartments in proper order, and perform the ordinary business of the house and stables; an establishment very well proportioned to the President's salary. The lighting of the apartments, from the kitchen to the parlors and chambers, is a tax indeed; and the fires we are obliged to keep to secure us from daily agues is another very cheering comfort. To assist us in this great castle, and render less attendance necessary, bells are wholly wanting, not one single one being hung through the whole house, and promises are all you can obtain. This is so great an inconvenience, that I know not what to do, or how to do. . . . [I]f they will put me up some bells and let me have wood enough to keep fires, I design to be pleased. I could content myself almost anywhere three months; but, surrounded with forests, can you believe that wood is not to be had because people cannot be found to cut and cart it? . . .

You must keep all this to yourself, and when asked how I like it, say that I write you the situation is beautiful, which is true. The house is made habitable, but there is not a single apartment finished . . . If the twelve years, in which this place has been considered as

———————
* Washington, D.C.

the future seat of government, had been improved, as they would have been if in New England, very many of the present inconveniences would have been removed. It is a beautiful spot, capable of every improvement, and the more I view it, the more I am delighted with it.

—Abigail Adams

 **END OF SECTION II**

# ANSWERS AND EXPLANATIONS

## Quick-Score Answers

| | | | | |
|---|---|---|---|---|
| 1. C | 12. E | 23. D | 34. A | 45. E |
| 2. D | 13. B | 24. C | 35. B | 46. C |
| 3. B | 14. A | 25. B | 36. C | 47. C |
| 4. C | 15. B | 26. D | 37. C | 48. D |
| 5. B | 16. E | 27. E | 38. C | 49. C |
| 6. A | 17. B | 28. C | 39. A | 50. B |
| 7. B | 18. C | 29. B | 40. D | 51. A |
| 8. E | 19. B | 30. C | 41. C | 52. E |
| 9. E | 20. E | 31. B | 42. A | 53. E |
| 10. B | 21. D | 32. B | 43. D | 54. D |
| 11. E | 22. B | 33. B | 44. A | |

## DIAGNOSTIC TEST

1. **The correct answer is (C).** This is a main idea question. The word *fervent* should provide a clue. The tone of the selection is certainly passionate. Choice (A) is contrary to the theme of the selection. While the writer may hope that the future will be bright for women, choice (B), there is no evidence of this idea in the passage. Both choices (D) and (E) represent some truth, but both are too general to be the best answer, and choice (D) is not particularly supported by the passage.

2. **The correct answer is (D).** This is another type of main idea question in that you are asked the author's solution to the issue of inequality. Wollstonecraft argues that women may be the intellectual equal of men, but she does not say that they are their superior, choice (A). The emotional issue in choice (B) distorts the main point. Choices (C) and (E) are irrelevant to this question and illogical in relation to the selection.

3. **The correct answer is (B).** Being aware of consistency in answers (ideas) will help you with this question. If you answered questions 1 and 2 correctly, you recognized that developing rational powers is consistent with Wollstonecraft's theories about education and the unjust treatment of women by society. You might argue that choice (D) is also consistent, but the author does not mention business or politics. Choices (A) and (E) are inconsistent with Wollstonecraft's thesis, while choice (C) is not mentioned in the passage. Choice (E) is tricky, but Wollstonecraft is making the point that women should not depend on men; they need only depend on God, and they will find themselves equal to men in reason.

4. **The correct answer is (C).** If you did not know the meaning of *adamantine*, you could substitute the answer choices in the sentence to see which made the most sense. Consider that a chain is made of something hard and difficult to break, like iron, so that choices (B) and (E) would be inaccurate. Extensive, choice (A), is not a good fit then, nor is choice (D) consistent with the thesis. You probably also realized that the correct answer is very similar to *adamant*, a word that you probably know.

**Test-Taking Strategy**

*Be sure all parts of an answer are correct. A partially correct answer is a partially incorrect answer— and a quarter-point deduction.*

5. **The correct answer is (B).** Remember, a writer communicates the tone through diction. Tone reflects the writer's attitude toward the subject and the audience. You might think that choice (A) is a good possibility, especially if you do not agree with Wollstonecraft. However, her arguments are very logical, and her development is sound. The word choice, which might seem overwrought to you, is typical of the Romantic period. Choice (C) is incorrect; this piece is frank and forthright. Choice (D) is only partially correct. Choice (E) is illogical.

6. **The correct answer is (A).** This question is tricky, not because of what it asks but how it asks it. Did you notice that the question asked what society valued, not what the author valued? If you chose choices (B) or (C), you probably misread the question because these are qualities Wollstonecraft judged important. Choice (D) is illogical, not only in terms of the selection, but also in terms of real life. Very few, if any, societies value deceit. While the writer would heartily agree with choice (E), it is irrelevant and not supported by facts.

**Review Strategy**

*Be sure to review the* Glossary of Literary and Rhetorical Terms.

7.  **The correct answer is (B).** This question tests your knowledge of English literature. The reference, or allusion, is to Sir Thomas More's *Utopia.* If you did not know that, you could still eliminate answers and make an educated guess. An allegory, choice (A), is a story or tale with several levels of meaning, one literal and another symbolic. This is not a tale, and the meaning is plainly stated. An aphorism, choice (C), is a general truth or observation about life, usually stated concisely. While this selection qualifies by the first standard, it is hardly concise. A conundrum, choice (D), is a puzzling question or problem, most often in the form of a riddle. A synecdoche, choice (E), a figure of speech, occurs when a part is used for the whole. **HINT:** If you are sure you have never seen a word before, eliminate the choice. It was probably included to confuse you.

8.  **The correct answer is (E).** To answer this question correctly, you must first find the literary devices and identify them correctly. Then remember that both parts in an answer choice must be correct for the answer to be the right one. Choices (A) and (B) are partly correct (personification and simile) but not entirely (conundrum and allusion). Choices (C) and (D) are completely wrong.

9.  **The correct answer is (E).** If you were unfamiliar with the word, you could determine the correct answer by substituting the answer choices in the sentence. Also, the root word *-blind* is a clue. Yes, a blind can be a hiding place for hunters, but that makes no sense in the context of the sentence and the essay. Choice (B) is a noun, and, therefore, it does not fit. Choice (C) is incorrect because it modifies "us mortals," which includes women. Choice (D) contradicts the selection.

10. **The correct answer is (B).** Often on the Advanced Placement exam, you will find the same kinds of information tested in different ways. Remember that the test is really about comprehension and analysis, what you understand about what you read. Use the consistent idea strategy to help you answer this question. Choice (B) is consistent with the correct answers to questions 1, 2, and 3. Choice (A) is illogical because no facts support it. Choice (C) is contradictory to the writer's argument. Choices (D) and (E) are incorrect because both are distortions of Wollstonecraft's points.

11. **The correct answer is (E).** This question tests your knowledge of grammar and the conventions of writing. First, review the elements in each point against the sentence. The word *when* is a subordinating conjunction joining two complete ideas by making one of the ideas dependent on the other, and the phrase *to have* is an infinitive. Both elements are in the sentence, so item I cannot be the answer. Because participles end in *-ing*, at first glance, you may think that the sentence contains a participial phrase; however, *acquiring* is part of the main verb of the clause beginning with *who*, and the sentence does not have any subjunctive verbs, so point II is one response that you know is not correct. Keep going through the points to see if any others are also incorrect. Both *assert* and *recommend* are transitive verbs and *are acquiring* is progressive tense, so III is correct and not a possible answer. The sentence contains neither an appositive nor alliteration, several words beginning with the same sound, so point IV is also incorrect. Now you need to see which answer choices include points II and IV—choice (E).

12. **The correct answer is (E).** While the passage touches on the beauty of the United States, that is not the main focus, so choice (A) is eliminated. Nothing really is said about poetry as literature, so choice (B) is incorrect. The past and the present are discussed, but not in terms of literature, so choice (C) cannot be the answer. Choice (D) has virtually nothing to do with the passage. That leaves choice (E).

13. **The correct answer is (B).** There is no mention of poetry in the paragraph, which eliminates choice (A). Slough, choice (C), literally means the skin of a snake that is cast off; figuratively, it means a layer is cast off. You might not know that, but from the context, you could at least figure out that slough was something extraneous—maybe like fuzz—that stuck to something else. It would not seem important enough to be a corpse. Choice (D) is related to choice (C). Line 2 mentions politics but in the context of creating the past. Choices (C), (D), and (E) all relate in some way to the past, which is choice (B).

**14. The correct answer is (A).** Whitman suggests that America accepts the lesson of the past with calmness and that the past informs and educates the present, so point I seems to be a correct statement about the passage. Points II and III are incorrect restatements of the passage's theme. Point IV has a subtle implication that the past is always present, whereas Whitman suggests that the past nurtures the present for a time and then leaves, so point IV is also incorrect. Only choice (A) has item I, so it is the correct answer.

**15. The correct answer is (B).** Using the process of elimination, choice (A) is out because the writer plainly states that the United States is large. Choices (C) and (D) contradict Whitman's assertions that diversity makes the nation unique. Certainly, the United States is a nation that is changing, so choice (E) is not the answer. That leaves choice (B), and nowhere does the writer speak of Americans' ability to read.

**16. The correct answer is (E).** When Whitman writes about the past, he calls it a corpse. Personification, choice (A), gives human characteristics to nonhuman things, including concepts, but in this instance, metaphor is a more accurate identification of how Whitman uses the figure of speech in context. The passage is prose, so choice (B) is incorrect. Oxymoron, choice (C), combines two contradictory ideas and is wrong in this context. A conceit, choice (D), is an extended metaphor comparing two or more ideas and is, therefore, incorrect.

**17. The correct answer is (B).** The poet states that the nation is a poem. The only answer that indicates the same thing is choice (B), that the nation is poetic. While choices (A), (B), (D), and (E) mention poetry, they do not indicate that it is the United States itself that is the poem.

**18. The correct answer is (C).** This is a difficult question. By logically examining the choices, you can see that choice (E) is much too simplistic. Humanity is not Whitman's subject, choice (A), nor are emotions, choice (B). A contrast is possible but not between easy and difficult, choice (D), which do not relate to the passage. That leaves the physical and cultural landscape.

**Test-Taking Strategy**

*Use educated guessing when you know something about the question and can eliminate some of the answers.*

19. **The correct answer is (B).** To choose the right answer here is really an issue of vocabulary. Even if you do not know what choice (B) means, choices (A) and (E) can be eliminated because they contradict what Whitman says about the United States. He does not mention education, so eliminate choice (C). Whitman's tone in the passage is one of exuberance, choice (D), but he does not characterize the nation that way. That leaves choice (B), which means that something is not rigid and can be changed and molded.

20. **The correct answer is (E).** Whitman stresses the diversity of the United States, which he finds positive. While aspects of choices (A), (B), (C), and (D) may be true, they are not points that Whitman makes in this selection.

21. **The correct answer is (D).** The tone of this paragraph is neither ponderous, choice (A), nor formal, choice (C), but joyous. The repetition of the word *here* helps develop that tone. One might argue that the repetition is stylistically poetic, choice (E), the writer using it purposely to create unity and a sense of rhythm, but that better fits the definition of parallelism.

22. **The correct answer is (B).** Because the construction *to* and a verb form is not part of the sentence, there is no infinitive, thus eliminating choices (C) and (D). A gerund is a form of the verb that acts as a noun. No verbal form functions as a noun in this sentence, so choice (A) can be eliminated. There are several participles, forms of a verb acting as an adjective, and several participial phrases, participles modified by an adverb or adverbial phrase or that have a complement, choice (B). Since there are participial phrases, choice (E) is incorrect.

23. **The correct answer is (D).** This is a very complex sentence, but you can eliminate choices (A), (B), and (C) because a compound verb has the same tenses for both or all verbs. *Crowds* and *showers*, choice (E), could be *nouns* or *verbs*, but in this sentence, *crowds* is a noun, the object of the preposition *of*.

24. **The correct answer is (C).** Choice (E) may sound important but has no relationship to the passage. Choice (A) is too simplistic. Choices (B) and (D) may be true but do not relate to the passage.

**Test-Taking Strategy**

*When all the answer choices seem to be correct, see if one may be the main idea or theme and the others, supporting details.*

**25. The correct answer is (B).** Because all of these answer choices are touched on in the passage, the answer that covers the broadest portion of the selection is the correct response. Diction deals with the choice of words in written or spoken language, and, therefore, choice (B) is the most encompassing of the available responses.

**26. The correct answer is (D).** The question asks for the primary concern of the passage. The author discusses all of these answers at some point in the passage, but he spends most of his time listing and discussing some rules for better writing.

**27. The correct answer is (E).** The best approach to this question is to work through the answers, eliminating the incorrect answers. Orwell does not propose the expanded use of the English language, the introduction of new grammar rules, or the teaching of creative writing, choices (A), (B), and (C). He may imply a search for new means of expression, choice (D), but he clearly states a predilection for word and sentence simplification, choice (E).

**28. The correct answer is (C).** Orwell states that he is an advocate of simple, direct word selection. Each of the remaining four responses are counter to his fundamental thesis of simplicity.

**29. The correct answer is (B).** The question asks the reader to determine the feel or tone of the excerpt. The passage cannot be viewed as humorous, choice (A); ironic, choice (C); satirical, choice (D); or dramatic, choice (E). Orwell is quite serious in his concern for language, and his essay is meant to be persuasive, choice (B).

**30. The correct answer is (C).** The author lists six rules that he believes will improve writing. The last of these states "Break any of these rules sooner that say anything outright barbarous." That rule is consistent with choice (C). He does not advocate irresponsible or unreasoned breaking of rules, choices (A) and (D), nor does he advocate rigid adherence to rules, choice (B). Choice (E) is a statement of opinion that Orwell would probably agree with, but it is not the most accurate restatement of the essay. Be careful of such distracters that seem to be reasonable answers; check to see if they most accurately reflect the content.

**31. The correct answer is (B).** In the second paragraph, Orwell says, "But one can often be in doubt about the effect of a word or a phrase, and one needs rules that one can rely on when instinct fails." Only choice (B) reflects Orwell's statement.

32. **The correct answer is (B).** In the last sentence of the second paragraph, the author expresses the sentiment that these rules will not make bad writing good, the opposite of choice (A). On the other hand, good writing does not employ these rules. Choices (B) and (D) are similar. The difference is that components other than following the rules are needed to make writing "as good as possible," choice (D). Regardless of the other components, writing will be "easier to follow" if the writer follows the rules. Choice (C) is irrelevant to the passage.

33. **The correct answer is (B).** The author is stating that what a writer intends to say should determine word selection. The chosen words should not alter the writer's meaning. Choices (A) and (C) incorrectly deal with the definitions of words. Orwell does not address the responses contained in choices (D) and (E) in the lines cited.

34. **The correct answer is (A).** In the sentence given, there is figurative language that is a cliché, "go down the drain." Orwell would also object to the redundant phrase "rich treasury." However, there is no response that deals with redundancy. Choice (C) deals with wordiness, not redundancy. The given sentence has no long words, choice (B); is not in the passive voice, choice (D); and contains no foreign phrases, scientific words, or jargon, choice (E). A cliché is not jargon.

35. **The correct answer is (B).** At first, you might think that several of these are possible answers. Remember that the writer states that it is acceptable to break rules if the meaning becomes clearer by doing so. Orwell wants the reader to pay close attention here, so he directly addresses the audience. The other responses do not make sense in context.

**Review Strategy**

*Check the Quick Review of Literary and Rhetorical-Terms, p. 173.*

36. **The correct answer is (C).** The definition of personification is a figure of speech in which inanimate objects or abstractions are endowed with human characteristics. In this sentence, *words* is given a human characteristic that suggests that a person can surrender to them. A simile uses *like* or *as* for comparison, choice (A), while a metaphor states that something is something else, choice (B). Words that sound like their meanings are onomatopoeia, choice (D), and words in a series that repeat an initial consonant sound are examples of alliteration, choice (E).

37. **The correct answer is (C).** The readers of your essays may not agree with Orwell, but he states in the second paragraph, "It has nothing to do with correct grammar and syntax, which are of no importance so long as one makes one's meaning clear . . ." The context does not support choices (A), (D), or (E). Choice (B) is only half right. The statement from Orwell has the qualifier "so long as one's meaning is clear," thus eliminating choice (B).

38. **The correct answer is (C).** Orwell lists some phrases that were popular at the time he wrote this article. He suggests that they be thrown in the trash can. Choice (A) is the opposite of what Orwell is saying. Choice (B) would be correct only if you were asked a question about metaphor. Orwell may be advocating choice (D) at some point in the essay, but the question asks what Orwell is saying in the last sentence, and choice (C) restates his idea. Choice (E) is irrelevant to the sentence.

39. **The correct answer is (A).** The tone of the passage could not be considered serious or deep. Any answer with that sense would be incorrect, so choices (B), (C), and (D) can be eliminated. Humor and wit are more evident in the writing than questioning or curiosity, choice (E), so choice (A) is the better response.

40. **The correct answer is (D).** Each of the five answers has an element of Twain's commentary in them; therefore, you must look for the response that best matches or sums up the main idea. Much of the selection links Lake Tahoe with improving health. Choice (D) is the only choice that recognizes the recuperative powers of the area. Choices (A) and (E) focus more on the scenic beauty, and choices (B) and (C) touch on aspects of the area that might be helpful to good health, and thus support choice (D).

41. **The correct answer is (C).** This selection should not be viewed as a serious piece of writing, and any response that suggests that view is incorrect. That includes choices (A), (B), and (E). Of the two remaining answers, the passage is an anecdote, a short narrative, choice (C), rather than a myth, a story once believed to be true, choice (D).

**42.** **The correct answer is (A).** The speaker is not a teacher or an advocate, so choices (B), (C), and (D) must be eliminated. Choice (E) suggests a more indirect approach, but there is nothing subtle about the speaker; he tells his audience what they should do. The simple answer, to amuse and entertain, is the best response.

**Test-Taking Strategy**

*If you don't immediately know the answer, try eliminating wrong answers. If you are down to two answers that you are not sure about, choose the one that seems most likely to be correct.*

**43.** **The correct answer is (D).** The possible correct answers can quickly be reduced by two, choices (A) and (E), because the excerpt states that Lake Tahoe is on the California-Nevada border. The locale is not set in a desert, so that eliminates choice (C). Mark Twain wrote in the 1800s, choice (B), and the lake is in the mountains. This identifies choice (D) as the correct answer.

**44.** **The correct answer is (A).** The correct answer can be determined by the process of elimination. Twain's diction could not be called erudite, choice (B), and his style is not sophisticated, choice (C). Although he chooses words of common speech, he does so with care to paint vivid images, thus eliminating choice (D). The passage is dynamic rather than static, so choice (E) can be eliminated. Examples like "brim full of friskiness" (line 5) support choice (A) as the correct answer.

**45.** **The correct answer is (E).** This is not a romantic passage, choice (A); it does not express great emotion or devotion, even though nature is prominently featured. Considering the amount of exaggeration, it certainly is not realistic, choice (B). Neither is it an example of naturalism or classicism, choices (C) and (D). The focus of this passage is clearly on a specific area of the country. This type of advocacy for a territory is known as regionalism.

**46.** **The correct answer is (C).** It is important to put the question in context. The phrase represents a transition from Twain's listing of health benefits at Lake Tahoe to other approaches that were then in vogue. The reference to slowness shows that the author was indicating that it will take time for people to learn about something new and to change. Choices (A) and (E) have no relationship to the passage. On a quick reading, you might think that choice (D) could be correct, but choice (D) relates to real movement. In the context of the question, the author is not speaking about literal movement. Choice (B) might seem correct, but the author is implying that people have to change their ways—rather than that the information about new things will be delayed.

47. **The correct answer is (C).** As Mark Twain often does, he is using an exaggerated comparison to make a point about Lake Tahoe. In this case, he uses a figure of speech that includes a long-dead mummy to make the point that Lake Tahoe has significant recuperative powers. Choices (A) and (B) are incorrect because the author mentions neither the region's dryness nor the lake's age. Nor does he refer to spiritual aspects of the area, choice (D), or its beauty, choice (E).

48. **The correct answer is (D).** The question is asking about sleep, the topic of the sentence. The items to note in reading the sentence are the antecedent of *its* (Lake Tahoe) and the recuperative powers of the lake. These elements identify choice (D) as the answer. Choices (A), (B), and (C) do not mention the lake, while choice (E) does not mention sleep.

49. **The correct answer is (C).** While delicious may mean tasty, it does not mean tasteful, so you can eliminate choice (A). Both sets of words in choices (D) and (E) mean *bracing*, so they can be eliminated. Although *bracing* can mean supportive, choice (B), *invigorating,* is a better meaning in the context of air, and *delicious* when referring to the senses means enjoyable, choice (C).

50. **The correct answer is (B).** The identification of the correct answer requires you to make an inference about the author's feelings. It is clear from Twain's comments that he has a positive feeling for the area. Points I and II reflect this attitude, whereas point III negatively compares Lake Tahoe with the East. Only choice (D) has both I and II.

51. **The correct answer is (A).** Taken with the phrase "the air up there in the clouds," the reference to angels points directly to height as an element in the correct answer. Since angels are said to be "up" in the heavens, altitude, choice (A), is the answer. Choices (D) and (E) may distract you, but the question asks about the environment—in the mountains. Choices (B) and (C) do not relate to angels.

52. **The correct answer is (E).** If you do not readily see that Twain does not use classical Shakespearean sentence structure, try the process of elimination. The author uses both specific details, choice (A), and local color, choice (B), to make his points. The speaker is also an ordinary person using common speech, choices (C) and (D).

53. **The correct answer is (E).** On a quick reading, you might select choice (A) without bothering to read a sentence or two above and below the cited lines. Avoid this temptation and go back to the selection. If you do, you will see that choice (A) is a distracter. Choice (C) can also be considered a distracter. It, too, is a very literal answer, and Twain is not to be taken literally, so eliminate choice (C). While brief, the example Twain gives should not be taken literally, so eliminate choice (B), which asks you to consider this example as a nonfiction account. Choice (D) is incorrect because there is no skit involved.

54. **The correct answer is (D).** You must choose which of the answer choices is not found in the passage. The passage is personal, as evidenced by the use of the first person pronoun, and fits the definition of an anecdote, making choice (A) a true statement about the passage and, therefore, an incorrect answer. There are several figures of speech, so choice (B) is not the answer. The entire passage is a tall tale, so choice (C) is also incorrect. There are several simple sentences—for example, sentence 3 and the final sentence—so choice (E) is also incorrect. Although Twain is known for using colloquialisms in his writing, none appear in this passage.

# SUGGESTIONS FOR ESSAY QUESTION 1

The following are points you might have chosen to include in your essay on Faulkner's speech to the graduating class. Consider them as you complete your self-evaluation. Revise your essay once, using points from this list to strengthen it.

## Form or Mode
- Prose; a speech
- Persuasive

## Theme
- Individuals can and must choose to change the world for the better.
- "It is man himself, created in the image of God so that he shall have the power and the will to choose right from wrong, and so be able to save himself because he is worth saving."

## Characters
- Faulkner, the speaker
- Audience, the graduating high school students

## Conflict/Issue/Challenge
- Good versus evil

## Content/Important Points
- Beginning quotation
- Youth has power to rid the world of war and injustice
- Fear danger in the world
- Danger in those who use human fear to control humankind
- Right and duty to choose justice, courage, sacrifice, compassion
- If people choose right actions, tyrants will disappear.

## Setting
- Speech given at graduation
- Contemporary times—the bomb

## Point of View
- First person

## Diction/Syntax/Style

- Offers no proof to support opening quotation; abandons point in third paragraph
- Speaking directly to students; use of second person, *you*
- Long, complex sentences
- Much parallel construction: "giving him free food which he has not earned, easy and valueless money which he has not worked for"
- Cadence ministerial, almost musical
- Word choice sophisticated but comprehensible: "glib," "baffled," "aggrandizement"

*Peterson's AP Success:
English Language & Composition*

# SUGGESTIONS FOR ESSAY QUESTION 2

The following are points you might have chosen to include in your essay on Carnegie's comments about the responsibilities of the wealthy. Consider them as you complete your self-evaluation. Revise your essay once, using points from this list to strengthen it.

## Form or Mode

- Persuasive essay

## Theme

- The extra wealth of the few should become the property of all

## Conflict/Issue/Challenge

- How to resolve the unequal distribution of wealth and reconcile the rich and the poor

## Content/Important Points

- The wealthy should spend their excess wealth for public purposes and for the public good.
- Not Communist because the change that Carnegie advocates requires an evolution, not an overthrow of existing civilization
- The concept is based on the American ideal of individualism.
- Wealth should be administered by the few for the public good.
- Such a system is more beneficial to the poor than direct distribution of small sums of money to them.
- The result is a powerful force that will improve public conditions.

## Point of View

- First person plural to include all readers

## Diction/Syntax/Style

- Long, complicated sentences with many clauses or prepositional phrases
- Persuasive language: "only one mode," "true antidote," "ideal state," "in the best sense"
- Use of active and passive voices
- Sentence variety
- Some parallel structure: "to see this, and to agree that"
- Strong adjectives: "ideal," "surplus," "potent," "great," "principal," "trifling"

# SUGGESTIONS FOR ESSAY QUESTION 3

The following are points you might have chosen to include in your essay about Abigail Adams's letter to her daughter. Consider them as you complete your self-evaluation. Revise your essay once, using points from this list to strengthen it.

## Form or Mode
- Prose; a letter
- Descriptive

## Theme
- The new executive mansion, the White House, leaves much to be desired.
- The people of New England are more competent than those in Washington, D.C.

## Characters
- The author
- Her daughter
- Individuals working in the White House

## Conflict/Issue/Challenge
- Making a home in the unfinished White House

## Content/Important Points
- Washington, D.C., is not a city.
- Lack of conveniences; the many inconveniences
- Difficulties in getting things done
- The loveliness of the place

## Setting
- Washington, D.C.
- The White House

## Point of View
- First person, singular

## Diction/Syntax/Style

- Highly descriptive, many details
- Creates a sense of place; a picture, similar to a snapshot
- Sense of an unsettled, unfinished area
- Strong, definite vocabulary, more than vivid word choice
- Amusing and intimate tone
- Directly addresses her audience, her daughter *you*
- Elegant sentence structure

# SELF-EVALUATION RUBRIC FOR THE ADVANCED PLACEMENT ESSAYS

| | 8–9 | 6–7 | 5 | 3–4 | 1–2 | 0 |
|---|---|---|---|---|---|---|
| **Overall Impression** | Demonstrates excellent control of the literature and outstanding writing competence; thorough and effective; incisive | Demonstrates good control of the literature and good writing competence; less thorough and incisive than the highest papers | Reveals simplistic thinking and/or immature writing; adequate skills | Incomplete thinking; fails to respond adequately to part or parts of the question; may paraphrase rather than analyze | Unacceptably brief; fails to respond to the question; little clarity | Lacking skill and competence |
| **Understanding of the Text** | Excellent understanding of the text; exhibits perception and clarity; original or unique approach; includes apt and specific references | Good understanding of the text; exhibits perception and clarity; includes specific references | Superficial understanding of the text; elements of literature vague, mechanical, overgeneralized | Misreadings and lack of persuasive evidence from the text; meager and unconvincing treatment of literary elements | Serious misreadings and little supporting evidence from the text; erroneous treatment of literary elements | A response with no more than a reference to the literature; blank response, or one completely off the topic |
| **Organization and Development** | Meticulously organized and thoroughly developed; coherent and unified | Well organized and developed; coherent and unified | Reasonably organized and developed; mostly coherent and unified | Somewhat organized and developed; some incoherence and lack of unity | Little or no organization and development; incoherent and void of unity | No apparent organization or development; incoherent |
| **Use of Sentences** | Effectively varied and engaging; virtually error free | Varied and interesting; a few errors | Adequately varied; some errors | Somewhat varied and marginally interesting; one or more major errors | Little or no variation; dull and uninteresting; some major errors | Numerous major errors |
| **Word Choice** | Interesting and effective; virtually error free | Generally interesting and effective; a few errors | Occasionally interesting and effective; several errors | Somewhat dull and ordinary; some errors in diction | Mostly dull and conventional; numerous errors | Numerous major errors; extremely immature |
| **Grammar and Usage** | Virtually error free | Occasional minor errors | Several minor errors | Some major errors | Severely flawed; frequent major errors | Extremely flawed |

Using the rubric on the previous page, rate yourself in each of the categories below for each essay on the test. Enter on the lines below the number from the rubric that most accurately reflects your performance in each category. Then calculate the average of the six numbers to determine your final score. It is difficult to score yourself objectively, so you may wish to ask a respected friend or teacher to assess your writing for a more accurate reflection of its strengths and weaknesses. On the AP test itself, a reader will rate your essay on a scale of 1 to 9, with 9 being the highest.

Rate each category from 9 (high) to 0 (low).

# QUESTION 1

**SELF-EVALUATION**

Overall Impression     _____

Understanding of the Text     _____

Organization and Development     _____

Use of Sentences     _____

Word Choice (Diction)     _____

Grammar and Usage     _____

TOTAL     _____

    Divide by 6 for final score     _____

**OBJECTIVE EVALUATION**

Overall Impression     _____

Understanding of the Text     _____

Organization and Development     _____

Use of Sentences     _____

Word Choice (Diction)     _____

Grammar and Usage     _____

TOTAL     _____

    Divide by 6 for final score     _____

# QUESTION 2

**SELF-EVALUATION**

Overall Impression     _____

Understanding of the Text     _____

Organization and Development     _____

Use of Sentences     _____

Word Choice (Diction)     _____

Grammar and Usage     _____

TOTAL     _____

    Divide by 6 for final score     _____

**OBJECTIVE EVALUATION**

Overall Impression     _____

Understanding of the Text     _____

Organization and Development     _____

Use of Sentences     _____

Word Choice (Diction)     _____

Grammar and Usage     _____

TOTAL     _____

    Divide by 6 for final score     _____

# QUESTION 3

**SELF-EVALUATION**

Overall Impression     _____

Understanding of the Text     _____

Organization and Development     _____

Use of Sentences     _____

Word Choice (Diction)     _____

Grammar and Usage     _____

TOTAL     _____

    Divide by 6 for final score     _____

**OBJECTIVE EVALUATION**

Overall Impression     _____

Understanding of the Text     _____

Organization and Development     _____

Use of Sentences     _____

Word Choice (Diction)     _____

Grammar and Usage     _____

TOTAL     _____

    Divide by 6 for final score     _____

# Chapter 1

## ABOUT ANSWERING MULTIPLE-CHOICE QUESTIONS

The questions in the multiple-choice section of the AP English Language and Composition exam ask you about passages from a variety of sources, rhetorical modes, historical eras, literary periods, and disciplines. You may read passages from commentaries, autobiographies, diaries and journals, biographies, historical accounts, or passages from essays about politics, science, nature, and the arts. In this chapter, you will find some basic information about Section I of the test, and you will develop an effective strategy for acing the multiple-choice section of the test.

On the Advanced Placement examination, you will discover that most of the multiple-choice questions assess how carefully you read, how well you interpret what you read, and how well you analyze literature. Some questions will ask you about grammar, mechanics, rhetorical modes of writing, structure, organization, or development.

You may have taken hundreds of multiple-choice tests during your time in school. The multiple-choice questions on the AP English exam really are not that different. Of course, there is a lot riding on the AP test, but just like any other standardized test, if you have studied and you know some test-taking techniques, you can do well.

## PRACTICE PLAN

### Study Strategy

*Check the* Practice Plan for Studying for the AP English Language and Composition Test, *pp. 10–14.*

Chapter 1 presents some general strategies for taking the objective portion of the Advanced Placement test. In addition, you will learn some special techniques that will allow you to score your highest. You will also have opportunities to practice what you are learning.

Use the *Diagnostic Test* and *Practice Test 1* as tools to improve your objective test-taking skills. Use the techniques explained in this chapter to practice answering multiple-choice questions on the selections. Correct your responses with the *Quick-Score Answers* provided for each test. If you do not understand why an answer is correct, refer to the explanations given after the *Quick-Score Answers*. It is a good idea to read the answer explanations to all the questions—even the ones you answered correctly—because you may find ideas or tips that will help you better analyze the answer choices to questions on the next *Practice Test* that you take and on the real test.

After you have finished reviewing all the answers, ask yourself what your weak points are and what you can do to improve. Review the strategies in this chapter. Then try taking the next *Practice Test.* Remember the following test-taking tips:

- Carefully apply the test-taking system that you will be learning in this chapter.

- Work the system to get more correct responses.

- Pay attention to your time, and strive to answer more questions in the time period.

See how much you can improve your score each time you take a *Practice Test.*

# BASIC INFORMATION ABOUT THE MULTIPLE-CHOICE SECTION

## FAST FACTS

1. Section I consists of 50 to 55 multiple-choice questions, with five choices for each.

2. Section I has four to five prose passages, and each selection has approximately 10 to 15 questions.

3. You will have 60 minutes to answer all of the questions.

4. The multiple-choice questions require the ability

   - to analyze rhetorical and linguistic choices.

   - to identify stylistic effects that result from word choice.

   - to critically examine prose selections.

   - to understand an author's meaning and purpose.

   - to recognize structural organization.

   - to comprehend rhetorical modes.

   - to analyze syntax, figurative language, style, and tone.

5. The test requires that you understand the terms and conventions of English and use the skills of critical reading and literary analysis.

**Red Alert!**

*You will have approximately 1 minute to answer each multiple-choice question.*

6. You receive 1 point for each correct answer you give. You receive no points for each question you leave blank. If you answer incorrectly, one-quarter point is subtracted. This is the guessing penalty. We will discuss this penalty in detail later in this chapter.

7. Section I accounts for 45 percent of your final composite score.

Besides the obvious importance of understanding the material, you have probably discovered during your educational career that there are three significant considerations when taking multiple-choice tests:

- Effective reading and analysis of test material

- Time management

- Educated guesses

The consequences of failing to do any of these can affect your score:

- If you fail to read the selections or the questions skillfully, you may make errors that are unnecessary.

- If you neglect time, you may miss opportunities for showing what you know.

- If you do not make educated guesses to answer questions about which you are not positive, then you are missing out on a higher score.

How do you prevent these things from happening and ensure your highest score? You need to develop a plan to read effectively, to manage your time well, and to use all your knowledge to the best possible effect.

# CREATING A PLAN OF ATTACK

Consider the following steps to help you create an effective plan of attack for Section I:

1. Be aware of the time, and pace yourself.

2. Select the order in which to tackle the passages.

3. Read the passages.

4. Answer the questions.

Let's examine the steps in detail.

# PACING YOURSELF

The first part of the strategy for acing the multiple-choice section is time awareness. Since you have 60 minutes for Section I, give yourself approximately 11 to 14 minutes for each of the passages, depending on whether there are four or five selections. (You will see under *Setting Priorities* why it's not 12 to 15 minutes.) Use that 11-to-14-minute time period as a guideline. If you find you are spending significantly more time per section, speed up. In the event that you finish with time to spare, revisit any problem passages to see if you can answer questions that you left blank.

If, as the hour comes to an end, you find that you have only 5 or so minutes and another passage to complete, try this technique. Do not read the passage; read the questions instead. Some questions, such as those that ask about vocabulary, can be answered by reading the lines identified and a few lines above and below to understand the context. Other questions ask specific information about specific portions of the selection. Answer these sorts of questions when time is short.

# SETTING PRIORITIES

The first active step to take is prioritizing the passages. Quickly scan the passages (this is where the extra 4 to 5 minutes come in) to find which ones seem difficult to you and which seem easier. You do not have to complete questions or passages in the order they appear on the test. Do the most difficult one last and the easiest one first. Read and answer the other passages according to how difficult they seem. Don't spend time agonizing over the order, or you'll lose your advantage in answering the easiest selection first.

# EFFECTIVE STRATEGIES FOR READING SELECTIONS

The first step is obvious: Read the selections. The passages can vary from a few short paragraphs to lengthy sections. Some selections may be from fictional works, but more than likely, the passages will be taken from essays, articles, letters, histories, and other types of nonfiction.

- Begin by skimming the selection. Take only 30 seconds or so to do this. You want an overview at this point; don't worry about the details.

- Then, concentrate and read the selection carefully. Read for a clear, specific understanding of the writer's main idea—the underlying communication that the writer is trying to make. It is not details but the fundamental message that you, the reader, are supposed to receive.

# CRITICAL READING SKILLS

**Test-Taking Strategy**

*Devise a system for highlighting the key elements you read, such as circling, underlining, using brackets and parentheses, or using codes (e.g., "F" for fact and "O" for opinion).*

To do well on the AP test, however, you must do more than understand what you read. The test asks you to make judgments about what you are reading, analyze such elements as purpose and style, and evaluate the selections. A critical reader uses the following skills to read effectively:

- Establishing the facts

- Analyzing the reasoning

- Identifying the elements of style

- Recognizing your own response

- Evaluating the literature

- Determining its significance

- Comparing and contrasting the work to other literature

# ANALYZING THE TYPES OF QUESTIONS

The ideal is to know the correct answer as soon as you read the question, but that does not always happen. If you can identify the type of question you are facing, you can employ the best strategies to answer it correctly.

## COMPREHENSION QUESTIONS

Most of the multiple-choice questions will test how carefully you read and how well you interpret what you read. These comprehension questions fall into several categories: main idea, rhetoric, modes of discourse, definitions, meaning and purpose, form, organization, structure, and development.

- **Main Idea Questions.** This type of question frequently appears on the AP English Language Test. The question measures your ability to identify the author's ideas, attitude, and tone. A main idea question may also require you to identify the subject of the passage or to select the choice that best tells what the passage is about. Often, you must piece together facts and make an inference based on those facts.

Most inference questions will include one of these key words: *think, predict, indicate, feel, probably, seem, imply, suggest, assume, infer,* and *most likely.* When you come upon a question that contains one of these terms, return to the selection to find specific sentences that the question refers to, and make a sound generalization based on the clues. Skimming the first and last paragraphs of a passage is another helpful technique for answering these questions because writers often state their topic in the beginning or the end of a selection. Remember that in answering an inference question, you are making a guess, but the best guess is based on facts from the selection.

- **Rhetoric Questions.** A great many of the questions on the exam are in this category. Questions about rhetoric might ask about syntax, point of view, or figurative language. To answer these questions, you must know how language works within a given passage. Not only must you be able to recognize these devices, but you must understand the effects these elements have on the piece of writing.

- **Mode Questions.** A few questions ask you to identify the various rhetorical modes that writers employ. You must understand the differences among narration, exposition, description, and persuasion. Knowing why an author is particularly effective at using a specific mode will help you with other types of questions.

**Study Strategy**

*As you answer multiple-choice questions in the* Practice Tests, *try to identify the category of each one. Knowing the question type will help you to identify the best strategy to use for answering the question.*

- **Definition Questions.** These are basically vocabulary questions about difficult words in a passage or about ordinary words that are used with a special meaning. Use the context surrounding the word or phrase in the question to arrive at its meaning. Reread the sentence in which the word appears, and then substitute each of the possible choices to see which is closest in meaning. To get the full sense of the idea, you may need to read the sentences that surround the one containing the word or phrase in question. Avoid choosing a word or phrase that looks or sounds like the word to be defined, unless you have checked it in context.

- **Tone or Purpose Questions.** These frequently asked questions ask you to determine how or why the author wrote the material. The tone reflects the writer's attitude toward the subject and the audience. The purpose defines the effect the author wants to have upon the audience. Understanding the tone helps you to understand the purpose. Writers convey purpose through their choice of words and the impression those words create. Some possible tones are *admiration, adoration, optimism, contempt, pride, objectivity, disappointment, respect, surprise, anger, regret, irony, indignation, suspicion, pessimism,* and *amusement.*

- **Form Questions.** Form is the method of organization that a writer uses. As you read, observe the patterns of organization used. While some authors will use only one form, others may use a combination. Be aware of structure, organization, and development. Look for comparison and contrast, cause and effect, order of importance, logical sequence of events, and spatial order.

## FACTUAL KNOWLEDGE QUESTIONS

There may be a few other question types that appear on the test.

- **English Language Questions.** These questions may test your knowledge of English grammar, punctuation, or mechanics, or they may test your understanding of literary terminology.

- **Cultural Questions.** This kind of question tests your knowledge of facts that are a part of our civilization. Well-educated people should know this type of information.

# ATTACKING THE QUESTIONS: STRATEGIES FOR ACING THE MULTIPLE-CHOICE SECTION

Remember that the more multiple-choice questions you answer correctly, the less pressure you will have to do exceptionally well on the three essays. The following test-taking strategies, combined with your use of critical reading skills, will help you do well on Section I.

## READING THE SELECTIONS

- Most passages have no titles. If a selection is titled, think about what it tells you about the work. You may get a sense of the subject and theme just from the title.

- If there is no title, and there probably won't be, look for the topic sentence or thesis statement. In most writing, you will find it near the beginning. However, since AP exams ask you about challenging literature, you may find the topic sentence at the end or in the middle of the selection. Or you may find that the thesis is implied as opposed to stated.

- Scan the passages to decide the order in which you want to answer them. You do not have to answer the selections in the order presented. You can and should answer the selections and then the questions for each selection in the order that works for you. By showing yourself that you know answers, you build self-confidence.

- After you have decided the order in which you wish to answer the selections, skim for an overall impression of the selection. Then, read the selection carefully. Do not skip over confusing sentences. Repeat this process each time you begin a new selection.

- As you read, highlight words and sentences that seem significant. However, don't spend a great deal of time on this.

- As you read, observe patterns of organization that the writer employs. Patterns may follow a certain sequence or order, set up a compare-and-contrast situation, offer a problem and solution, show cause and effect, or offer a series of examples. Some authors may use more than one system of organization across paragraphs.

- Mentally paraphrase the passages. Paraphrasing helps you to discover the subject and the organization of the selection or the thesis and supporting arguments. The writer's style, transitions, sentence types, language, and literary devices become clear. You can see the framework of the passage in a paraphrase.

- Recall what you can about the author, the literary form, and the historical period.

## IDENTIFYING THE QUESTION TYPE

- Remember that there are six major types of multiple-choice questions: *main idea, rhetoric, mode, definition, tone* or *purpose,* and *form.* You may also find a few factual knowledge or cultural questions.

- When answering a main-idea question, the correct choice must be entirely true and include as much relevant information as possible. In many questions, two or three choices might be correct. However, the answer that is most complete is the one to choose.

- When you are asked to make judgments about what is inferred or implied in a selection, you must put together clues from the passage. You must be able to support your answer with specific facts or examples from the selection.

- Questions that ask about the meaning of words or phrases are best answered by substituting your choice in the sentence or paragraph. If the choice makes sense, you have the correct answer.

- In answering a question about tone or purpose, pay attention to word choice. This type of question asks you to determine how or why the writer created the selection. Authors convey that information through diction.

## ANSWERING THE QUESTIONS

- Reread lines, sentences, or paragraphs that are identified in the questions. In fact, scan or reread any selection if you do not immediately know the answer to a question.

- Just as you choose the order to attack the passages, choose how you wish to answer the multiple-choice questions. If you understand the passage, answer the questions in order.

- If you are not confident about a passage, skip difficult questions, and answer the easy ones first. Be sure to mark in the test booklet the ones you have not answered. If you skip questions, check to be sure that you also skip that number on your answer sheet.

## STRATEGIES FOR ANSWERING OBJECTIVE QUESTIONS/ MAKING EDUCATED GUESSES

| ANSWER CHOICE | REASON TO ELIMINATE |
|---|---|
| 1. too narrow | too small a section of the selection covered, based on the question |
| 2. too broad | an area wider than the selection covered, based on the question |
| 3. irrelevant | • nothing to do with the passage<br>• relevant to the selection but not the question |
| 4. incorrect | • distortion of the facts in the selection<br>• contradiction of the facts in the selection |
| 5. illogical | • not supported by facts in the passage<br>• not supported by cited passage from the selection |
| 6. similar choices | GO BACK AND REVIEW 1-5 TO TEASE OUT THE DIFFERENCES. |
| 7. *not/except* | answers that correctly represent the selection |

- Read the question stem carefully, and be sure to read all the answer choices. Since the directions often ask for the best answer, several choices may be logical. Look for the most inclusive answer or the generalization.

- Look for consistency in the answers to the questions about a passage. If a choice seems contradictory to other answers you have given, rethink that choice.

- Many times, the key to finding the correct answer is to narrow the choices and to make an intelligent guess. Eliminate some answers by finding those that are obviously unrelated, illogical, or incorrect. Having reduced the number of choices, you can make an educated guess from among the remaining possibilities. Use the techniques presented in the chart above to reduce the number of choices.

The *not/except* questions are tricky. You can forget what it is you are looking for and choose a correct answer for the selection but the wrong answer for the question. Convoluted? Yes; as you go through each answer, ask yourself, "Is this statement true about the selection?" If you answer "yes," cross off the answer and keep going until you find a choice to which you can answer "no."

# LEARN THE DIRECTIONS NOW

It is a good idea to familiarize yourself with the instructions for each part of the test before the real test day. Knowing ahead of time what you have to do can save you time on the day of the test—perhaps enough to answer another one or two questions.

## GENERAL DIRECTIONS FOR THE AP ENGLISH LANGUAGE AND COMPOSITION TEST

On the front page of your test booklet, you will find some information about the test. Because you have studied this book, none of it should be new to you, and much of it is similar to other standardized tests you have taken.

The page will tell you that the following exam will take 3 hours—1 hour for the multiple-choice section and 2 hours for the three essays—and that there are two booklets for this exam, one for the multiple-choice section and one for the essays.

The page will also tell you that SECTION I—

- is 1 hour.

- has 50 questions (or some number from 50 to 60).

- counts for 45 percent of your total grade.

Then, you will find a sentence in capital letters that tells you not to open your exam booklet until the monitor tells you to open it.

Other instructions will tell you to be careful to fill in only ovals 1 through 50 (or whatever the number is) in Section I on your separate answer sheet. Fill in each oval completely. If you erase an answer, erase it completely. You will not receive any credit for work done in the test booklet, but you may use it for making notes.

You will find not only a paragraph about the guessing penalty—deduction of one-quarter point for every wrong answer—but also words of advice about guessing if you know something about the question and can eliminate several of the answers.

The final paragraph will remind you to work effectively and to pace yourself. You are told that not everyone will be able to answer all the questions. The page suggests that you skip questions that are difficult and come back to them if you have time—just what we have been telling you.

## DIRECTIONS FOR THE MULTIPLE-CHOICE SECTION

The specific directions for Section I read like this:

---

### Section I
### Time—60 minutes

**Directions:** This section consists of selections of literature and questions on their content, style, and form. After you have read each passage, select the response that best answers the question, and mark the space on the answer sheet.

---

In general, the directions for each selection and its accompanying multiple-choice questions read like this:

> **Questions 1 through 15.** Read the passage carefully and then choose the answers to the questions.

# A FINAL WORD OF ADVICE: EDUCATED GUESSING

One technique that is especially helpful for achieving your best score is educated guessing. Use this technique when you do not immediately know the correct answer.

- Ignore answers that are obviously wrong. See the table on page 71, "Strategies for Answering Objective Questions/Making Educated Guesses," for reasons why you should eliminate certain types of answer choices.

| **Test-Taking Strategy** |
|---|

*A partially correct answer is a partially incorrect answer—and a quarter-point deduction.*

- Discard choices in which part of the response is incorrect.

- Revisit remaining answers to discover which seems more correct. Remember to eliminate any response that has anything wrong about it.

- Choose the answer you feel is right. Trust yourself. Your subconscious usually will guide you to the correct choice. Do not argue with yourself.

You're probably thinking about the quarter-point penalty for an incorrect answer, and are wondering if taking a chance is worth the possible point loss. Recognize that if you use this technique, your chances of scoring higher are excellent. You are not guessing but making an educated guess. You will have to answer 4 questions incorrectly to lose a single point, but answering even 1 question out of 4 correctly that you are not sure about will give you a quarter-point edge. If you have an idea about which choice is correct, act on it. Even the College Board suggests that you try—as long as you can eliminate some answer choices.

# PRACTICE

Now, take the time to practice what you have just learned. Read the selection below that was written in the eighteenth century by Hector St. John de Crèvecoeur. Apply the suggestions and strategies to determine the right answer. Circle the correct answer, and then write out your reasoning on the lines provided below each question.

If you do not understand the question, you may check the explanation immediately. You may refer to the answers question by question, or you may wish to score the entire section at one time. No matter which method you choose, read all the explanations against your own. See where your reasoning and ours differ. If your answer is incorrect, what is the flaw in your reasoning? If your answer is correct, is your reasoning the same as ours, or did we add to your understanding of the question and the process of arriving at the answer?

**Directions:** This section consists of selections of literature and questions on their content, style, and form. After you have read each passage, choose the best response to each question.

**Questions 1 through 10.** Read the passage carefully, and then choose the answers to the questions.

## FROM THE THIRD ESSAY OF
## *LETTERS FROM AN AMERICAN FARMER*

Line  What attachment can a poor European emigrant have for a country where he had nothing? The knowledge of the language, the love of a few kindred as poor as himself, were the only cords that tied him: his country is now that which gives him land, bread, protection, and
5  consequence. *Ubi panis ibi patria** is the motto of all emigrants. What then is the American, this new man? He is either an European, or the descendant of an European, hence that strange mixture of blood, which you will find in no other country. I could point out to you a family whose grandfather was an Englishman, whose wife was
10  Dutch, whose son married a French woman, and whose present four sons have now four wives of different nations. *He* is an American, who, leaving behind him all his ancient prejudices and manners, receives new ones from the new mode of life he has embraced, the government he obeys, and the new rank he holds. He becomes an

---

* Where bread is, there is one's country.

15    American by being received in the broad lap of our great *Alma
      Mater.*** Here individuals of all nations are melted into a new race of
      men, whose labors and posterity will one day cause great changes in
      the world. Americans are the western pilgrims, who are carrying
      along with them that great mass of arts, sciences, vigor, and industry
20    which began long since in the east; they will finish the great circle.
      The Americans were once scattered all over Europe; here they are
      incorporated into one of the finest systems of population which has
      ever appeared, and which will hereafter become distinct by the
      power of the different climates they inhabit. The American ought
25    therefore to love this country much better than that wherein either
      he or his forefathers were born. Here the rewards of his industry
      follow with equal steps the progress of his labor; his labor is founded
      on the basis of nature, *self-interest;* can it want a stronger allurement?
      Wives and children, who before in vain demanded of him a morsel of
30    bread, now, fat and frolicsome, gladly help their father to clear those
      fields whence exuberant crops are to arise to feed and to clothe them
      all; without any part being claimed, either by a despotic prince, a rich
      abbot, or a mighty lord. Here religion demands but little of him; a
      small voluntary salary to the minister, and gratitude to God; can he
35    refuse these? The American is a new man, who acts upon principles;
      he must therefore entertain new ideas, and form new opinions. From
      involuntary idleness, servile dependence, penury, and useless labor,
      he has passed to toils of a very different nature, rewarded by ample
      subsistence.—This is an American.

1.    Which of the following best describes the author's view of
      American society?

      (A)  A melting pot
      (B)  Lacking in prejudices
      (C)  Devoid of principles
      (D)  Class conscious
      (E)  Lawless

      _____

      _____

      _____

      _____

      _____

_____

** Beloved mother

2. Considering diction, tone, and rhetorical mode, how can this selection best be characterized?

   (A) An eloquent expression of the American dream
   (B) A charming narrative
   (C) An ironic discourse
   (D) A subtle criticism of the new American nation
   (E) A commentary directed at reforming European countries

   _____

   _____

   _____

   _____

   _____

3. Which of the following is not a reason for Americans to love this country more than that of their ancestors?

   (A) Religion demands little of them.
   (B) Rewards follow their labor.
   (C) Abbots, princes, or lords do not set a levy on crops.
   (D) The labor of Americans is founded on their own self-interest.
   (E) Charity is freely given.

   _____

   _____

   _____

   _____

   _____

**4.** In the next to the last sentence of the excerpt (line 37) what is the meaning of the word "penury"?

(A) Largess
(B) Imprisonment
(C) Destitution
(D) Hard work
(E) Corporal punishment

_____

_____

_____

_____

_____

**5.** The semicolon after the word "Europe" in line 21 serves which of the following purposes?

(A) It sets off two or more independent clauses.
(B) It separates items in a series.
(C) It separates parenthetical elements.
(D) It establishes a new thought.
(E) It sets off an introductory phrase.

_____

_____

_____

_____

_____

6. What literary device is used to describe the new American in this sentence, "He becomes an American by being received in the broad lap of our great *Alma Mater*"?

   (A) Simile
   (B) Personification
   (C) Metaphor
   (D) Apostrophe
   (E) Hyperbole

   _____

   _____

   _____

   _____

   _____

7. The organization of the selection could best be characterized as

   (A) stream of consciousness
   (B) comparison
   (C) order of importance
   (D) contrast
   (E) argumentation

   _____

   _____

   _____

   _____

   _____

8. Which of the following is the literary form that the writer has chosen to employ?

   (A) Narrative
   (B) Personal letter
   (C) Expository article
   (D) Epistle
   (E) Dialogue

   _____

   _____

   _____

   _____

   _____

9. What is the best synonym for the word "exuberant" in line 31?

   (A) Sparse
   (B) Abundant
   (C) Harvested
   (D) Withered
   (E) Enthusiastic

   _____

   _____

   _____

   _____

   _____

10. Which of the following statements best presents the writer's theme?

    (A) Americans will become self-absorbed.
    (B) The new nation will become an imperialist power.
    (C) America will cause worldwide changes.
    (D) American citizens will develop a rigid class structure.
    (E) The people will destroy their own country because of their excesses.

    _____

    _____

    _____

    _____

    _____

## Quick-Score Answers

| | | | | |
|---|---|---|---|---|
| 1. A | 3. E | 5. A | 7. C | 9. B |
| 2. A | 4. C | 6. B | 8. D | 10. C |

**Test-Taking Strategy**

*Did you recognize this as a tone question? Asking for the author's view is another way of asking what his or her attitude is toward the subject of the piece.*

1.  **The correct answer is (A).** The challenge on this question is to sift through the responses to select the one that most accurately describes the author's vision of America. Choice (E) is not mentioned in the selection and can be eliminated immediately. The information in each of choices (A) through (D) is mentioned in the passage in one form or another, so you might select one of these four because they sound familiar. A scanning of the passage, however, shows that the only response that truly reflects the author's words is choice (A), "a melting pot." Choice (B) is a detail that supports choice (A). Choices (C) and (D) contradict the attitude of the passage.

2.  **The correct answer is (A).** Sometimes, the obvious choice is the correct answer. Choices (C), (D), and (E) do not reflect the tone, mode, or subject matter that is addressed by the author. Your decision should have been between choices (A) and (B). Choice (B) is in the running only because of the word *charming*. The style is arguably charming, but it is not a narrative.

3.  **The correct answer is (E).** The key to choosing the correct answer for this question is in noting the word *not* in the question. You are looking for the one answer in the series that is either opposite to or not included in the writer's thesis. In this case, the subject of "charity," choice (E), is never mentioned in the passage.

**Test-Taking Strategy**

*Substituting the definitions in context will help you figure out definition questions.*

4.  **The correct answer is (C).** This is a straightforward vocabulary question, which makes it easy if you know the meaning of the word. If you are uncertain of the meaning, find the given word in context, and substitute each of the answer choices. By doing so, some answers may be eliminated, and one may clearly stand out as the correct answer. In this case, inserting the answer choices in context of line 37 easily eliminates choices (A) and (D) because gifts and hard work would not logically appear in the same series as involuntary idleness and useless labor. Because involuntary idleness might mean either imprisonment or unemployment, eliminate choices (B) and (E) because the author would probably not repeat the same idea. Also corporal punishment, choice (E), does not seem to fit in a series about working or not working. That leaves choice (C), which means destitute or penniless.

5. **The correct answer is (A).** Choice (B) can be eliminated because there is neither a series nor a parenthetical element that eliminates choice (C). Choice (D) does not follow any grammar rule, and there is no introductory phrase, choice (E), in the sentence. There are, however, two independent clauses, choice (A).

**Test-Taking Strategy**

*Read all the answer choices. Don't jump too quickly at an answer because it seems right. Be sure it is right by reviewing all the choices.*

6. **The correct answer is (B).** Using the process of elimination is a good strategy to use for determining the answer when you are not sure about the responses. You can eliminate choice (A) immediately because a simile is a figure of speech that includes *as* or *like*. Choice (B) might be correct because the author is attributing a lap to America, which seems like it is personification, but keep reading the answer choices. Reject choice (C) because a metaphor is an implied comparison. Apostrophe, choice (D), is a literary device of calling out to an imaginary, dead, or absent person; to a place, thing, or personified abstraction; or to begin a poem or make a dramatic break. Neither that nor choice (E), hyperbole, an obvious, lavish exaggeration or overstatement, fits the sentence. That leaves choice (B) as the only correct response.

7. **The correct answer is (C).** This question tests your ability to recognize types of organization and structure. Eliminate choices (A) and (E) because they do not apply to the selection. There is nothing that could be considered stream of consciousness about the selection. It might be persuasive, a form of argumentation, but argumentation is a mode of discourse, not a form of organization. While the writer does seem to compare, choice (B), and contrast, choice (D), he has arranged his thoughts to rise in power and conclude on a very strong note.

8. **The correct answer is (D).** The author is writing an epistle, or literary letter, which is a formal composition written in the form of a letter that is addressed to a distant person or group of people. Unlike personal letters, choice (B), which are more conversational and private, epistles are carefully crafted literary works that are intended for a general audience. Your best hint for this is in the title of the selection. Eliminate choices (A) and (E) since there is no story being told and no discussion among people. While you may have considered choice (C), the passage is less expository than persuasive.

9. **The correct answer is (B).** This is not so much a vocabulary drill as it is a test of your comprehension. None of the responses are an exact synonym for the word *exuberant* as we use the word today. You must determine the definition from the context of the sentence. Substitute each of the proposed responses, and select the one that makes the most sense, keeping in mind the tone and theme of the author. Neither *sparse*, choice (A), nor *withered*, choice (D), would likely be the correct response given the rest of the sentence. *Harvested*, choice (C), does not make sense before the crops grow. *Enthusiastic*, choice (E), is a synonym for *exuberant*, but it does not make sense in context. *Abundant*, choice (B), best captures the author's meaning.

10. **The correct answer is (C).** You can eliminate all but the correct answer in this question by keeping in mind the general tone of the author. The writer is very positive about America and America's future. Four of the five possibilities, choices (A), (B), (D), and (E), are negative. A clue to the answer can be found in the sentence, "Here individuals of all nations are melted into a new race of men, whose labors and posterity will one day cause great changes in the world." (lines 16–18)

Now that you have a sense of the logic involved in acing Section I of the test, try *Practice Set 1* and *Practice Set 2*. Study the explanations for choosing the correct answers. If you are still unsure of your ability with multiple-choice questions, continue on with *Practice Set 3* and *Practice Set 4*.

# PRACTICE SET 1

> **Directions:** This section consists of selections of literature and questions on their content, style, and form. After you have read each passage, choose the best response to each question.

**Questions 1 through 10.** Read the passage carefully, and then choose the answers to the questions.

## From *The Law of the Great Peace* from the Iroquois Confederacy

Line When a candidate is to be installed, he shall furnish four strings of
shells or wampum one span in length bound together at one end.
Such will constitute the evidence of his pledge to the chiefs of the
League that he will live according to the Constitution of the Great
5 Peace and exercise justice in all affairs. When the pledge is furnished,
the Speaker of the Council must hold the shell strings in his hand and
address the opposite side of the Council Fire, and he shall begin his
address saying:

Now behold him. He has now become a chief of the League. See
10 how splendid he looks.

An address may then follow. At the end of it he shall send the
bunch of shell strings to the opposite side, and they shall be received
as evidence of the pledge. Then shall the opposite side say:

We now do crown you with the sacred emblem of the deer's
15 antlers, the emblem of your chieftainship. You shall now
become a mentor of the people of the Five Nations. The
thickness of your skin shall be seven spans, which is to say that
you will be proof against anger, offensive actions, and criticism.
Your heart shall be filled with peace and good will. Your mind
20 shall be filled with a yearning for the welfare of the people of
the League. With endless patience you shall carry out your duty
and your firmness shall be tempered with tenderness for your
people. Neither anger nor fury shall find lodging in your mind.
All your words and actions shall be marked with calm delibera-
25 tion. In all your deliberations in law-making, in all your official
acts, self-interest shall be cast away. Do not cast over your
shoulder behind you the warnings of your nephews and nieces
should they chide you for any error or wrong you may do, but
return to the way of the Great Lake which is right and just. Look
30 and listen for the welfare of the whole people, and have always

in view not only the present, but also the coming generations, even those whose faces are yet beneath the surface of the ground—the unborn of the future Nation.

1. According to this passage, which of the following is conduct that the leaders would be least likely to encourage in a new chief?

   (A) Punish criticism and offensive behavior.
   (B) Be mindful of future generations.
   (C) Be calm in words and actions.
   (D) Consider the welfare of all people.
   (E) Be a stern but fair lawmaker.

2. The clause "The thickness of your skin shall be seven spans" (lines 16–17) is an example of which of the following?

   (A) Simile
   (B) Analogy
   (C) Visual imagery
   (D) Metaphor
   (E) Alliteration

3. How does the speaker use rhetoric and style in the second speech of the selection to communicate the conduct expected of a new chief?

   (A) Declarative sentences, formal diction
   (B) Declarative sentences, future tenses
   (C) Imperative sentences, formal diction
   (D) Imperative sentences, future tenses
   (E) Imperative sentences, active verbs

4. In the context of this passage, the best interpretation of the word "span" (line 17) is:

   (A) span of a life
   (B) span of a hand
   (C) span of an arrow
   (D) the wing span of an eagle
   (E) span of an arm

5. Which of the following is the best interpretation of the sentence "Neither anger nor fury shall find lodging in your mind" (line 23)?

   (A) A chief does not become angry.
   (B) A chief does not rule with anger.
   (C) A chief does not remain angry.
   (D) A chief does not display anger.
   (E) A chief does not let anger rule him.

6. Which of the following can you infer about Native American culture from the imperatives and admonitions included in the installation ceremony?

   I. Family is important.
   II. A chief's conduct is important.
   III. Anger is offensive.

   (A) I only
   (B) II only
   (C) III only
   (D) I and II
   (E) I and III

7. The mode of this selection as a whole is best described as

   (A) argumentative
   (B) narrative
   (C) exposition
   (D) historical treatise
   (E) description

8. After careful rhetorical analysis of the selection, which of the following best describes the genesis of the speech?

   (A) Tribal customs
   (B) Logic
   (C) Ethics
   (D) Emotion
   (E) Spirituality

9. The sentence "With endless patience you shall carry out your duty and your firmness shall be tempered with tenderness for your people" contains all of the following EXCEPT

(A) a verb in the passive voice
(B) parallel structure
(C) specific details
(D) a participial phrase
(E) courtly diction

10. In the sentence "Do not cast . . . right and just" (lines 26–29), what is the best meaning of the word "chide"?

(A) Judge
(B) Blame
(C) Reprove
(D) Criticism
(E) Reprimand

# ANSWERS AND EXPLANATIONS FOR PRACTICE SET 1

| Quick-Score Answers | | | | |
|---|---|---|---|---|
| 1. A | 3. C | 5. E | 7. C | 9. D |
| 2. C | 4. B | 6. B | 8. C | 10. C |

**Test-Taking Strategy**

*Did you note the word* least *in the question stem? This question is a type of* not/except *question.*

**Study Strategy**

*See Chapter 4 for a quick review of literary and rhetorical terms.*

1. **The correct answer is (A).** This question asks you to find the one answer that is incorrect. You could return to the passage and skim to find the behaviors required. Or you could also use common sense to recognize that choices (B), (C), (D), and (E) are behaviors that are desirable in a leader, which eliminates those as the answer, because you are being asked to find the behavior that is least likely to be encouraged in a leader. Choice (A) is not behavior that is desirable in a leader, so it is the correct answer. If you found the probable answer by using this logic, you could confirm your answer choice by scanning the selection.

2. **The correct answer is (C).** This question requires your knowledge of literary elements. Choice (A), simile, is a comparison that requires the word *like* or *as*, so it can be eliminated. Choice (B), an analogy, or comparison of similar things, is incorrect because there is no comparison in the sentence. A metaphor, choice (D), is another type of comparison in which one thing is referred to as another; it, too, is incorrect. Choice (E), alliteration, requires a series of words beginning with the same sound, so it can be eliminated.

3. **The correct answer is (C).** This question tests your knowledge of English grammar. The sentence is imperative; the use of *shall* instead of the usual *will* indicates a demand. *Shall* is not a form of the verb *to be*, but it is a helping verb. A declarative sentence, choices (A) and (B), simply states an idea, which is not the case here. One clue that the sentences are not exclamatory, choice (D), is the lack of an exclamation point as the end mark. Because the sentences do not ask a question, they cannot be interrogative, choice (E).

4. **The correct answer is (B).** This question asks you to be logical. Thickness of skin could not relate to life span, making choice (A) incorrect. Choices (C), (D), and (E) are illogical, too; seven times the span of either an arrow, a wing, or an arm would not related to the depth of skin. As you probably have learned through your study of history, the hand was commonly used as a measure, making choice (B) the most logical interpretation.

**Test-Taking Strategy**

*When a question asks for the "best" characterization, description, etc., look for the most inclusive answer choice.*

5. **The correct answer is (E).** This is a comprehension question. Choices (B), (C), and (D) all seem appropriate, but the question is asking you for the "best interpretation." Choice (E) is the best because it includes the ideas in choices (B), (C), and (D). Choice (A) is a distracter because the selection does not say a chief cannot become angry, only that that anger should not affect his rule.

6. **The correct answer is (B).** Although anger and family (nephews and nieces) are mentioned in the passage, the fundamental message is the importance of a chief's conduct. Therefore, only choice (B), which mentions the chief's conduct, can be correct. Choice (A), family, and choice (C), the offensiveness of anger, are incorrect because they do not mention conduct. Choice (D) is only partially correct because only conduct is correct. Choice (E) is entirely wrong.

7. **The correct answer is (C).** The question asks you to identify the type of discourse used in the selection. If you recognized that the purpose is to explain how a candidate is installed as a chief of the Iroquois, selecting choice (C), exposition, is easy. If you did not see that, you could use the process of elimination to find the best choice. There is no argument or persuasion occurring, so choice (A) can be ruled out. A narrative, choice (C), tells a story, which is not the mode used here. While there is a great deal of description, choice (E), the purpose of the selection is to present the stages of the ceremony. Choice (D) is a distracter; this is a not a mode of discourse.

8. **The correct answer is (C).** Don't be fooled. This is obviously a tribal custom, choice (A), and there may be some unspoken spiritual overtones, choice (E), but remember the conventions of rhetoric—logic, ethics, and emotion. This passage discusses the conduct that is expected of new chiefs and, hence, clearly evolves from ethics.

**Test-Taking Strategy**

*For a* not/except *question, ask yourself if an answer is correct in relation to the selection. If it is, cross it off and go on to the next answer choice.*

9. **The correct answer is (D).** This question tests your understanding of rhetoric and the conventions of English. You must identify what is NOT in the sentence. The sentence contains a verb, "shall be tempered," in the passive voice, so choice (A) is wrong. The coordinating conjunction, *and,* which joins two independent clauses, establishes parallel structure, thus eliminating choice (B). There are specific details, and the language is courtly, formal, and elegant, so choices (C) and (E) are incorrect. A participial phrase, choice (D), is a verb form that functions as an adjective or adverb. There is no such structure, which makes the only incorrect choice the right answer!

10. **The correct answer is (C).** This is a difficult vocabulary question. Most of the choices make sense in the context of the sentence. Think about the sense of the sentence, and use the process of elimination to find the best definition. You can eliminate choice (D) immediately because, while it suggests a very good possibility, it is a noun, and *chide* is a verb. Look for a verb among the other four choices that is similar in meaning to *criticism*. Since the youth are chiding a chief, you can safely assume that choices (A), (B), and (D) are too harsh. *Reprove,* close in meaning to criticize, is gentler and the best choice.

# PRACTICE SET 2

**Directions:** This section consists of selections of literature and questions on their content, style, and form. After you have read each passage, choose the best response to each question.

**Questions 1 through 10.** Read the passage carefully, and then choose the answers to the questions.

## FROM DECLARATION OF SENTIMENTS

Line When in the course of human events, it becomes necessary for one
portion of the family of man to assume among the people of the
earth a position different from that which they have hitherto occupied, but one to which the laws of nature and nature's God entitle
5 them, decent respect to the opinions of mankind requires that they
should declare the causes that impel them to such a course.

We hold these truths to be self-evident: that all men and women
are created equal; that they are endowed by their Creator with
certain inalienable rights, that among these are life, liberty, and the
10 pursuit of happiness; that to secure these rights governments are
instituted, deriving their just powers from the consent of the governed. When any form of government becomes destructive of these
ends, it is the right of those who suffer from it to refuse allegiance to
it, and to insist upon the institution of a new government, laying its
15 foundation on such principles, and organizing its powers in such
form as to them shall seem most likely to effect their safety and
happiness. Prudence, indeed, will dictate that governments long
established should not be changed for light and transient causes;
accordingly, all experiences hath shown that mankind are more
20 disposed to suffer, while evils are sufferable, than to right themselves
by abolishing the forms to which they are accustomed. But when a
long train of abuses and usurpations, pursuing invariably the same
object evinces a design to reduce them under absolute despotism, it
is their duty to throw off such government, and to provide new
25 guards for their future security. Such has been the patient sufferance
of the women under this government, and such is now the necessity
which constrains them to demand the equal station to which they are
entitled.

The history of mankind is a history of repeated injuries and
30 usurpations on the part of man toward women, having in direct
object the establishment of an absolute tyranny over her. . . . [An
explanation of fifteen specific grievances follows this paragraph.]

He has endeavored, in every way that he could, to destroy her confidence in her own powers, to lessen her self-respect, and to

35 make her willing to lead a dependent and abject life. Now, in view of this entire disfranchisement of one-half the people of this country, their social and religious degradation, — in view of the unjust laws above mentioned, and because women do feel themselves aggrieved, oppressed, and fraudulently deprived of their most sacred rights, we

40 insist that they have immediate admission to all the rights and privileges which belong to them as citizens of the United States. . . .

—Elizabeth Cady Stanton

1. At the end of the second paragraph, in the sentence beginning "Such has been the patient . . ." (lines 25–28), which of the following is the best meaning for the word "constrains"?

   (A) Restrains
   (B) Coerces
   (C) Encourages
   (D) Demands
   (E) Entitles

2. From your reading of this selection, what does the writer believe about the origin of women's rights?

   (A) They come from government.
   (B) They come from nature.
   (C) They come from God
   (D) They come from society.
   (E) They come from men.

3. The syntax and organization of the passage serve to

   I. establish an extended analogy to the Declaration of Independence
   II. create a powerful argument supporting the writer's position
   III. point out the effects of disenfranchisement

   (A) I only
   (B) I and II
   (C) II and III
   (D) I and III
   (E) I, II, and III

4. In the sentence beginning "He has endeavored . . ." (lines 33–35), the repetition of the infinitive phrases serves which of the following rhetorical functions?

   I. Provides parallel structure to intensify the message
   II. Details the list of grievances
   III. Creates an intellectual tone

   (A) I only
   (B) II only
   (C) III only
   (D) I and II
   (E) II and III

5. The writer emphasizes the evils experienced by women in order to further her argument for

   (A) abolishing all government
   (B) writing powerful statements
   (C) holding demonstrations
   (D) amending the constitution
   (E) demanding equal rights

6. To what does the writer liken the plight of women in the United States?

   (A) To the universal plight of women
   (B) To the plight of wives
   (C) To the plight of all oppressed people
   (D) To America's plight as a colony
   (E) To the plight of slaves

**7.** Which of the following best describes the tone of this passage?

(A) Inspiring, powerful
(B) Serious, angry
(C) Objective, informative
(D) Emotional, pretentious
(E) Dramatic, portentous

**8.** This passage is an example of which of the following modes of discourse?

(A) Argument
(B) Persuasion
(C) Exposition
(D) Narrative
(E) Description

**9.** The passage as a whole can best be described as which of the following?

(A) A commentary about women's suffrage
(B) An indictment of men's tyranny over women
(C) A declaration of independence for women
(D) A feminist diatribe
(E) A political lament

**10.** In the sentence beginning "We hold these truths to be self-evident: . . ." (lines 7–12), the best meaning for the word "inalienable" is

(A) undeniable
(B) fundamental
(C) natural
(D) God-given
(E) not to be taken away

# ANSWERS AND EXPLANATIONS FOR PRACTICE SET 2

| Qick-Score Answers | | | | |
|---|---|---|---|---|
| 1. B | 3. B | 5. E | 7. A | 9. C |
| 2. C | 4. D | 6. D | 8. A | 10. E |

1. **The correct answer is (B).** This vocabulary question presents a challenge. All the choices, with the exception of choice (A), which is an antonym for *constrains* in this context, make sense in the sentence. You want the strongest choice because the sentence needs a word meaning "forces." Choices (C) and (E) are weaker than choices (D) and (B), so you can eliminate them. Choice (D) creates a repetition in the sentence ("which demands them to demand"), so it is not the best choice. Choice (B) remains as the strongest verb and best response.

2. **The correct answer is (C).** The question, which is rather easy, asks you to recall a detail and interpret it. The author, Elizabeth Cady Stanton writes, ". . . they are endowed by their Creator with certain inalienable rights." Ask yourself, what is the Creator? You know that the Creator is not the government, choice (A); society, choice (D); or men, choice (E). You might be able to make a case for nature, choice (B). However, nature is rarely if ever called the Creator, so that choice is not the most accurate.

### Test-Taking Strategy

*For these multiple-response questions, figure out which of the point(s) marked with Roman numerals is correct. Then see which answer choice has the correct Roman numeral(s).*

3. **The correct answer is (B).** Don't be misled. Point III, a part of choices (C), (D), and (E), is a distracter. The effects of disenfranchisement are mentioned, but the question revolves around syntax and organization. Choice (B) is the correct answer because both I and II are used to support the syntax and organization of the passage.

4. **The correct answer is (D).** Point III is a distracter. The repetition of infinitive phrases provides both point I, parallel structure, and point II, a list of grievances, so choice (D) is the correct answer because it is the only answer that has both points I and II.

5.  **The correct answer is (E).** This comprehension question asks for the main idea. Ask yourself, what point is the writer making? Stanton certainly does not advocate the overthrow of all governments; she wants the rules of the U.S. government to apply fairly to all citizens, so choice (A) is incorrect. The writer might feel that choices (B) and (C) are good methods for spotlighting the problem, but neither reflect the main purpose of the passage. Choice (D) would be required to gain equal rights, but that is implied in the passage and is not the main idea.

6.  **The correct answer is (D).** This is a cultural question that relies on your knowledge of U.S. history. Just as the British colonists felt that they were denied their rights as citizens by the British, Stanton and her peers felt that U.S. women were denied their rights as citizens by the U.S. government. The remaining choices, (A), (B), (C), and (E), have little or no relationship to the Declaration of Independence.

7.  **The correct answer is (A).** While the article has some elements of choices (B) and (E), neither choice is entirely correct. The document is serious but not necessarily angry, choice (B), and portentous but not necessarily dramatic, choice (E). The passage is argumentative, not objective, so choice (C) is not the answer. Although based on the Declaration of Independence, some readers of the Declaration of the Sentiments might have considered it emotional and pretentious, choice (D), but that is not the tone the author set out to create. That leaves choice (A) as the correct answer.

8.  **The correct answer is (A).** You can immediately eliminate choices (C), (D), and (E) because the selection is not simply informative, does not tell a story, and does not describe a person, place, thing, event, or idea. The answer hinges on your understanding of the difference between persuasion and argumentation. Argumentation is a more powerful type of writing than persuasion. That eliminates choice (B), because this is a very strong piece of writing.

**Test-Taking Strategy**

*Look for clues and consistency among answers in other questions.*

9. **The correct answer is (C).** If you remembered question 6, about the Declaration of Independence, you had a good idea about how to answer this question. The selection advocates female suffrage, not just comments on it, so choice (A) is incorrect. The writer discusses men's tyranny over women, but that is only part of the argument, so you can eliminate choice (B). You can eliminate choices (D) and (E) as inappropriate descriptions of this passage. The word *diatribe*, choice (D), has a negative connotation, and *lament* has a connotation of weakness.

10. **The correct answer is (E).** All the answers for this question make sense. You must pick the best one. While human rights may be undeniable, choice (A); fundamental, choice (B); natural, choice (C); and God-given, choice (D), the most important aspect is that they cannot be made alien; that is, they cannot be taken away, choice (E).

# PRACTICE SET 3

> **Directions:** This section consists of selections of literature and questions on their content, style, and form. After you have read each passage, choose the best response to each question.

**Questions 1 through 10.** Read the passage carefully, and then choose the answers to the following questions.

Line Washington, April 14, 1865
Published in the *New York Herald*, April 15, 1865

Washington was thrown into an intense excitement a few minutes before eleven o'clock this evening, by the announcement
5  that the President and Secretary Seward had been assassinated and were dead.

The wildest excitement prevailed in all parts of the city. Men, women, and children, old and young, rushed to and fro, and the rumors were magnified until we had nearly every member of the
10  Cabinet killed. Some time elapsed before authentic data could be ascertained in regard to the affair.

The President and Mrs. Lincoln were at Ford's theatre, listening to the performance of The American Cousin, occupying a box in the second tier. At the close of the third act a person entered the box
15  occupied by the President, and shot Mr. Lincoln in the head. The shot entered the back of his head, and came out the temple.

The assassin then jumped from the box upon the stage and ran across to the other side, exhibiting a dagger in his hand, flourishing it in a tragical manner, shouting the same words repeated by the
20  desperado at Mr. Seward's house, adding to it, "The South is avenged," and then escaped from the back entrance to the stage, but in his passage dropped his pistol and his hat.

Mr. Lincoln fell forward from his seat, and Mrs. Lincoln fainted.

The moment the astonished audience could realize what
25  happened, the President was taken and carried to Mr. Peterson's house, in Tenth street, opposite the theatre. Medical aid was immediately sent for, and the wound was at first supposed to be fatal, and it was announced that he could not live, but at half-past twelve he is still alive, though in a precarious condition.

1.  This passage is an example of which of the following modes of discourse?

    (A) Description
    (B) Exposition
    (C) Narration
    (D) Persuasion
    (E) Argument

2.  Which of the following best describes the tone of this passage?

    (A) Angry
    (B) Objective
    (C) Dramatic
    (D) Solemn
    (E) Emotional

3.  The sentence from the second paragraph beginning "Men, women, and children, old and young, rushed to and fro. . . ." (lines 7–10) is an example of which of the following?

    (A) Parallelism
    (B) Simple sentence
    (C) Run-on sentence
    (D) Archaic English
    (E) Exaggeration

4.  In the first two paragraphs, the writer's rhetoric and syntax combine to create an impression of

    I.   excitement and chaos
    II.  fear and tragedy
    III. terrible news and uncertainty

    (A) I only
    (B) II only
    (C) III only
    (D) I and II
    (E) I and III

5.  In the fourth paragraph, what is the best meaning of the word "tragical" (line 19)?

    (A) Sorrowful
    (B) Dramatic
    (C) Terrible
    (D) Threatening
    (E) Deadly

6.  In this passage, which of the following rhetorical devices is most evident?

    (A) Appealing to authority
    (B) Massing of factual information
    (C) Abstract generalizations
    (D) Emotional appeal
    (E) Anecdotal information

7.  Which of the following best summarizes the purpose of the passage?

    (A) To discuss the reason for the city's excitement
    (B) To report the news of President Lincoln's death
    (C) To clarify the report of the assassination attempt on President Lincoln
    (D) To report that President Lincoln is still alive
    (E) To give an account of the events at Ford's Theatre

8.  Reviewing the diction of the passage, which of the following best characterizes the writer's style?

    (A) Informal diction
    (B) Colloquial diction
    (C) Slang diction
    (D) Formal diction
    (E) Pretentious diction

9. In this selection, which of the following patterns of organization is most in evidence?

(A) Development by details
(B) Chronology
(C) Cause and effect
(D) Analysis
(E) Synthesis

10. In the last sentence of the last paragraph (lines 26–29), what is the best meaning for the word "precarious"?

(A) Risky
(B) Dangerous
(C) Vulnerable
(D) Uncertain
(E) Treacherous

# ANSWERS AND EXPLANATIONS FOR PRACTICE SET 3

## Quick-Score Answers

| | | | | |
|---|---|---|---|---|
| 1. B | 3. A | 5. B | 7. C | 9. B |
| 2. B | 4. E | 6. E | 8. D | 10. D |

1. **The correct answer is (B).** The passage explains what happened at Lincoln's assassination. A clue is offered in the introduction, where the selection is identified as a newspaper article. News articles almost always are expository; answering who, what, where, when, why, and how. There is no effort to persuade in the selection, so choices (D) and (E) can be eliminated. While there are some descriptive elements, the purpose is to inform, thus excluding choice (A). You might have thought twice about choice (C), but the factual nature of the piece eliminates narration, the telling of a story.

**Test-Taking Strategy**

*Look at other questions for clues to the correct answer. You probably recognized that this question is linked to question 1.*

2. **The correct answer is (B).** To answer this question correctly, you need to identify the feeling that the article gives you, not the feeling of the event reported. That people were angry and emotional is true, but the tone is neither angry, choice (A), nor emotional, choice (E). The event is very dramatic, choice (C), yet the writer presents the situation in an informative and impersonal manner, making choice (C) incorrect. Consequent events were solemn, not this article, choice (D). That leaves choice (B) as the correct answer.

3. **The correct answer is (A).** You probably recognized several examples of parallel construction in the sentence. If not, you could discover the answer by the process of elimination. The sentence is a grammatically correct compound-complex sentence, so choices (B) and (C) are incorrect. This sentence is certainly not archaic English. To be so, it would read like *Beowulf* or *The Canterbury Tales*, making choice (D) invalid. There is no exaggeration in this factual reporting of a very distressing event. Thus, choice (E) is incorrect.

**Test-Taking Strategy**

*For these multiple-choice questions, figure out which of the point(s) marked with Roman numerals is correct. Then, see which answer choice has the correct Roman numeral(s).*

4. **The correct answer is (E).** The question is about rhetoric and its effect in creating an impression in the first two paragraphs. Don't be carried away by what you know about the historical event. Although the assassination of Lincoln was indeed a tragedy and undoubtedly generated fear (point II), that is not the sense that was related in the first two paragraphs. They talk about excitement and rumors and people rushing to and fro. These facts relate to points I and III. The only answer choice that includes both points is choice (E).

5. **The correct answer is (B).** Did you notice that several of these answers made sense in the sentence, but only one made sense in the context of the article? This is why in order to choose the correct answer, you need to read a few lines above and below the line that is identified. The assassin waved a dagger after he shot Lincoln. The gesture was dramatic, choice (B), more than terrible, choice (C), and not very threatening, choice (D), or deadly, choice (E). Choice (A), sorrowful, is illogical.

6. **The correct answer is (E).** This question may seem difficult, but you can eliminate the incorrect answers through logical thinking. Does the article appeal to authority? No, authorities are not cited, let alone addressed. Therefore, choice (A) is incorrect. Is there a mass of information? Yes, the article presents information, but it is not an overwhelming amount, so choice (B) is invalid. The article is a factual report, containing neither abstractions nor appeals to emotion, so choices (C) and (D) are incorrect.

**Test-Taking Strategy**

*Look for the most inclusive response in answering a main-idea, theme, or purpose question.*

7. **The correct answer is (C).** You may have found this main-idea question fairly easy. All responses except choice (B) are truthful. However, choices (A), (D), and (E) are support for the purpose of the article—to give the facts about the assassination attempt on the president.

8. **The correct answer is (D).** Several of the answers, choices (A), (B), and (C), are redundant, so you can conclude that these are incorrect. The article is not affected or ostentatious, which eliminates choice (E).

9. **The correct answer is (B).** Choices (C), (D), and (E) are easily ruled out because although they may be in evidence in parts of the article—cause and effect in the description of why rumors were flying—none of them predominate in the article. The selection offers details, but in terms of the pattern of organization, choice (B), chronology, is the most important feature.

**Test-Taking Strategy**

*If you are not certain of the meaning of the word, use the context surrounding the word to arrive at its meaning.*

10. **The correct answer is (D).** For vocabulary questions, substitute in the sentence each of the possible choices to see which is closest in meaning. Using this process, choices (A), (B), and (E) don't quite fit the context. Choice (C) is tempting, but the actual definition of the word precarious is "uncertain, insecure."

# PRACTICE SET 4

> **Directions:** This section consists of selections of literature and questions on their content, style, and form. After you have read each passage, choose the best response to each question.

**Questions 1 through 10.** Read the passage carefully, and then choose the answers to the questions.

## FROM *EXTINCT ANIMALS* WRITTEN BY L. H. HELLER IN 1908

Line  Many animals which inhabited the earth in bygone periods have entirely disappeared, leaving not even a modern representative of their race. Others, no doubt, were known to pre-historic peoples, concerning which no record has come down to us. But within the

5     period of recorded observation, many animals have lived and died out; various causes contributing to their extermination, not least among these being in the presence of mankind. Man reconstructs the face of the earth to suit his needs; he cuts down forests, plows or burns over prairie lands, changes the course of rivers, drains the

10    swamps, and thus destroys the natural environment of many of nature's wild children. Then, too, he destroys creatures directly; he kills them for food, for clothing, or for other utilitarian purposes; he hunts them because he fears them, as dangerous foes to himself, or to his agricultural pursuits; he destroys them for sport; and finally he

15    draws them from feral conditions by domestication. Not only thus does man directly injure by exterminating influences, but his coming accompanied by exterminating influences, kills out certain other creatures. These, when man has destroyed their natural prey, practically die of starvation before they can adapt themselves to

20    changed conditions. Then the domestic dogs, cats, etc. help on the work of slaughter in certain ways, by preying upon wild life.

1. Which of the following best characterizes the tone of this passage?

    (A) Reproachful
    (B) Serious
    (C) Scholarly
    (D) Impassioned
    (E) Objective

2. What is the function of the first sentence of the passage?

    I. To state the main topic of the selection
    II. To state the author's opinion
    III. To arouse interest in the thesis

    (A) I only
    (B) II only
    (C) III only
    (D) I and II
    (E) I and III

3. The mode of discourse for this passage may best be characterized as

    (A) descriptive
    (B) narrative
    (C) expository
    (D) argumentative
    (E) persuasive

4. The best meaning for the word "feral" (line 15) is

    (A) primitive
    (B) untamed
    (C) deadly
    (D) fierce
    (E) tricky

5. The first sentence of the passage (lines 1–3) contains all of the following EXCEPT

    (A) a coordinating conjunction
    (B) a negative adverb
    (C) a prepositional phrase
    (D) a participial phrase
    (E) an intransitive verb

6. Which of the following best describes the theme of the passage?

    (A) Humankind as a destructive force in nature
    (B) The extinction of wild animals
    (C) Human beings' effect on wild animals
    (D) Humankind's responsibility for extinction of wild animals
    (E) Humankind's role in halting the extinction of wild animals

7. In this passage, which of the following rhetorical devices is most evident?

    (A) Stereotyping
    (B) Emotional appeal
    (C) Statement of facts
    (D) Causal relation
    (E) Simile

8. In the final sentence of the passage, which phrase(s) intensifies the mood of the selection?

    I. Domestic dogs, cats, etc.
    II. The work of slaughter
    III. Preying upon wild life

    (A) I only
    (B) II only
    (C) III only
    (D) I and II
    (E) II and III

9. In the sentence beginning "Not only thus does man . . ." (lines 15–18), to what does "thus" refer?

   (A) The direct and indirect actions of humans
   (B) Humankind's hunting of animals
   (C) The previous sentence
   (D) Humankind's fear of some animals
   (E) Humankind's alteration of the environment

10. In the clause "[man] destroys the natural environment of many of nature's wild children" (lines 10–11), "wild children" is an example of which of the following?

   (A) Simile
   (B) Metaphor
   (C) Personification
   (D) Analogy
   (E) Figurative language

# ANSWERS AND EXPLANATIONS FOR PRACTICE SET 4

## Quick-Score Answers

| | | | | |
|---|---|---|---|---|
| 1. C | 3. D | 5. A | 7. D | 9. C |
| 2. D | 4. B | 6. D | 8. E | 10. C |

1. **The correct answer is (C).** The key to this question is to sift through the choices to select the one that is best. Choice (E) is easily eliminated because the author examines only one side of the issue, people's negative effect on the environment. Choices (A), (B), and (D) are somewhat true, but choice (C) best characterizes the author's attitude and, therefore, most accurately reflects the tone of the passage.

2. **The correct answer is (D).** Evaluate the Roman numeral points first to see which one(s) may be true in relation to the question. Does the sentence state the main topic of the passage? Yes. Does it state the author's opinion? Yes. Does it arouse interest in the thesis? Not really. The rhetoric and style of this sentence is not exciting; it does not provide a "hook" to entice readers to read on. This means that you can eliminate any response with point III in it, choices (C) and (E). The sentence functions to state both the main topic and the author's view; therefore, choice (D), which includes both I and II, is the correct answer.

**Study Strategy**

*See Chapter 4 for a quick review of literary and rhetorical terms.*

3. **The correct answer is (D).** This is a question about the mode of discourse of this selection. Using the process of elimination, choice (A) is wrong because the writer is not simply describing something. Choice (B) is incorrect because the author is not telling a story. You can eliminate choice (C) because the author is not simply telling or explaining something. Choice (E) may be tempting because the author does indeed want you to think as he does, but choice (D) is the best response because the author's primary purpose is to give the reader information from which to draw certain conclusions.

4. **The correct answer is (B).** This is a vocabulary question. Use the context of the sentence to help you make your choice. Reread the sentence in which the word appears, and then substitute each of the possible choices to see which is closest in meaning. In context, Choices (C), (D), and (E) are easily eliminated because they do not make sense in the context of the sentence. Choice (A) is incorrect because primitive can be applied to an animal or its condition only if the connotation is prehistoric. Choice (B) is the correct answer, given the context and the fact that it modifies *conditions*.

**Study Strategy**

*See Chapter 3 for a quick grammar review.*

5. **The correct answer is (A).** This question tests your knowledge of English grammar. Sift through each of the grammatical applications in the sentence until you identify all that are present. There is a negative adverb, choice (B), "not even." There is a prepositional phrase, choice (C), "of their race." There is a participial phrase, choice (D), "leaving not even." There is an intransitive verb, choice (E), "have disappeared." What remains? Choice (A). There is no coordinating conjunction.

6. **The correct answer is (D).** This kind of question asks that you select the choice that best tells what the passage is about. Choice (E) is eliminated because the idea, although implied, is not actually stated in the passage. Choices (A), (B), and (C) are touched on in the passage, but choice (D) is the strongest message to the reader.

7. **The correct answer is (D).** The writer makes a number of statements as if they were factual, but they may actually be opinions, so choice (C) can be eliminated. In a simile, a writer says *something is like something else;* there is no evidence of that figure of speech in this piece, so choice (E) can also be eliminated. Depending on whether or not you agree with the author, you may see stereotyping in the passage, but that was not the author's intent, so cross off choice (A). The author is building his case on a series of reasons, so choice (B) is incorrect. That leaves causal relation, choice (D). Even though all the causes contributing to extinction may not be mentioned, the device is still causal relation.

8. **The correct answer is (E).** Point I, part of choices (A) and (D), contains no words that would intensify the mood. The words *slaughter* and *preying* in points II and III have emotional connotations that would intensify the mood of the sentence and assist the author in achieving his purpose. Only choice (E) has both points and is, therefore, the correct answer.

9. **The correct answer is (C).** The antecedent of *thus* refers to the previous sentence and all the actions of humankind described in it, choice (C). Choices (B) and (E) are too narrow. The remaining choices do not make sense in context.

10. **The correct answer is (C).** This is a language question that tests your knowledge of figures of speech. You can eliminate choices (A), (B), and (D) immediately because each refers to some kind of comparison, and there is no comparison in the clause. Figurative language, choice (E), a kind of vivid imagery, is generally true but not appropriate. This is a specific example of personification, the giving of human qualities to nonhumans, i.e., wild animals.

# Chapter 2

## ABOUT WRITING THE ESSAYS

### Red Alert!

*Remember that you do not need three "9" essays to get a "5" for your composite score.*

Section II of the Advanced Placement exam for English Language and Composition contains three essays asking you to analyze literary style, discuss rhetorical usage, and defend a position. There are several things to remember about the test. First, usually when you work on an essay, you have adequate time to brainstorm, prewrite, revise, and edit. On the AP exam your time is limited. Second, most of the essays you have written in English class involve literature you and your classmates have studied. In this exam you most probably have not seen the selections previously. Finally, you know your English teacher. You know what he or she thinks is important. You recognize your teacher's preferences in organization, mechanics, sentence structure, and so forth. You do not know the individuals who will score your AP essays, so you cannot write to the audience. If you are wondering how you are going to be succesful, this chapter will help.

Chapter 2 lays out some basic information about the essay portion of the test and about good writing in general. In addition, this chapter will help you to understand what the essay questions ask and how to answer each specific type of question. Now is the time to plan and practice, so you will have the self-confidence to excel, not panic.

## PRACTICE PLAN

### Study Strategy

*Check the* Practice Plan for Studying for the AP English Language and Composition Test *on pp. 10–14.*

In Chapter 2 you will explore the different types of essays on the AP test. You will have ample opportunities to practice writing sample essays. Use the rubric and scoring guide to pinpoint your weaknesses and to improve as you write each subsequent essay.

Use the *Diagnostic Test* and *Practice Tests* as tools to improve your writing, too. Use the techniques described in this chapter to write each of your practice essays in about 40 minutes. Then turn to the *Answers and Explanations* section after each test. Compare each essay to the list of suggested points that you might have developed in that essay. Score your essay with the *Self-Evaluation Rubric*. Ask a reliable friend, an AP classmate, or a teacher to holistically evaluate your essay also. Where are you weak? What can you improve? Take several of the points from the list and rework your essay with those points, strengthening the weak areas.

Reevaluate your essay. Again, compare the points you made with the ones we suggest. Did our suggestions help you to better understand what the question is asking? Is your rewritten essay more tightly focused on the question and more clearly developed as a result of incorporating some of our points? Still need work on your weak points? How much did you improve?

Now, stop. Do not keep working on the same essay to polish it to perfection. You won't have that opportunity during the test. The purpose of reworking your essay is to help you pinpoint what the question is really asking and how you can best answer it with a clear, coherent, and unified essay. Keep in mind what you learned on your first try and go on to the next essay.

# BASIC INFORMATION ABOUT THE ESSAY SECTION

## FAST FACTS

1. Section II has three essay questions. They will probably ask you to analyze literary style, discuss rhetorical usage, and defend a position.

2. You will have 2 hours to write the three essays. The College Board suggests you allot approximately 40 minutes to each essay.

3. Each essay is scored from 1 to 9, with 9 being the highest.

4. A different reader with knowledge of the literary work that you discuss will read each of your essays.

5. Each essay counts for one third of your total essay score. If you do the math, each essay is worth approximately 18 percent of your total score.

6. The essays together account for 55 percent of your final composite score.

**Test-Taking Strategy**

*You will need a pen to write your essays. Be safe: take at least two.*

**Study Strategy**

*Time yourself as you do the practice essays. That way you will be comfortable with the time limit during the actual AP exam.*

What does all this mean? It means that you need to do some planning and practicing.

**1 and 2.** If you have 2 hours—120 minutes—to write all three essays, you cannot spend 90 minutes on one and 15 minutes apiece on the other two. When you practice, take five or so minutes to read each question and selection and to plan what you will say. Use the remaining time to write and revise your essay.

**3, 4, and 5.** Because none of the essays counts for more than the others, you don't have to worry about doing an outstanding job on a certain essay question. However, you have to do a good job on all three.

Skim the three questions and then put them in the order in which you want to answer them. Begin with the easiest, then move to the next hardest, and finally, write the most difficult.

**4.** Because your three essays will be read by three different people, you don't have to worry that one weaker essay will pull down the scores for the other two essays. Instead, you can be confident that your clear, coherent, unified—and neatly written—essays will brighten each grader's pile of vague, incoherent, fragmented, and illegible essays.

You are probably thinking that our mentioning a neatly written paper is a bit fatuous. While neatness does not count, it does matter. Why? Neatness affects legibility. You cannot expect a reader faced with hundreds of papers to score to take time to puzzle over your handwriting. Write as neatly as you can. If your cursive style is tiny and cramped or large and ill-defined, try printing. You will not have time for much revision, but if you do revise, do it neatly and clearly.

# STRATEGIES FOR ACING THE ESSAYS

**Test-Taking Strategy**

*Remember to use present tense when you analyze writing.*

Analyzing and evaluating literature requires skill and thoughtfulness. It is important to read the material carefully. You also must make the effort to understand the writers and be sensitive to their meaning. Writing good essays about language and literature requires the realization that your reader and evaluator can only receive what you place on your paper, not your unstated ideas. If your thesis is clear in your mind, you can state it clearly on paper. If you fully support that thesis with interesting, apt, and logical information that is well-organized, fully developed, coherent, and unified, your reader has a far better chance of understanding your message. If you also include good word choice and tone, you will ace the essay questions.

## CREATING A PLAN OF ATTACK

**Test-Taking Strategy**

*Write the essay that you feel most confident about first. Save the most difficult for last.*

As you practice writing the essays in this chapter, schedule your time according to the following breakdown:

- One to two minutes: Skim the selections and questions to determine the order in which you will write them.

- Five to seven minutes: Read the selection and the writing prompt. Plan your essay.

- Twenty-eight to thirty-two minutes: Write the essay.

- Two to three minutes: Revise and edit the essay.

# STEP 1: READ THE MATERIAL

Once you have skimmed the selections and questions and decided the order in which you will answer them, you have to go back and read each question and passage carefully—probably more than once. The mistake that students often make is writing an essay about something other than the question they are asked to answer. It may be a fabulous "9" essay in all other ways, but if it does not answer the question, it will earn you a low score.

- First, identify the type of essay question you are being asked to answer. Is it asking you for interpretation, analysis, and/or evaluation of the selection?

- Underline the important points or key words in the question. Are you being asked to explain how the writer's use of a motif affects the mood? Underline *explain*, *motif*, and *mood*. You now know that one of the things you will need to look for as you read is a motif.

- Restate the question to yourself—paraphrase it—to be sure you understand what you are being asked to do.

Once you know what you will need to write about, you are ready to read the selection, and you will need to read it several times. Remember, you have about 5 minutes to read and plan, but the selections are short. Follow these steps to get the most out of each reading:

- Regardless of what the question is asking, you need to determine the theme or meaning of the piece first. In order to talk about elements of the selection, you need to know what the piece is about.

- The first time you read, skim the passage.

- The second time, read carefully.

- Be aware of language and diction, person, tone, the writer's intentions and purpose, the selection's impact, and special techniques.

- As you read, underline words and sentences that seem significant and that you might want to quote in your essay. Jot down notes. However, do not spend a lot of time doing this.

**Test-Taking Strategy**

*You will be given paper for your essay, and you will be able to use your test booklet for scratch paper.*

# STEP 2: PLAN AND WRITE YOUR ESSAY

**Study Strategy**

*If you developed an Idea Bank of words and phrases to describe literary works, draw on it to help you develop your thesis. See Chapter 3.*

**Writing Strategy**

*Don't forget to use transitions between ideas and paragraphs.*

**Study Strategy**

*For more about concluding paragraphs, see "Your Style" in this chapter, p. 130.*

- After you have completed your reading, take a few minutes to plan what you will write. Brainstorm or list ideas and thoughts, but do not outline. Outlining wastes time. What you want to do is analyze the passage. List how each literary element enhances the communication in the passage. Make another list of examples and supporting evidence from the passage. Review anything you underlined in the passage to include in the lists.

- Check through your notes and lists and develop your thesis.

- Organize your ideas and begin writing.

- Periodically reread your introductory paragraph to be sure you stay on track to prove your thesis. Do more than summarize. Include your insights, reactions, and emotions.

- Be sure to include examples from the selection to support your points. However, don't try to use copious quotations to fill up the sheets. You don't need to use complete sentences; you can use ellipses.

- Write an effective concluding paragraph. Restate your thesis and summarize how your essay supports it.

- Plan your time so you can proofread and revise your essay.

The chart "Analyzing Literature" on pp. 112-113 suggests questions to ask yourself to help you analyze literary elements to find the meaning in what you read. Use this chart to prepare the practice essay questions in this chapter. Try it for the essays you have to write about prose selections in school, too, and see how much easier it is to organize and develop your thoughts.

# STEP 3: REVISE YOUR ESSAY

**Study Strategy**

*Time yourself as you plan and write your practice essays. That way you will become comfortable with the time limits on the actual AP test.*

Pace yourself so that you have at least two minutes to reread your essay for proofreading and revision. Cross out any irrelevant ideas or words and make any additions—neatly. If you have been following your informal plan to develop your thesis, you can use this time to make sure your grammar and mechanics are correct and your handwriting is legible.

# ANALYZING LITERATURE

**IDENTIFICATION**
**Genre/Mode of Discourse**
  1. What type of prose is it—fiction or nonfiction? Exposition, persuasion, argument, description, narrative, or drama?
  2. Are points developed by definitions, examples, facts, events, or quotations and citations?

**Author**
  1. Who is the author?
  2. What do you know about the writer?
  3. What do you know about the time period or literary period in which the passage was written?

**Title**
  1. If there is a title, what does it tell you?
  2. What does it suggest about the subject or the theme (meaning) of the passage?

**Subject**
  1. What is the subject of the passage?
  2. What is this selection about?

**Theme/Thesis**
  1. What is the theme, or central idea, of the selection?
  2. How is the theme conveyed?

**LITERARY ELEMENTS**
**Setting**
  1. Where and when does the selection take place?
  2. What details does the writer use to create the setting?
  3. Does the setting create a mood or feeling?
  4. Is the setting a symbol for an important idea the writer wants to convey?
  5. Does the setting play a role in the central conflict?

**Point of View**
  1. Is the passage told from the first-person or from the third-person point of view?
  2. Is the narrator limited or omniscient?
  3. What effect does the point of view have on the way you experience the selection?

**Central Conflict**
  1. In what struggle is the protagonist involved?
  2. Is the central conflict internal, within the main character's mind, or external, with another character, society, or nature?
  3. How is the conflict resolved?

**Development**
  1. What events take place in the selection?
  2. Does the piece have an introduction?
  3. If so, what does the reader learn in the introduction?
  4. What is the inciting incident?
  5. What happens during the development?

# ANALYZING LITERATURE—*continued*

**Development—*continued***
6. When does the climax occur?
7. What events mark the resolution?
8. Does the selection have a denouement?
9. Are there special plot devices, such as a surprise ending, foreshadowing, or flashbacks?

**Characterization**
1. Who is the protagonist or speaker?
2. Who are the other major and minor characters?
3. Is there conflict among characters?
4. How does the writer develop each of the characters or the speaker?
5. Which characters change and which are flat?

**LANGUAGE AND STYLE**
**Rhetorical Elements**
1. What words does the writer choose?
2. Are there denotative words, connotative words, abstract words, or inclusive words?
3. What is the tone?

**Organization and Structure**
1. What kinds of sentence structure are present?
2. Is there sentence variety?
3. Does sentence length vary?
4. How is the passage organized?
5. What type of structure did the writer use?

**Literary Devices and Figures of Speech**
1. Does the writer make use of devices such as euphony or alliteration?
2. Does the passage contain any examples of figurative language, such as hyperbole, metaphor, or simile?
3. Is there symbolism? What is it?

**Diction**
1. Is there a specialized vocabulary?
2. Does the writer employ irony to communicate meaning?
3. Are overstatement or understatement used?
4. Is the language inflated by scholarly, technical, or scientific words or overly long phrases?
5. Does the selection contain jargon or euphemisms?
6. What are some of the writer's best-worded phrases?
7. Is the word choice colloquial, idiomatic, scientific, formal, informal, or concrete?

**NOTE:** These questions are general. You will need to adapt them to the type of prose you are reading. Some questions are more appropriate for fiction, while others work better with nonfiction. By using them throughout the chapter, you will become so familiar with the questions that you will know automatically which ones to use with each prose passage on the test.

# THE ESSAY: A QUICK REVIEW

You will recall that an essay is a group of paragraphs that work together to present a main point, or thesis. An essay contains an introductory paragraph, separate paragraphs that develop the thesis, and a concluding paragraph. You can see the parts of a five-paragraph essay—the beginning, called the introduction; the middle, called the body; and the ending, called the conclusion—diagrammed on the next page.

To communicate clearly and precisely, you must determine who your audience is, what your purpose is, and what the appropriate tone is. Your writing must be clear and coherent. For the AP essays, consider the following suggestions.

## AUDIENCE

You have an audience of one—a College Board-trained reader who teaches high school or college English and who will be reading hundreds of similar papers. She or he has knowledge of the literary work you have written about and will have a scoring guide or rubric to evaluate your paper. He or she will score your essay holistically, that is, there is no single score for things like grammar and punctuation. The reader will consider every aspect of writing for its impact on the overall impression of your essay. (Our rubric singles out the various descriptors so you can pinpoint your weaknesses to work on and increase your overall score.)

## PURPOSE

Your purpose is to get a score of 5 or better. To do that, you need to write a unified, coherent, and consistent essay that answers the question. A well-written essay that misses the point of the question will not get you a good score.

## TONE

Your tone is the reflection of your attitude toward the subject of the essay. A writer's tone, for example, may be lighthearted, brusque, or serious. The safest tone to adopt is formal and subjective, since you are being asked your opinion. You do not want to be stuffy and pretentious by using phrases such as "one understands" or "we can surmise." On the other hand, do not be too casual either by writing things like "you know what I mean." Most students, however, err on the side of "faux" erudition, using big words and convoluted constructions. When is doubt, write what you mean simply and directly.

*Peterson's AP Success:
English Language & Composition*

**INTRODUCTION**

Interesting Material and Background Information On Topic

**Thesis Statement**

*The introduction should catch the reader's attention, establish the purpose and tone, and present the thesis statement, or the main idea.*

**Body Paragraph 1**

**Supporting Information**

*Each paragraph within the body of the essay should develop a subtopic of the main point by providing strong supporting information.*

**Body Paragraph 2**

**Supporting Information**

*Each paragraph within the body of the essay should develop a subtopic of the main point by providing strong supporting information.*

**Body Paragraph 3**

**Supporting Information**

*Each paragraph within the body of the essay should develop a subtopic of the main point by providing strong supporting information.*

**CONCLUSION**

Reminder of Thesis Statement

**Summary or Final Remarks**

*The conclusion of an essay should bring the essay to a satisfactory close and remind the reader of the main point.*

How do you develop the proper tone? Through style. Your style should be your own natural style that you use for school essays. That means:

- using proper grammar and punctuation.

- choosing words that convey your meaning in an interesting rather than a pedestrian or vague way: "The author created a dynamic personality in Tom Jones" versus "The main character is interesting."

- avoiding the use of several words when one will do: "There are a number of aspects to the character that are dynamic such as . . ." versus "Jones is both a rascal and . . ."

- avoiding hackneyed phrases and clichés such as "The writer was on cloud nine" versus "The writer's tone showed her enthusiasm."

**Test-Taking Strategy**

*Whenever possible, write in the active voice. Your essay will seem stronger.*

# UNITY

Your style adds interest to the paper. Interesting words and phrasing as much as a unique point of view about a subject can make a paper interesting to read.

Unity is another word for clarity. All of your essay's ideas and information must belong together and be essential to the development of the thesis. The parts of the essay—the introduction, the body, and the conclusion—should all focus on the main idea. Each paragraph must relate to every other, and every paragraph must support the overall thesis. In addition, each paragraph within the essay must be unified. Each paragraph must have a topic sentence, and every sentence in the paragraph must relate to every other and add to the development of the topic sentence. In other words, a unified paper is one that is clearly developed. The introduction and the conclusion work together to create unity. The introduction establishes the main point. Then the conclusion echoes the ideas or key words of the introduction.

Perhaps the most important element creating unity in an essay is the clarity of the thesis statement. Remember that your thesis statement contains the central idea that you have developed from brainstorming ideas to respond to the essay prompt. As the *Harbrace College Handbook,* that venerable college English manual, states: "[Your thesis statement] is basically a claim statement, that is, it indicates what you claim to be true, interesting, or valuable about your subject."

If the thesis statement is focused and clear, it outlines the scope of the essay and the boundaries separating the relevant from the irrelevant. In the same way, the subtopics must logically grow out of the thesis. When the subtopics represent significant aspects of the main point and relate to each other, in all probability you will write a unified essay.

Although you can place your thesis statement anywhere in your essay, it is probably safest to put it in the introduction, even as the first sentence, so you can refer to it as you write to be sure that everything you are writing develops and supports it. Putting the thesis first also gets you started writing.

## COHERENCE

In a coherent essay, a reader can move smoothly and logically from one thought to another. A coherent essay is one in which the ideas within each paragraph and within the essay as a whole are in logical order and their connections flow. Coherence depends on clear, relevant ordering of ideas and the introduction of transitional words and phrases. Many methods exist for organizing ideas logically. The following chart offers five methods for organizing your work.

| Organization of Supporting Information | |
|---|---|
| Chronological order | Information arranged in time sequence |
| Spatial order | Information arranged according to space relationships |
| Order of importance | Information arranged from least important to most important, or vice versa |
| Compare and contrast | Information arranged according to similarities and differences between two or more subjects |
| Developmental order | Information arranged so that one point leads logically to another |

# TRANSITIONS

Besides being logically organized, a coherent essay moves smoothly from one thought to the next because its ideas are connected by transitions, repetitions of key words, synonyms, and pronouns. Transitions indicate how one idea relates to another, while repetition of words ties ideas together. The following are some transitions that help establish logical order.

| Time Relationship | | |
| --- | --- | --- |
| after | finally | later |
| before | first | meanwhile |
| during | second | next |
| earlier | third | then |

| Spatial Relationship | | |
| --- | --- | --- |
| above | beneath | near |
| ahead | beyond | outside |
| before | here | over there |
| behind | inside | |

| Comparison or Contrast | | |
| --- | --- | --- |
| although | indeed | nonetheless |
| conversely | in like manner | similarly |
| however | instead | whereas |
| in contrast | likewise | yet |

| Cause and Effect | | |
| --- | --- | --- |
| accordingly | inevitably | then |
| as a result | on account of | therefore |
| because of | since | thus |
| consequently | | |

| Addition | | |
| --- | --- | --- |
| also | furthermore | not only |
| as well | in addition | too |
| besides | moreover | |

| Emphasis | | |
| --- | --- | --- |
| indeed | in other words | |
| in fact | most of all | most significantly |

| Examples | | |
| --- | --- | --- |
| also | for example | specifically |
| as an illustration | in particular | that is |
| for instance | namely | |

# ADEQUATE DEVELOPMENT

What is an "adequate development"? You have 20 minutes to read, plan and develop your ideas—neatly. In addition to the thesis statement, your essay must contain enough specific information to explain your main idea. Support consists of examples, details, facts, reasons, or events. The following chart presents five types of supporting information that you can use to develop your thesis.

| KINDS OF SUPPORT | | |
|---|---|---|
| **Type of Support** | **Definition** | **Example** |
| **Examples** | Particular instances of a general idea or principle | An essay about the best movies of the year might include a discussion of three or four films. |
| **Details** | Small items or pieces of information that make up something larger | An essay about an author might describe details about his or her career. |
| **Facts** | Specific pieces of information that can be verified | An essay about the tone and style of a selection might include quotations. |
| **Reasons** | Explanations, justifications, or causes, often answering the question *why?* about the main idea | An essay advocating gun control might include an explanation of ineffective current laws. |
| **Events** | Incidents or happenings | An essay about a travel memoir might include one or two amusing anecdotes |

A well-developed essay must contain enough support to meet the expectations established by your introduction and thesis statement. In addition, the supporting information must make the essay seem complete.

# TYPES OF ESSAYS ON THE AP EXAM

On previous tests, almost all of the essays have been either expository, persuasive, or argumentation, so most probably you will be called on to write at least two of these kinds of essays. Expository writing is meant to inform your reader of something. Argumentation and persuassion essays are meant to influence your reader's opinion and, in the case of persuasive writing, to lead your reader to act. Knowing the elements of each mode of writing ensures that you can work effectively in that manner.

## EXPOSITORY ESSAYS

**Review Strategy**

*Review literary and rhetorical terms on pages 173–179.*

If the essay prompt asks you to present information, to explain style, to define a concept or idea, or to analyze rhetoric, you are being asked to write an expository essay. Expository essays are usually objective and straightforward. The distinguishing characteristics of exposition are an explanatory purpose and an informative tone, because expository essays are intended to communicate factual material.

An expository essay should follow the standard three-part essay structure. However, the essay's thesis statement should be clearly explanatory, presenting a factual statement that the body of the essay elaborates upon, clarifies, and explains.

The supporting information furthers the explanatory purpose by providing sufficient examples and details to give your reader an understanding of your main point. Such information should be verifiable, so avoid controversial statements. Your support should be organized logically in subtopics that develop important elements of your main point. These guidelines will help you plan, write, and revise an expository essay.

---

### GUIDELINES FOR EXPOSITION

1. Limit your main point, so it can be developed in the 40-minute time period.

2. Be sure that your main point lends itself to a factual treatment.

3. Brainstorm supporting information that you will need in order to explain your main idea thoroughly to your reader.

4. Develop a thesis statement and break it down into several subtopics.

5. Organize the subtopics and their supporting information for clarity.

6. Concentrate on explaining as you write.

---

As you write your expository essay, focus on explaining your topic to the audience. Move logically through the steps of the process or through the supporting details for a concept by providing all the information a reader needs to understand what you are presenting. Be sure to use transitions to assist your audience in following your explanation. If time remains, revise your essay, checking for unity and coherence. Review your word choices to ensure an objective, informative tone.

# ARGUMENT AND PERSUASION

**Test-Taking Strategy**

*Vary your sentence structure by:*

- *beginning with a prepositional phrase*
- *using adverbs and adverbial phrases*
- *starting with dependent clauses*
- *using various conjunctions—not only, either, yet, so*
- *including infinitives and participles*
- *beginning with adjectives and adjective phrases*
- *employing inversions*

If you are asked to defend an opinion or convince your readers of your position on a social, an intellectual, or a political issue, you will be writing a persuasive essay. Persuasive writing is often subjective. However, it must contain logical reasoning and forceful factual information in order to defend your opinion effectively. A persuasive composition differs from other kinds of essays because of its persuasive purpose and tone.

Like exposition, persuasive essays should employ the three-part essay format. The thesis statement should present the stand you are defending and be reasonable in tone. The thesis should reveal the opinion that the entire essay defends. Unlike an expository essay, a persuasive thesis may be a controversial statement.

In a persuasive essay, supporting material provides convincing evidence for the thesis statement. Support may consist of logical reasons or examples, facts, and details. Your supporting information should never be based on unsubstantiated opinions. Your evidence should be solid, authoritative, rational, and believable, appealing even to those readers who disagree with you. You want to show your readers that you are well informed and have thought about opposing arguments.

Your tone should be persuasive but reasonable, forceful but respectful of opposing viewpoints. In writing a persuasive essay for class, you would adjust your tone to your audience and take into consideration whether your audience might be sympathetic, apathetic, or strongly opposed to your position. You might choose a humorous, lighthearted approach or a serious, intellectual one. Do the same in writing your essay for the AP exam, and be sure to maintain whatever tone you choose throughout the essay.

When you advocate a highly controversial opinion, an effective method for developing supporting information is to list the principal arguments for your position and then marshal the strongest arguments against your viewpoint. After each opposing argument, present counterarguments for your side.

You may be asked to write an argument for or against a position. Don't worry. An argument is simply the first part of persuasion. In an argument, the writer leads the audience to conclusions based on premises and inferences. Persuasion takes the process one step further. A persuasive essay convinces the reader with logic, reason, and facts that certain beliefs or actions are indeed the best or the most intelligent course of action. The guidelines below will help you to write either type of essay.

---

**GUIDELINES FOR PERSUASION**

1. Use your knowledge and beliefs to choose an opinion/topic that you can support.

2. Decide how persuasive you must be to make your points—the intensity of your purpose and tone.

3. Determine your readers' probable response to your position.

4. Brainstorm for specific examples, facts, details, reasons, and events that support your thesis statement.

5. If your opinion is controversial, consider the opposing arguments and list evidence for and against your position.

6. State your opinion in a thesis statement that is direct, significant, and supportable.

7. Organize your support in order of importance.

8. Consider conceding one or two points to the other side if your main point is highly controversial.

9. Use concrete, specific words. Be sure your language is reasonable but compelling. Don't be emotional.

10. Employ smooth, logical transitions.

11. Revise your paper by examining your word choices to ensure a balanced, forceful, and consistent tone.

---

**Test-Taking Strategy**

*To build a strong conclusion, add an insight, a solution, a humorous touch, or a poignant thought.*

As you write your persuasive essay, focus on winning the reader's agreement. Capture the reader's interest without antagonizing. Imagine that you are speaking directly to your reader and that you want to hold his or her attention. Use transitions to create a roadmap for your arguments. In the conclusion, rephrase your main point and end confidently.

# A Word about Logic

**Study Strategy**

*Applying logic can help you with the multiple-choice section as well as the essay questions.*

When you write persuasively or argumentatively, you must think critically. First, you must analyze and evaluate the information so you can decide if it is reliable. Second, you must distinguish between valid and invalid forms of reasoning to determine if a position holds up under scrutiny.

To determine if material is reliable, you must distinguish fact from opinion. A fact, of course, is a statement that can be verified by objective means. An opinion is subjective and must be supported by relevant facts before it can be considered valid. An opinion may express personal feelings about an idea or condition, or it may reflect a judgment or prediction based on facts. No matter which, an opinion is not valid if the facts supporting it are insufficient.

After you have verified facts and determined that the opinions are valid, you must analyze how the information is presented. To draw valid conclusions, you must think logically and reasonably about the material. There are two types of formal reasoning, inductive and deductive. Each produces valid conclusions when used properly, but each can lead to invalid conclusions when used incorrectly.

Inductive reasoning moves from specific facts to a conclusion, or a generalization, based on those facts. A valid generalization is supported by evidence and holds true in a majority of circumstances. If the reasoning is illogical, the result is a logical fallacy. Errors in logic can take the form of the following:

- A hasty generalization or statement that is made about a large number of cases or a whole group on the basis of a few examples, without taking into account qualifying factors.

   **Example:** Teenage drivers have poor skills; therefore, they cause most of the automobile accidents

- A non sequitur is an idea or conclusion that does not follow logically from the preceding idea.

   **Example:** Vladimir would be a great history teacher because he was born in Europe and has traveled extensively on three continents.

Deductive reasoning moves from the generality that is assumed to be true to specific cases. Logical fallacies occur when deduction is used incorrectly.

- Begging the question occurs when a general statement is restated without supporting evidence or facts, assuming as true something that needs to be proved or explained.

  **Example:** The lawyer said he is qualified to try the case because he has tried other cases.

In addition to inductive and deductive reasoning, two other forms of reasoning can be used to reach valid conclusions: cause and effect and analogy. A cause-and-effect sequence is one in which something is affected by one or more events that occurred before it.

- A false cause results when one thing preceding another is assumed to have caused a second event.

  **Example:** If I sleep eight hours tonight, I can run five miles in the morning.

An analogy is a comparison between two things that are similar in some ways but are essentially unalike.

- A false analogy is one that overlooks essential dissimilarities between two things being compared.

  **Example:** Debbie is like her sister because they both have freckles.

When you apply logic to an analysis or to your own writing, use these questions to examine an author's logic.

---

**QUESTIONS FOR VALID REASONING**

**Generalizations**

1. What facts are being presented as evidence to support the general statement?

2. Are there any exceptions to the statement?

3. Are enough cases or examples presented to lead you to a solid conclusion, or does the material lead you to jump to hasty generalizations?

**Cause and Effect**

1. What evidence is there that the first event or situation could have caused the second, or does the cause-and-effect sequence reveal a non sequitur?

2. What other events might have caused the second event?

3. Could the second event have occurred without the first?

**Analogies**

1. How are the two things compared essentially different?

2. How are the things similar? Is the comparison logical or does it lead to a false analogy?

3. What is the truth that the comparison tries to show?

**NOTE:** These questions are general. You will need to adapt them to the type of prose you are reading. Some questions may be more appropriate for fiction, while others work better with nonfiction. By using them throughout this chapter, you will know automatically which ones are appropriate to use with a given prose passage.

---

# SOME PRACTICAL ADVICE ON WRITING YOUR ESSAYS

The following are some suggestions to help you write clear, well-organized, well-reasoned, coherent, and interesting essays. If you keep these suggestions in mind as you write your practice essays, these steps will come naturally to you on the day of the test.

### Test-Taking Strategy

*Do not forget the simple things such as capitalization, punctuation, and spelling. See Chapter 3 for a quick review.*

- Begin writing your first paragraph by stating the thesis clearly. Take a full 5 minutes to be sure that you are writing a clearly stated and interesting introduction.

- At the end of the first paragraph, read it to be sure that your ideas are logically following each other and supporting the thesis.

- Write a transition into the second paragraph. Check your list of ideas.

- Do more than summarize. Include your insights, reactions, and emotions.

- Keep writing until you have used all the RELEVANT ideas on your list. If a new idea comes from the flow of your writing, use it if it fits.

- Use transitions.

- Periodically reread your introductory paragraph to be sure you are staying on track to prove your thesis. If you must change something, cross it out neatly.

- Do not be concerned about perfection. No essay can be perfect in just 40 minutes.

- Allow time to write a solid concluding paragraph. There are several ways to approach the conclusion: rephrasing the thesis, summarizing the main points, or referring in some way back to your opening paragraph. Do not leave the reader wondering, "So what?"

# PRACTICE ESSAYS

The following question and selection are very similar to those that you will find on the actual AP exam. Apply the suggestions and strategies you have just read and write about the excerpt from Ralph Waldo Emerson's *Self Reliance*. Then check your essay by reading the suggested points of discussion that follow. Evaluate yourself by using the *Self-Evaluation Rubric* on p. 140.

# SAMPLE ESSAY

**Study Strategy**

*When you practice, limit yourself to 40 minutes— about 5 minutes to read and plan and 35 minutes to write and revise—so you will become comfortable with writing on demand.*

(Suggested time—40 minutes)

> **Directions:** Read the following passage carefully. It was written by Ralph Waldo Emerson, one of the most influential of the Transcendentalists. Discuss how the author's style contributes to his arguments espousing transcendental ideas. Consider such elements as literary devices, tone, and rhetoric.

## FROM *SELF-RELIANCE*

Line There is a time in every man's education when he arrives at the conviction that envy is ignorance; that imitation is suicide; that he must take himself for better, for worse, as his portion; that though the wide universe is full of good, no kernel of nourishing corn can
5 come to him but through his toil bestowed on that plot of ground which is given to him to till. The power which resides in him is new in nature, and none but he knows what that is which he can do, nor does he know until he has tried. Not for nothing one face, one character, one fact makes much impression on him, and another
10 none. This sculpture in the memory is not without preestablished harmony. The eye was placed where one ray should fall, that it might testify of that particular ray. We but half express ourselves, and are ashamed of that divine idea which each of us represents. It may be safely trusted as proportionate and of good issues, so it be faithfully
15 imparted, but God will not have his work made manifest by cowards. A man is relieved and gay when he has put his heart into his work and done his best; but what he has said or done otherwise, shall give him no peace. It is a deliverance which does not deliver. In the attempt his genius deserts him; no muse befriends; no invention, no
20 hope.

Trust thyself: every heart vibrates to that iron string. Accept the place the divine providence has found for you; the society of your contemporaries, the connection of events. Great men have always done so and confided themselves childlike to the genius of the age,
25 betraying their perception that the absolutely trustworthy was stirring at their heart, working through their hands, predominating in all their being. And we are now men, and must accept in the highest mind the same transcendent destiny; and not minors and invalids in a protected corner, but guides, redeemers, and benefactors, obeying
30 the Almighty effort and advancing on Chaos and the Dark. . . .

Society everywhere is in conspiracy against the manhood of every one of its members. Society is a joint-stock company in which

the members agree for the better securing of his bread to each shareholder, to surrender the liberty and culture of the eater. The
35 virtue in most request is conformity. Self-reliance is its aversion. It loves not realities and creators, but names and customs.

Whoso would be a man must be a nonconformist. He who would gather immortal palms must not be hindered by the name of goodness, but must explore if it be goodness. Nothing is at last sacred
40 but the integrity of our own mind. Absolve you to yourself, and you shall have the suffrage of the world. . . .

A foolish consistency is the hobgoblin of little minds, adored by little statesmen and philosophers and divines. With consistency a great soul has simply nothing to do. He may as well concern himself
45 with his shadow on the wall. Speak what you think now in hard words and tomorrow speak what tomorrow thinks in hard words again, though it contradict everything you said today. "Ah, so you shall be sure to be misunderstood?"—Is it so bad, then, to be misunderstood? Pythagoras was misunderstood, and Socrates, and Jesus, and
50 Luther, and Copernicus, and Galileo, and Newton, and every pure and wise spirit that ever took flesh. To be great is to be misunderstood. . . .

—Ralph Waldo Emerson

> Before you turn the page and read our suggestions for an essay on this selection, score your essay using the *Self-Evaluation Rubric* on p. 140.

# SUGGESTIONS FOR SAMPLE ESSAY ON EMERSON'S SELF-RELIANCE

**Test-Taking Strategy**

*Remember to read and analyze the question before you do anything else.*

The following are points that you might have chosen to include in your essay on a passage from *Self-Reliance*. Consider them as you perform your self-evaluation. You will notice that we discuss elements of literature that are not called for in the essay question. However, by identifying the author, naming the type of literature, and writing the title you have a place to begin and you give yourself an opportunity to include information that should impress your readers.

## MODE OF DISCOURSE

This selection is a persuasive essay, a piece of nonfiction. While you were not asked about this point directly in the question, by being specific about what type of literature you read, you appear to know literature.

## AUTHOR

A philosopher, poet, orator, and writer, Ralph Waldo Emerson became the most influential member of the Transcendentalists, a group of Massachusetts intellectuals of the mid-nineteenth century. The Transcendental philosophy is one of responsible individualism. Adherents believed that all forms of being are united through a shared universal soul. They believed that God and the human spirit were reflected in nature. By studying nature, Transcendentalists thought they would come to know themselves and discover universal truths. The Transcendentalists valued intuition, individuality, and self-reliance.

Of course, you cannot find this in the selection, but you might remember some of this from your study of American literature. The information may help you understand the selection better.

## TITLE

This selection is excerpted from *Self-Reliance*. The title speaks to one of Emerson's core beliefs, the importance of self-reliance, which, along with intuition and individuality, form the heart of the philosophical system known as Transcendentalism.

## SUBJECT

The subject, obviously, is self-reliance, Emerson's profound conviction that each person must count one's self, count for one's self, account to one's self, and nurture the seeds of greatness to be found within. Emerson advises each person to trust one's self, to accept one's self and one's place in life, to resist conformity, and to think little of society's regard, in fact, many great and wise spirits were misunderstood.

## LITERARY DEVICES AND FIGURES OF SPEECH

In the first paragraph, Emerson uses an analogy, "kernel of . . . corn," comparing the effort needed to produce corn to the effort people must make to reach their potential. He uses imagery when he says "every heart vibrates to that iron string." He employs a number of metaphors—"Society is a joint-stock company," "immortal palms," and "a foolish consistency is the hobgoblin." Emerson makes reference to individuals who made important contributions in the fields of mathematics, philosophy, religion, and science and who were also nonconformists and misunderstood. They were great spirits and self-reliant, as we must be.

## THEMES AND THESES

Emerson's thesis is that people (and, therefore, society) would be better served by espousing a creed of responsible individualism. He has immense faith in human potential, and he advocates that one must obey internal dictates only and that one must resist the pressures of society to conform. He conveys these beliefs directly and clearly throughout the essay.

## STYLE

The author's tone is one of heartfelt emotion, and yet at the same time he writes in a logical and erudite manner, with an educated diction. He develops his ideas point by point, in order of importance. He uses a positive denotation for words proposing self-reliance (*nourishing, harmony, trust*) and negative ones for words describing conformity (*dark, conspiracy, foolish*). He uses a variety of sentence structures and employs a rhetorical question in the conclusion of the last paragraph.

## YOUR STYLE

### Study Strategy

*If you have not already started an Idea Bank, see Chapter 3, p. 162, for information on how to get a head start on developing an effective vocabulary for your essays.*

You have just read some important points that you might have included in your essay. Now review your introductory paragraph. If it seems a little dry, consider trying one of these types of openings to punch it up: more forceful or vivid language, a quotation, a rhetorical question, an anecdote, or perhaps one of Emerson's images. But whatever you add has to relate to your thesis.

Look at your concluding paragraph. A simple summary of your major points creates an effective conclusion. You can also end an essay with a relevant quote. A specific suggestion works well in a persuasive essay. If you have organized your writing around a problem/solution, consider a vivid image of the consequences.

## Study Strategy

*See* "Practice Plan for Studying for the AP English Language and Composition Test" *pp. 10–14.*

Once you have evaluated your essay with the *Self-Evaluation Rubric* on p. 140 and reviewed our points, you may choose to revise your essay using the points suggested here. However, do not spend a great deal of time trying to make it perfect. Revise it simply to see how adding some of our points may make it stronger. Whether you revise or not, ask a classmate or your teacher to evaluate your essay for you using the *Self-Evaluation Rubric*. How does your own evaluation match with a more objective view? Keep the differences in mind as you write and score more essays.

Now that you have a sense of the logic involved in acing the essay questions of Section II, try *Practice Set 1*. Study the points for evaluation and use the self-evaluation rubric. If you are still unsure about writing essays, continue with *Practice Set 2* and *Practice Set 3*.

# PRACTICE SET 1

**Study Strategy**

*When you practice, limit yourself to 40 minutes— about 5 minutes to read and plan and 35 minutes to write and revise—so you will become comfortable with writing on demand.*

(Suggested time—40 minutes)

**Directions:** James Boswell stated: "to write, not his panegyric, which must be all praise, but his Life; which, great and good as he was, must not be supposed to be entirely perfect . . . in every picture there should be shade and light." Read the following passage carefully. Write an essay analyzing how Boswell's style contributed to success or failure in achieving his goal. Consider such literary and rhetorical elements as diction, point of view, and tone.

## FROM *THE LIFE OF SAMUEL JOHNSON*, "FEELINGS"

Line  [Said Johnson:] "Pity is not natural to man. Children are always cruel. Savages are always cruel. Pity is acquired and improved by the cultivation of reason. We may have uneasy sensations from seeing a creature in distress, without pity; for we have not pity unless we
5     wish to relieve them. When I am on my way to dine with a friend, and finding it late, have bid the coachman make haste, if I happen to attend when he whips his horses, I may feel unpleasantly that the animals are put to pain, but I do not wish him to desist. No, sir, I wish him to drive on."
10        Johnson's love of little children, which he discovered upon all occasions, calling them "pretty dears," and giving them sweetmeats, was an undoubted proof of the real humanity and gentleness of his disposition.
          His uncommon kindness to his servants, and serious concern,
15    not only for their comfort in this world, but their happiness in the next, was another unquestionable evidence of what all, who were intimately acquainted with him, knew to be true.
          Nor would it be just, under this head, to omit the fondness which he showed for animals which he had taken under his protec-
20    tion. I never shall forget the indulgence with which he treated Hodge, his cat; for whom he himself used to go out and buy oysters, lest the servants, having that trouble, should take a dislike to the poor creature. I am, unluckily, one of those who have an antipathy to a cat, so that I am uneasy when in the room with one; and I own I
25    frequently suffered a good deal from the presence of this same Hodge. I recollect him one day scrambling up Dr. Johnson's breast, apparently with much satisfaction, while my friend, smiling and half-whistling, rubbed down his back and pulled him by the tail; and when I observed he was a fine cat, saying, "Why, yes, sir, but I have

30   had cats whom I liked better than this;" and then, as if perceiving Hodge to be out of countenance, adding, "but he is a very fine cat, a very fine cat indeed."

This reminds me of the ludicrous account which he gave Mr. Langton of the despicable state of a young gentleman of good
35   family. "Sir, when I heard of him last, he was running about town shooting cats. " And then, in a sort of kindly reverie, he bethought himself of his own favorite cat, and said, "But Hodge shan't be shot; no, no, Hodge shall not be shot."

—James Boswell

> Use the *Self-Evaluation Rubric* on p. 140 to help you assess your progress in writing your essays.

# SUGGESTIONS FOR PRACTICE SET 1

## Background Information
- Mode: nonfiction; excerpt from biography
- Author: James Boswell, mid- to late 1700s,
- Title: a biography, one of the fullest records of a man's life ever written; character of Johnson revealed
- Subject: attitude toward animals, characterization of Johnson

## Point of View
- First person
- Author as narrator
- Personal knowledge and experience
- Accounts of personal dialogues

## Characterization
- Two characters: Johnson and Boswell
- Boswell: admiration of Johnson, respect, almost idolatry, conscientious record, frank
- Examples: allergy to cats, story of Langton
- Johnson: fondness for animals, kind feelings, humor, idiosyncratic
- Examples: getting oysters himself, thinking Hodge could understand language

## Theme or Thesis
- People are made of contradictory qualities. A man as great as Johnson has quirks and idiosyncracies just as others do.
- Johnson is a man to be admired.

## Style
- Most biographers are objective; Boswell is not.
- Diction shows admiration: fondness, indulgence, kindly reverie.
- Tone: admiration, respect, approval, amusement
- Sentences: direct quotes from conversation, varied, complex, but clear
- Examples: "But Hodge shan't be shot; no, no, Hodge shall not be shot."
- Use of specific details: pulling Hodge's tail, half-whistling
- Organization: anecdotal

# PRACTICE SET 2

(Suggested time—40 minutes)

**Study Strategy**

*When you practice, limit yourself to 40 minutes— about 5 minutes to read and plan and 35 minutes to write and revise—so you will become comfortable with writing on demand.*

**Directions:** Read the following work carefully. Then write a well-organized essay in which you discuss how the selection uses humor to comment on human nature and human conduct. Consider such literary elements as diction, narrative pace, satire, and point of view.

## "ADVICE TO LITTLE GIRLS"

Line  Good little girls ought not to make mouths at their teachers for every trifling offense. This retaliation should only be resorted to under peculiarly aggravated circumstances.

5  If you have nothing but a rag-doll stuffed with sawdust, while one of your more fortunate little playmates has a costly China one, you should treat her with a show of kindness nevertheless. And you ought not to attempt to make a forcible swap with her unless your conscience would justify you in it, and you know you are able to do it.

10  You ought never to take your little brother's "chewing-gum" away from him by main force; it is better to rope him in with the promise of the first two dollars and a half you find floating down the river on a grindstone. In the artless simplicity natural to his time of life, he will regard it as a perfectly fair transaction. In all ages of the

15  world this eminently plausible fiction has lured the obtuse infant to financial ruin and disaster.

If at any time you find it necessary to correct your brother, do not correct him with mud—never, on any account, throw mud at him, because it will spoil his clothes. It is better to scald him a little,

20  for then you obtain desirable results. You secure his immediate attention to the lessons you are inculcating, and at the same time your hot water will have a tendency to move impurities from his person, and possibly the skin, in spots.

If your mother tells you to do a thing, it is wrong to reply that

25  you won't. It is better and more becoming to intimate that you will do as she bids you, and then afterward act quietly in the matter according to the dictates of your best judgment.

You should ever bear in mind that it is to your kind parents that you are indebted for your food, and your nice bed, and for your
30 beautiful clothes, and for the privilege of staying home from school when you let on that you are sick. Therefore you ought to respect their little prejudices, and humor their little foibles until they get to crowding you too much.

Good little girls always show marked deference for the aged.
35 You ought never to "sass" old people unless they "sass" you first.

—Mark Twain

> Use the *Self-Evaluation Rubric* on p. 140 to help you assess your progress in writing your essays.

# SUGGESTIONS FOR PRACTICE SET 2

The following are points you might have chosen to include in your essay on Mark Twain's "Advice to Little Girls." Consider them as you perform your self-evaluation. Revise your essay using points from this list to strengthen it.

**Form or Mode**
- Humorous essay

**Theme**
- Facetious advice telling girls how to behave

**Characters**
- Narrator, Mark Twain
- Addressing girls in general

**Dialogue**
- No specific dialogue
- Chatty and familiar style

**Conflict**
- Girls versus convention

**Plot/Development**
- Basically, advice on how girls can actually do what they want while appearing to be ever so proper

**Setting**
- Mid-1800s

**Point of View**
- Written to the second person

**Diction**
- Very informal
- Much humor
- "And you ought not to attempt to make a forcible swap with her unless your conscience would justify you in it, and you know you are able to do it."
- Tone: tongue in cheek
- Folksy language

# PRACTICE SET 3

**Study Strategy**

*When you practice, limit yourself to 40 minutes—about 5 minutes to read and plan and 35 minutes to write and revise—so you will become comfortable with writing on demand.*

(Suggested time—40 minutes)

Many behavioral scientists and psychologists have come to believe that success in school, in the workplace, on the playing field, and elsewhere in life is not so much determined by intellect but by social intelligence—the ability to work with others, lead and motivate others, and inspire team spirit.

Write a persuasive essay that either qualifies, agrees with, or disagrees with these social scientists' assertion.

# SUGGESTIONS FOR PRACTICE SET 3

**Study Strategy**

*Ask a friend, AP classmate, or teacher to evaluate your practice essays.*

The following are some of the points you might have chosen to include in your persuasive essay. Consider them as you perform your self-evaluation. Did you fall into any of the traps of illogical reasoning? Revise your essay using points from this list to strengthen it.

- A thesis that states your stand or point of view on the reasons for success. It must be supported by valid evidence

- Evidence that the reader should be willing to accept as true without further proof

- Evidence comprising a major portion of the essay, especially if you have created a controversial or complex thesis. Bear in mind that the more commonly acknowledged or the more widely shared an experience, the fewer examples you need.

- Evidence in the form of statistics, illustrations, specific examples, personal experience, occurrences reported by authorities

- Perhaps demonstration of proof, showing the connection between the truth of the supporting evidence and the truth of the assertion; often signaled by words *because* or *as well*

- Definition of any term whose exact meaning is essential to clearly communicating your position

- Soundly reasoned with no distortions of evidence

- Answers to objections from the opposition

- Matching of structure to your audience and goal

# SELF-EVALUATION RUBRIC FOR THE ADVANCED PLACEMENT ESSAYS

| | 8–9 | 6–7 | 5 | 3–4 | 1–2 | 0 |
|---|---|---|---|---|---|---|
| **Overall Impression** | Demonstrates excellent control of the literature and outstanding writing competence; thorough and effective; incisive | Demonstrates good control of the literature and good writing competence; less thorough and incisive than the highest papers | Reveals simplistic thinking and/or immature writing; adequate skills | Incomplete thinking; fails to respond adequately to part or parts of the question; may paraphrase rather than analyze | Unacceptably brief; fails to respond to the question; little clarity | Lacking skill and competence |
| **Understanding of the Text** | Excellent understanding of the text; exhibits perception and clarity; original or unique approach; includes apt and specific references | Good understanding of the text; exhibits perception and clarity; includes specific references | Superficial understanding of the text; elements of literature vague, mechanical, overgeneralized | Misreadings and lack of persuasive evidence from the text; meager and unconvincing treatment of literary elements | Serious misreadings and little supporting evidence from the text; erroneous treatment of literary elements | A response with no more than a reference to the literature; blank response, or one completely off the topic |
| **Organization and Development** | Meticulously organized and thoroughly developed; coherent and unified | Well organized and developed; coherent and unified | Reasonably organized and developed; mostly coherent and unified | Somewhat organized and developed; some incoherence and lack of unity | Little or no organization and development; incoherent and void of unity | No apparent organization or development; incoherent |
| **Use of Sentences** | Effectively varied and engaging; virtually error free | Varied and interesting; a few errors | Adequately varied; some errors | Somewhat varied and marginally interesting; one or more major errors | Little or no variation; dull and uninteresting; some major errors | Numerous major errors |
| **Word Choice** | Interesting and effective; virtually error free | Generally interesting and effective; a few errors | Occasionally interesting and effective; several errors | Somewhat dull and ordinary; some errors in diction | Mostly dull and conventional; numerous errors | Numerous major errors; extremely immature |
| **Grammar and Usage** | Virtually error free | Occasional minor errors | Several minor errors | Some major errors | Severely flawed; frequent major errors | Extremely flawed |

Using the rubric on the previous page, rate yourself in each of the categories below for each essay on the test. Enter on the lines below the number from the rubric that most accurately reflects your performance in each category. Then calculate the average of the six numbers to determine your final score. It is difficult to score yourself objectively, so you may wish to ask a respected friend or teacher to assess your writing for a more accurate reflection of its strengths and weaknesses. On the AP test itself, a reader will rate your essay on a scale of 1 to 9, with 9 being the highest.

Rate each category from 9 (high) to 0 (low).

# QUESTION 1

**SELF-EVALUATION**

Overall Impression _____

Understanding of the Text _____

Organization and Development _____

Use of Sentences _____

Word Choice (Diction) _____

Grammar and Usage _____

TOTAL _____

Divide by 6 for final score _____

**OBJECTIVE EVALUATION**

Overall Impression _____

Understanding of the Text _____

Organization and Development _____

Use of Sentences _____

Word Choice (Diction) _____

Grammar and Usage _____

TOTAL _____

Divide by 6 for final score _____

# QUESTION 2

**SELF-EVALUATION**

Overall Impression _____

Understanding of the Text _____

Organization and Development _____

Use of Sentences _____

Word Choice (Diction) _____

Grammar and Usage _____

TOTAL _____

Divide by 6 for final score _____

**OBJECTIVE EVALUATION**

Overall Impression _____

Understanding of the Text _____

Organization and Development _____

Use of Sentences _____

Word Choice (Diction) _____

Grammar and Usage _____

TOTAL _____

Divide by 6 for final score _____

# QUESTION 3

**SELF-EVALUATION**

Overall Impression _____

Understanding of the Text _____

Organization and Development _____

Use of Sentences _____

Word Choice (Diction) _____

Grammar and Usage _____

TOTAL _____

Divide by 6 for final score _____

**OBJECTIVE EVALUATION**

Overall Impression _____

Understanding of the Text _____

Organization and Development _____

Use of Sentences _____

Word Choice (Diction) _____

Grammar and Usage _____

TOTAL _____

Divide by 6 for final score _____

# Chapter 3

# QUICK REVIEW: PARTS OF SPEECH, GRAMMAR, MECHANICS, AND USAGE TIPS

This chapter has four parts: (1) a quick review of parts of speech for the multiple-choice section, (2) a quick overview of the mechanics and punctuation that you are mostly likely to need in order to write a grammatically correct essay, (3) some recommendations for refining your diction, and (4) suggestions for avoiding the top 98 usage problems.

## GRAMMAR FOR THE MULTIPLE-CHOICE QUESTIONS

Any grammar questions on the AP English Language Test are really disguised comprehension questions. They will ask you to identify one of the parts of speech—nouns, verbs, adjectives, adverbs, prepositions, conjunctions, and interjections—or they will ask you to classify parts of a sentence—subjects, predicates, complements, modifiers, or an antecedent of a word. To answer questions in the multiple-choice section, remember:

### FUNCTIONS OF NOUNS AND PRONOUNS

- For the subject, look for nouns, pronouns, or word groups (gerunds, participial phrases, or clauses) acting as essential nouns that tell you *who* or *what* the sentence is about.

    **What I have described in the Frenchman** was merely the result of an excited, or perhaps of a diseased, intelligence.
    —*The Murders in the Rue Morgue*, Edgar Allen Poe

    Note: The subject will not be stated if the sentence or clause is imperative.

    "Do talk to me as if I were one," said Lord Warburton.
    —*Portrait of a Lady*, Henry James

- A gerund is a verbal that ends in *-ing* and serves as a noun. It may take objects, complements, and modifiers.

    **Describing the Frenchman** was a tour de force for Poe.

- A participle is a verb that ends in either *-ing* or *-ed* and modifies a noun or pronoun. A participle in a participial phrase may have objects, complements, and modifiers of its own.

  What I have described in the Frenchman was merely the result **of an excited**, or perhaps of a diseased, **intelligence**.
  —*The Murders in the Rue Morgue*, Edgar Allen Poe

- The direct object is a noun, pronoun, or group of words acting as a noun that receives the action of a transitive verb, the person or thing acted on. To find a direct object, rephrase the sentence by changing it into a *whom* or *what* question.

  I believe that I have omitted **mentioning** that in my first voyage from Boston to Philadelphia, being becalmed off Block Island, our crew employed themselves catching cod and hauled up a great number.
  —*Autobiography of Benjamin Franklin*,
  Benjamin Franklin

  Rephrased: I have omitted whom or what? The direct object is *mentioning*.

- An indirect object is a noun or pronoun that appears with a direct object and names the person or thing that something is given to or done for.

  Whichever way I turn, O I think you could give **me** my mate back again if you only would.          —"Sea-Drift," Walt Whitman

- A sentence can have both an object and an indirect object.

  Whichever way I turn, O I think you could give **me** my **mate** back again if you only would.
          —"Sea-Drift," Walt Whitman

- An antecedent is a noun or words taking the place of nouns for which a pronoun stands.

  No good novel will ever proceed from a superficial mind; that seems to me an **axiom** which, for the artist in fiction, will cover all needful moral ground: if the youthful aspirant take it to heart it will illuminate for him many of the mysteries of "purpose."

  —"The Art of Fiction," Henry James

## FUNCTIONS OF VERBS

- Verbs express action, occurrence (*appear*, *become*, *continue*, *feel*, *grow*, *look*, *remain*, *seen*, *sound*, and *taste*), or state of being (the verb *to be*).

  > Ye Angells bright, **pluck** from your Wings a Quill;
  >   **Make** me a pen thereof that best **will write**:
  > **Lende** me your fancy and Angellick skill
  >   To **treate** this Theme, more rich than Rubies bright.
  > — "Meditation Sixty: Second Series,"
  > Edward Taylor

- Verbs that express occurrence or state of being, also known as linking verbs, are intransitive verbs and have no objects.

  > The first time that the sun rose on thine oath
  > To love me, I **looked** forward to the moon
  > To slacken all those bonds which seemed too soon
  > And quickly tied to make a lasting troth.
  > —*Sonnets from the Portuguese*,
  > Elizabeth Barrett Browning

  *Looked* is an intransitive verb and, therefore, has no object. *Forward* is an adverb that answers the question "where," and the adverbial phrase "the first time" answers the question "when."

- Linking verbs may have predicate adjectives or predicate nominatives, also known as predicate nouns.

  > Of all historical problems, the nature of a national character **is the most difficult and the most important.**
  > — "American Ideals," Henry Adams

# VERB TENSES

It would also be useful to review the tenses and forms of verbs, not necessarily because you may find multiple-choice questions about them but because the review will help you when you write your own essays. Verbs have six tenses to reveal the time of an action or condition. Each tense has a basic, progressive, and emphatic form.

| Tenses and Forms of Verbs | | |
|---|---|---|
| | **Basic Form** | **Progressive Form** | **Emphatic Form** |
| **Present** | I talk a lot. | I am talking about it now. | I do talk more than most students. |
| **Past** | I talked with the group. | I was talking when you interrupted. | I did talk with you about that. |
| **Future** | I will talk to you Sunday. | I will be talking at the conference. | |
| **Present Perfect** | I have talked for almost an hour. | I have been talking too much. | |
| **Past Perfect** | I had talked to him a year ago. | I had been talking with you when he arrived. | |
| **Future Perfect** | I will have talked to the recruiter by the end of the week. | I will have been talking about this project for a month before I get approval. | |

# SOME PRACTICAL ADVICE ON WRITING YOUR ESSAYS

The basic grammar and punctuation we are talking about here will help you with writing. Review the following rules and tips before you write a practice essay, and then evaluate your finished essay against them. As you write your next essay, keep in mind any rules with which you had trouble. If necessary, focus on one rule at a time. It is important that you are comfortable with the rules of grammar and punctuation; that way, they flow naturally as you write, and you don't spend time thinking about where the commas should go.

# SENTENCE STRUCTURE

Good writing has a variety of sentence structures: simple, compound, complex, and compound-complex. Sentence combining is one way to be sure you have a varied sentence pattern that adds to the interest of your writing. Consider the following examples as possibilities that you have to choose from, and note the correct punctuation for each. All quotations are from Henry Adams's "American Ideals."

### Simple Sentence

Of all historical problems, the nature of a national character is the most difficult and the most important.

Ralph Waldo Emerson, a more distinct idealist, was born in 1780.

### Compound Sentence

After the downfall of the French republic, they (Americans) had no right to expect a kind word from Europe, **and** during the next twenty years, they rarely received one.

Probably Jefferson came nearest to the mark, **for** he represented the hopes of science as well as the prejudices of Virginia.

### Complex Sentence

Lincoln was born in 1809, the moment **when** American character stood in lowest esteem.

Jefferson, the literary representative of his class, spoke chiefly for Virginians, and dreaded so greatly his own reputation as a visionary **that** he seldom or never uttered his whole thought.

### Compound-Complex Sentences

Benjamin Franklin had raised high the reputation of American printers, **and** the actual President of the United States, **who** signed with Franklin the treaty of peace with Great Britain, was the son of a farmer, and had himself kept a school in his youth.

In the year 1800 Eli Terry, another Connecticut Yankee of the same class, took into his employ two young men **to help** him make wooden clocks, **and** this was the capital **on which** the greatest clock-manufactory in the world began its operation.

## PARALLEL CONSTRUCTION

In addition to using dependent and independent clauses to add variety, try using words, phrases, and clauses in parallel constructions. Parallelism reinforces equal ideas, contributes to ease in reading, and, most importantly, adds clarity and rhythm to your ideas. The most simple parallelism employs comparisons and contrasts.

Eli Whitney was **better** educated than Fitch, but had **neither wealth, social influence, nor patron to back his ingenuity.**

Review your own essays, and underline sentences that you could combine. Then try combining them on a separate sheet of paper. This is a good exercise to get you accustomed to varying your sentence structures as you write. But do not try for variety for the first time during the real test.

When combining sentences, do not fall prey to run-on sentences, sentence fragments, or comma splices.

# RUN-ON SENTENCES

A run-on sentence is a compound or compound-complex sentence in which neither a conjunction nor punctuation separates two or more independent clauses. You can fix a run-on sentence by using

1. a coordinating conjunction, if you are writing a compound sentence;

2. a coordinating adverb;

3. a transitional phrase;

4. and/or a semicolon in a complex or compound-complex sentence.

The following examples are taken, with our apologies, from "Milton" by John Babington Macaulay.

1. Milton was, like Dante, a statesman and a lover, **and,** like Dante, he had been unfortunate in ambition and in love.

2. Milton was, like Dante, a statesman and a lover; **moreover,** like Dante, he had been unfortunate in ambition and in love.

3. Milton was, like Dante, a statesman and a lover; **in addition,** like Dante, he had been unfortunate in ambition and in love.

4. Milton was, like Dante, a statesman and a lover; like Dante, he had been unfortunate in ambition and in love.
   (Macaulay's choice)

Did you notice that these sentences are also examples of both comparison and the use of independent clauses as parallelism?

# SENTENCE FRAGMENTS

A sentence fragment is just that—part of a sentence, a group of words that does not express a complete thought. If it has a verb form—a verbal such as a participle—it may look like a sentence, but it is not a sentence. You can avoid sentence fragments by always making sure that

- the verb is a verb—not a participial form (*-ing* or *-ed*) without its auxiliary (some form of *have* or *be*) or an infinitive (*to* plus a verb).

  Such as it was. When, on the eve of great events, he [Milton] returned from his travels, in the prime of health and manly beauty. Loaded with literary distinctions, and glowing with patriotic hopes. . . .

- there is a subject. If there is none, add one or attach the fragment to a sentence.

> Such as it was. When, on the eve of great events, he [Milton] returned from his travels, in the prime of health and manly beauty, **loaded** with literary distinctions, and glowing with patriotic hopes. . . .

- you remove any incorrectly used subordinating conjunctions, or you combine the fragment so it becomes a sentence.

> Such as it was. When, on the eve of great events, he [Milton] returned from his travels, in the prime of health and manly beauty. **He was** loaded with literary distinctions, and glowing with patriotic hopes. . . .

The following is Macaulay's choice:

> Such as it was **when**, on the eve of great events, he [Milton] returned from his travels, in the prime of health and manly beauty, **loaded** with literary distinctions, and glowing with patriotic hopes. . . .

| CONJUNCTIVE ADVERBS | | TRANSITIONAL PHRASES |
|---|---|---|
| also | meanwhile | after all |
| anyhow | moreover | as a consequence |
| anyway | nevertheless | as a result |
| besides | next | at any rate |
| consequently | nonetheless | at the same time |
| finally | now | by the way |
| furthermore | otherwise | even so |
| hence | similarly | for example |
| however | still | in addition |
| incidentally | then | in fact |
| indeed | therefore | in other words |
| likewise | thus | in the second place |
| | | on the contrary |
| | | on the other hand |

# COMMA SPLICES

Comma splices occur when two or more independent clauses are joined by a comma (1) when some other punctuation or (2) a coordinating conjunction or (3) subordinating conjunction should have been used. The following is an example of a comma splice.

> Euripedes attempted to carry the reform further, it was a task beyond his powers, perhaps beyond any powers.

You could correct it by any of the following:

1.  Euripedes attempted to carry the reform further; it was a task beyond his powers, perhaps beyond any powers.
    (Macaulay's choice)

2.  Euripedes attempted to carry the reform further, **but** it was a task beyond his powers, perhaps beyond any powers.

3.  **While** Euripedes attempted to carry the reform further, the task was beyond his powers, perhaps beyond any powers.

| COORDINATING CONJUNCTIONS | SUBORDINATING CONJUNCTIONS | |
|---|---|---|
| and | after | no matter how |
| but | although | now that |
| or | as far as | once |
| for | as soon as | provided that |
| nor | as if | since |
| so | as though | so that |
| yet | because | supposing that |
| | before | than |
| | even if | though |
| | even though | till, until |
| | how | unless |
| | if | when, whenever |
| | inasmuch as | where, wherever |
| | in case that | whether |
| | insofar as | while |
| | in that | why |

**RELATIVE PRONOUNS**
(used to introduce subordinate clauses that function as nouns)

| | |
|---|---|
| that | who, whoever |
| what | whom, whomever |
| which | whose |

You can also use subordinating conjunctions, conjunctive adverbs, and transitional phrases to link ideas between sentences and even paragraphs.

**Now** let us compare with the exact detail . . .
**Once more,** compare . . .
We venture to say, **on the contrary,** . . .

—"Milton," John Babington Macaulay

# MECHANICS AND PUNCTUATION

What do you need to know about mechanics and punctuation for the AP English Language and Literature test? Enough to be able to write and punctuate grammatically correct sentences. (This, by the way, is a sentence fragment. In your own writing, an occasional sentence fragment works, but do not take the chance in your essays. The reader may not understand that you wrote a sentence fragment for a purpose, not as a mistake.)

If you find any of the rules in the following brief review unfamiliar, go back to your English composition text and review the appropriate section in more depth. Do some of the practice exercises that the text undoubtedly has.

The test evaluators may not expect you to write a flawless essay, but you want to make sure that your mechanics and punctuation are as correct as possible. Everything you do well adds to the favorable impression necessary for a high score. The same is true about punctuation. Using the correct punctuation makes a good impression on the readers. Remember, too, that errors in punctuation may interfere with clarity.

## CAPITALIZATION

You have studied capitalization throughout your school years. The following list recaps the rules for capitalization you have learned.

### Nouns

- Capitalize the first word in interjections and incomplete questions.

- Capitalize the first word in a quotation if the quotation is a complete sentence.

- Capitalize the first word after a colon if the word begins a complete sentence.

- Capitalize geographical and place names.

- Capitalize names of specific events and periods of time.

- Capitalize the names of organizations, government bodies, political parties, races, nationalities, languages, and religions.

### Adjectives

- Capitalize most proper adjectives; for example *African* in *African American.*

- Do not capitalize certain frequently used proper adjectives; for example, *french fries, venetian blinds.*

- Capitalize a brand name used as an adjective but not the common noun it modifies; for example, *Jello pudding.*

- Do not capitalize a common noun used with two proper adjectives; for example, *Iron Age tools.*

- Do not capitalize prefixes attached to proper adjectives unless the prefix refers to a nationality; for example, *pre-Columbian art* but *Franco-American music.*

## Capitals in Titles

- Capitalize titles of people when used with a person's name or when used in direct address.

- Capitalize titles showing family relationships when they refer to a specific person, unless they are preceded by a possessive noun or pronoun.

- Capitalize the first word and all other key words in the titles of books, periodicals, plays, poems, stories, paintings, and other works of art.

# ABBREVIATIONS

Usually, you should not use abbreviations when you are writing formal English. However, sometimes abbreviations are appropriate. The following list reviews guidelines for using abbreviations.

## Names and Titles of People

- Use a person's full given name in formal writing, unless the person uses initials as part of his or her name; for example, the poet *A. E. Housman.*

- Abbreviations of social titles before a proper name begin with a capital letter and end with a period.

- Abbreviations of other titles used before proper names begin with a capital letter and end with a period.

- Abbreviations of titles after a name begin with a capital and end with a period.

- In formal writing, spell out numbers or amounts less than 100 and any other numbers that can be written in one or two words.

- Spell out all numbers found at the beginning of sentences.

- Use numerals when referring to fractions, decimals, and percentages, as well as addresses and dates.

### Writing Strategy

*Abbreviations for both traditional and metric measurements should only be used in technical and informal writing and only with numerals.*

# END MARKS

- Use a period to end a declarative sentence, a mild imperative, or an indirect question.

- Use a question mark to end an interrogative sentence, an incomplete question, or a statement intended as a question.

- Use an exclamation mark to end an exclamatory sentence, a forceful imperative sentence, or an interjection of strong emotion.

# COMMAS

- Use a comma before a conjunction that separates two independent clauses in a compound sentence.

- Use commas to separate three or more words, phrases, or clauses in a series.

- Use commas to separate adjectives of equal rank.

- Do not use commas to separate adjectives that must stay in a specific order.

**Common Error**

*Many writers overuse commas. Make certain that you know why you are adding a comma to a sentence.*

- Use a comma after an introductory word, phrase, or clause.

- Use commas to set off parenthetical expressions.

- Use commas to set off nonessential expressions.

- Use commas to set off a direct quotation from the rest of the sentence.

- Use a comma to prevent a sentence from being misunderstood.

# SEMICOLONS AND COLONS

- Use a semicolon to join independent clauses not already joined by a coordinating conjunction *(and, or, but, nor, so, yet)*.

- Use a semicolon to join independent clauses separated by either a conjunctive adverb or a transitional expression.

- Use a colon before a list of items following an independent clause.

- Use a colon to introduce a formal or lengthy quotation or one that is missing an introductory expression.

- Use a colon to introduce a sentence that summarizes or explains the sentence before it.

## QUOTATION MARKS AND UNDERLINING

If a word, a title, or a name would be italicized in printed material, then you need to underline it when you write it by hand. If you were writing your essay on a computer, you would use the *italics* function.

### Common Error

*Do not use quotation marks around an indirect quotation (a restatement of someone's words).*

- Use quotation marks to enclose a person's exact words.

- Place a comma or a period inside the final quotation mark.

- Place a semicolon or colon outside the final quotation mark.

- Place a question mark or exclamation mark inside the final quotation if the end mark is part of the quotation.

- Place a question mark or exclamation mark outside the final quotation if the end mark is not part of the quotation.

- Use three ellipsis marks in a quotation to indicate that words have been omitted.

- Use single quotation marks for a quotation within a quotation.

- Use quotation marks around titles of short written works, episodes in a series, songs, parts of musical compositions, or collections.

### Common Error

*Do not underline or place in quotation marks the titles of holy books such as the Koran or the Bible, or their parts.*

- Underline (italicize) titles of long written works, shows, films, and other works of art.

- Underline (italicize) words and phrases from a foreign language when not used commonly in English.

- Underline (italicize) numbers, symbols, letters, and words used as names for themselves.

## DASHES, PARENTHESES, AND BRACKETS

- Use dashes to indicate an abrupt change of thought, a dramatic interrupting idea, or a summary statement.

- Use dashes to set off a nonessential appositive, modifier, or parenthetical expression when it is long, already punctuated, or especially dramatic.

- Use parentheses to set off asides and explanations only when the material is not essential or when it consists of one or more sentences.

- Place all punctuation after the parentheses in a sentence with a set-off phrase.

- Use brackets to enclose words you insert into a quotation when you are quoting someone else.

# HYPHENS

- Use a hyphen when writing out the numbers *twenty-one* through *ninety-nine.*

- Use a hyphen with fractions used as adjectives.

- Use a hyphen in words with the prefixes *all-, ex-,* and *self-* and words with the suffix *-elect.*

- Use a hyphen to connect a compound modifier before a noun unless it includes a word ending in *-ly,* or is a compound proper adjective; for example, *beautifully dressed, Native American poem.*

- If a word must be divided at the end of a line, place a hyphen between syllables.

# APOSTROPHES

- Add an apostrophe and an *s* to show the possessive case of most singular nouns; for example, *cat's dish, the tomato's flavor.*

- Add an apostrophe to show the possessive case of plural nouns ending in *s* or *es;* for example, *the boys' club, the people's choice.*

- Add an apostrophe and an *s* to show possession with plural nouns that do not end in *s;* for example, *women's clothing, the mice's nests.*

- Add an apostrophe and an *s* or just an apostrophe (if the word is plural and ends in *s*) to the last word of a compound noun to form the possessive; for example, *the Joint Committee's decision, the mutual funds' investors.*

- To show joint ownership, make the final noun possessive. To show individual ownership, make each noun possessive; for example, *Marie and Leslie's apartment,* but *Mike's and Tom's cars.*

- Use an apostrophe and an *s* with indefinite pronouns to show possession; for example, *one's jacket, somebody's chair.*

- Use an apostrophe and an *s* to write the plurals of numbers, symbols, and letters; for example, *8's, &'s, p's.*

## Common Error

*Do not use an apostrophe with the possessive forms of personal pronouns; for example,* hers'.

# DICTION

Word choice speaks volumes about you. (That phrase is a cliché that would be best to avoid.) The following are some suggestions to help you refine your writing and polish your choice of words.

## REPLACE CLICHÉS WITH FRESHER IMAGES AND WORDS

A cliché is any stale, worn-out phrase that has been used so often it has become virtually meaningless. Clichés make your writing seem commonplace and secondhand. Some common clichés and trite expressions include the following:

| | |
|---|---|
| Ugly as sin | Like finding a needle in a haystack |
| Pretty as a picture | Like a bump on a log |
| Happy as a lark | Like a hot potato |
| Hard as a rock | Sky high |
| Fresh as a daisy | Sparkling clean |
| Skinny as a rail | Filthy rich |
| Sly as a fox | Dirt cheap |
| Stiff as a board | Costing an arm and a leg |
| Old as the hills | Heart of gold |
| Mad as a hornet | One in a million |
| Soft as silk | Between a rock and a hard place |
| Warm as toast | Out of the frying pan and into the fire |
| Dumb as a doorknob | When push comes to shove |
| Smart as a whip | Working fingers to the bone |
| Crazy as a loon | Come out smelling like a rose |
| Honest as the day is long | Tooting my/your/one's own horn |
| As much fun as a barrel of monkeys | In a New York minute |
| Quiet as a mouse | Variety is the spice of life. |
| Loose as a goose | Stand up and be counted. |
| Phony as a three-dollar bill | Raining cats and dogs |
| Pure as the driven snow | The sixty-four dollar question |
| Crystal clear | Day in and day out |
| True blue | Have a nice day. |
| Like pulling teeth | |
| Like a fish out of water | |

Replace clichés and trite expressions with livelier, more concrete language, for example:

> **Cliché:** I *was shaking in my boots* before the interview, but I was *happy as a lark* when the personnel manager offered me the job.

> **Improved:** I was *terrified* before the interview, but I was *ecstatic* when the personnel manager offered me the job.

> **Cliché:** Whether the author really believed what he wrote was the sixty-four-dollar question.

> **Improved:** Whether the author really believed what he wrote was difficult to determine from the answers he gave the interviewer.

## Avoid Euphemisms

A euphemism is a word or phrase that is less direct but that may be considered less offensive than another word or phrase with the same meaning; for example, saying someone is *no longer with us* instead of *dead.* Euphemisms can lead to wordiness, as in the above example, because you may need several words to say what one direct word could convey. Euphemisms also lessen the impact of a thought or idea, and they can mislead your readers. Occasionally you may choose to use a euphemism to protect someone's feelings—yours, the subject of your writing, or your audience—but eliminate euphemisms whenever possible so your writing does not seem insincere.

> **Euphemism:** Amit could not attend the meeting Thursday because he was *indisposed.*

> **Improved:** Amit could not attend the meeting Thursday because he was *sick.*

> **Euphemism:** Because she was constantly late to work, Leslie was *let go.*

> **Improved:** Because she was constantly late to work, Leslie was *fired.*

# Avoid Self-Important Language

**Writing Strategy**

*Polysyllabic, high-sounding words can make your writing sound pretentious rather than erudite.*

A writer who tries to impress readers with unnecessarily obscure words and lengthy, complicated sentences, often adopts self-important language. The result is bad tone and a confused message. When you write, avoid that type of language. Eliminate vague, general nouns and long verbs that end in *-ate* or *-ize*.

> **Self-important:** To facilitate input by the maximum number of potential purchasers, questionnaires were designed and posted well in advance of the launch of the promotional marketing campaign.

> **Improved:** Before we began advertising, we designed and mailed a marketing survey to find out what consumers were looking for.

# Avoid Flowery Language and Emotionally-Loaded Words

Good writing should include vivid modifiers and interesting phrases. However, your writing should never become overloaded with unnecessary adjectives and adverbs that serve only as decoration. Usually, a simpler way of expressing yourself is more effective.

> **Flowery:** The glimmering, golden rays of the brilliant orb of the sun shimmered above the white-hot sands of the vast desert, sere and lifeless.

> **Improved:** The rays of the sun shimmered above the hot, dry desert.

Similarly, overly emotional language can produce a harsh tone and make your readers reject your point of view. Avoid emotional language and substitute more rational diction.

> **Emotional:** The idiot who wrote that essay should have his head examined.

> **Improved:** The writer who developed that argument based it on a faulty assumption.

## AVOID WORDS THAT MAY NOT BE UNDERSTOOD

You should use only vocabulary and expressions that your readers will understand. No matter what your tone, some types of language can be confusing. In general, avoid slang words and expressions because you cannot be sure that your audience is familiar with current idioms. Also, remember that slang quickly becomes dated.

> **Slang:** Brian's mother reprimanded him for bombing his physics test.
>
> **Improved:** Brian's mother reprimanded him for failing his physics test.

**Review Strategy**

*Jargon is language aimed at specialists.*

Similarly, jargon can confuse readers and destroy your tone. Use it only if you are writing a highly technical report and must use special terms for the topic. Your readers may easily become lost if you do not replace jargon with concrete, understandable phrases.

> **Jargon:** Close-support, transport, and reconnaissance assistance is provided by the S-3X helicopter, which is the most cost effective in a crane configuration.
>
> **Improved:** The S-3X helicopter provides support, transportation, and reconnaissance. However, the helicopter is most cost effective when it works as a crane.

## ELIMINATE DEADWOOD

Check your essay for words that contribute nothing to your ideas. Discard these empty words that pad your sentences and create roundabout constructions. You will find some of the most common "empty words" in the following box.

| Commonly Used Empty Words and Phrases | | |
|---|---|---|
| a great deal of | due to | which is to say |
| is the one who is | it is a fact that | the area of |
| there is | the thing that | what I mean is |
| there are | of the opinion that | for the reason that |
| by way of | to the extent that | in a manner that |

> **Deadwood:** It is a fact that sunburn can cause skin cancer.
>
> **Improved:** Sunburn can cause skin cancer.

### Writing Strategy

*Be careful that you don't eliminate all hedging words in your writing. Sometimes you need to qualify what you are saying.*

Other deadwood you should eliminate are hedging words and phrases, or qualifiers. Writers use qualifiers to be noncommittal, but using them results in a vague and indefinite essay. However, don't eliminate all hedging words in your writing. For example, "Everyone in the stadium cheered the touchdown" needs to be qualified unless you know that the opposing team had no supporters in the stands. The following list contains words and phrases that unnecessarily qualify what you want to say:

| Commonly Used Hedging Words and Phrases | | |
|---|---|---|
| almost | rather | it seems |
| tends to | in a way | sort of |
| somewhat | kind of | that may or may not |

**Hedging:** A major earthquake that may or may not occur in this region can cause a great deal of damage.

**Improved:** If a major earthquake occurs in this region, it will cause a great deal of damage.

## AVOID REDUNDANCY

Redundancy occurs when you repeat an idea unnecessarily. It prevents writing from being concise. Saying the same thing repeatedly not only sounds awkward but adds deadwood to your essay. To eliminate redundancy in your writing, look for words or phrases that repeat the meaning of another word.

**Redundant:** Tamiko prefers the written letter to the telephone.

**Improved:** Tamiko prefers letters to telephone calls.

**Redundant:** The consensus of opinion in our community is that commercial building should be restricted.

**Improved:** The consensus in our community is that commercial building should be restricted.

# BE SUCCINCT

Less obvious than deadwood and redundant language are wordy phrases and clauses that can weaken the impact of your writing. Shorten wordy phrases and clauses if you can without changing the meaning of your sentence. Sentences can be rewritten by using appositives, prepositional phrases, adjectives, adverbs, or possessive nouns. Sometimes you can replace a phrase with a single word.

**Wordy:** Denee sang every Christmas carol in a loud voice.

**Improved:** Denee sang every Christmas carol loudly.

**Wordy:** Tourists from Germany and Canada love to vacation in the Caribbean.

**Improved:** Many German and Canadian tourists love to vacation in the Caribbean.

**Study Strategy**

*To review more about combining sentences, see page 147 in this chapter.*

If your essay has a great many adjective clauses, you can simplify sentences by dropping the clause's subject, verb, and other unnecessary words. Also substitute appositives, participial phrases, and compounds for wordy clauses.

**Wordy:** The painting, which hangs on the museum's third floor, accurately portrays the signing of the Declaration of Independence.

**Improved:** The painting, on the museum's third floor, accurately portrays the signing of the Declaration of Independence.

# CREATING AN IDEA BANK

**Test-Taking Strategy**

*Having this list in mind will keep you from having writer's block during the test.*

Before you begin practicing for the essay section of the test, brainstorm all the words and phrases you can think of to describe a literary work of nonfiction—critical essay, autobiography, biography, opinion piece, science article, and so on. Make categories under each. You might do the exercise with a friend, and then share lists to gather as many words as you can. Use this as your idea bank and your word bank, and consult it before you begin each practice essay. Here is a start to your list.

| Autobiography | |
|---|---|
| **Diction** | **Style** |
| verbose | convoluted |
| wordy | elegant |
| flowery | precise |

# 98 COMMON USAGE PROBLEMS

Many usage errors result from using colloquialisms, the language of everyday use, in formal written English. Others occur because words that are similar in meaning or spelling are confused. The following is a list of 98 common usage problems that you should avoid in your writing.

1. *a, an*
   Use the article *a* before consonant sounds and the article *an* before vowel sounds. Words beginning with *h*, *o*, and *u* can have either sound.

2. *accept, except*
   *Accept* is a verb meaning "to receive," and *except* is a preposition meaning "other than" or "leaving out."

3. *accuse, allege*
   *Accuse* means "to blame," whereas *allege* means "to state as fact something that has not been proved."

4. *adapt, adopt*
   *Adapt* means "to change," but *adopt* means "to take as one's own."

5. *advice, advise*
   *Advice,* a noun, means "an opinion." *Advise* is a verb that means "to express an opinion to."

6. *affect, effect*
   *Affect* is normally a verb meaning "to influence." *Effect* is usually a noun that means "result." Sometimes, *effect* is a verb that means "to cause."

7. *aggravate*
   *Aggravate* means "to make something worse"; it should not be used to refer to an annoyance.

8. *ain't*
   *Ain't* is nonstandard English.

9. *allot, a lot, alot*
   The verb *allot* means "to divide in parts" or "to give out shares." *A lot* is an informal phrase meaning "a great many," so you should not use it in formal writing. *Alot* is nonstandard spelling. It should never be used.

## 98 COMMON USAGE PROBLEMS—*continued*

**Writing Strategy**

*In formal writing, awful should be used to mean only "inspiring fear or awe."*

10. *all ready, already*
    *All ready,* which functions as an adjective, is an expression meaning "ready." *Already,* an adverb, means "by or before this time" or "even now."

11. *all right, alright.*
    *Alright* is a nonstandard spelling. Use the two-word version.

12. *all together, altogether*
    *All together* means "all at once." *Altogether* means "completely."

13. *A.M., P.M*
    *A.M.* refers to hours before noon, *P.M* to hours after noon. Numbers are not spelled out when you use these abbreviations, nor should you use phrases such as "in the morning" or "in the evening" with them.

14. *among, between*
    *Among* and *between* are prepositions. *Among* is used with three or more items. *Between* is generally used with only two items.

15. *amount, number*
    *Amount* is used with quantities that cannot be counted. Use *number* when items can be counted.

16. *anxious*
    *Anxious* means "worried" or "uneasy." It should not be used to mean "eager."

17. *anyone, any one, everyone, every one*
    *Anyone* and *everyone* mean "any person" and "every person." *Any one* means "any single person or thing," and *every one* means "every single person or thing."

18. *anyway, anywhere, everywhere, nowhere, somewhere*
    These adverbs should never end in *s.*

19. *as*
    *As* should not be used to mean "because" or "since."

20. *as to*
    *As to* is awkward. Substitute *about.*

21. *at*
    Eliminate *at* when used after *where.*

## 98 COMMON USAGE PROBLEMS—*continued*

**22.** *at about*
Eliminate *at* or *about* if you find them used together.

**23.** *awful, awfully*
*Awful* is used informally to mean "extremely bad." *Awfully* is also informal, meaning "very."

**24.** *awhile, a while*
*Awhile* is an adverb, meaning "for a while." *A while* is an article and a noun and is usually used after the preposition *for*.

**25.** *beat, win*
*Beat* means "to overcome." *Win* means "to achieve victory in." Replace *win* if the sentence sense is *beat*.

**26.** *because*
Eliminate *because* if it follows "the reason," or rephrase the sentence.

**27.** *being as, being that*
Replace either phrase with *since* or *because*.

**28.** *beside, besides*
*Beside* means "at the side of" or "close to." *Besides* means "in addition to." They are not interchangeable.

**29.** *bring, take*
*Bring* means "to carry from a distant place to a nearer one." *Take* means the opposite, "to carry from a near place to a more distant place."

**30.** *bunch*
*Bunch* means "a number of things of the same kind." Do not use *bunch* to mean "group."

**31.** *burst, bust, busted*
*Burst* is the present, past, and past participle of the verb *to burst*. *Bust* and *busted* are nonstandard English.

**32.** *but what*
*But what* is nonstandard English. Use *that*.

**33.** *can, may*
Use *can* to mean "to have the ability to." Use *may* to mean "to have permission to."

## 98 COMMON USAGE PROBLEMS—*continued*

**34.** *can't help but*
Use *can't help* plus a gerund instead of *can't help but;* for example, *can't help crying.*

**35.** *condemn, condone*
These words have nearly opposite meanings. *Condemn* means "to express disapproval of." *Condone* means "to pardon" or "excuse."

**36.** *continual, continuous*
*Continual* means "occurring over and over in succession," but *continuous* means "occurring without stopping."

**37.** *different from, different than*
The expression *different from* is more accepted.

**38.** *doesn't, don't*
Use *doesn't* with third-person singular subjects.

**39.** *done*
*Done*, the past participle of the verb *to do*, follows a helping verb.

**40.** *dove*
Use *dived* instead of *dove* for the past tense of the verb *dive*.

**41.** *due to*
Use *due to* only when the words *caused by* can be substituted.

**42.** *due to the fact that*
Use *since* or *because* instead.

**43.** *each other, one another*
Most of the time these expressions are interchangeable. Sometimes *each other* is used when only two people or things are involved, and *one another* is used when more than two are involved.

**44.** *emigrate, immigrate*
These are opposites. *Emigrate* means "to leave a country," and *immigrate* means "to enter a country." In both cases, it is a reference to establishing a residency.

**45.** *enthused, enthusiastic*
*Enthused* is nonstandard English; therefore, use *enthusiastic*.

## 98 COMMON USAGE PROBLEMS—*continued*

**Review Strategy**

*The principal parts of* lay *are* lay, laying, laid, *and* laid. *The principal parts of* lie *are* lie, lying, lay, *and* lain.

46. *farther, further*
    *Farther* is a reference to distance, but *further* means "to a greater degree."

47. *fewer, less*
    *Fewer* is properly used with things that are counted, and *less* is used with qualities or quantities that are not counted.

48. *former, latter*
    In referring to two items, *former* designates the first and *latter*, the second.

49. *get, got, gotten*
    Although these verbs are acceptable, it is better to select different verbs if possible, such as *become, became, have become.*

50. *gone, went*
    *Gone*, the past participle of the verb *to go*, requires a helping verb. *Went* is the past tense of *go*, and no helping verb is required.

51. *good, lovely, nice*
    Try to use more specific adjectives in their place.

52. *hanged, hung*
    *Hanged* means "executed," and *hung* means "suspended."

53. *healthful, healthy*
    *Healthful* is used with things (*healthful diet*), and *healthy* refers to people.

54. *if, whether*
    These conjunctions are interchangeable, except when the intention is to give equal stress to alternatives, in which case *if* won't work, and *whether* must be used with *or not*. "I'll go whether you come with me or not" is not the same as "I'll go if you come with me."

55. *in, into*
    *In* is a position reference (*the kitten drank the milk in the bowl*), but *into* implies movement (*the kitten stepped into the bowl of milk*).

56. *irregardless*
    This is nonstandard English. Use *regardless* instead.

## 98 COMMON USAGE PROBLEMS—*continued*

**57.** *judicial, judicious*
*Judicial* refers to a legal system. *Judicious* means "to show wisdom."

**58.** *just*
Place *just*, when it is used as an adverb meaning "no more than," immediately before the word it modifies.

**59.** *kind of, sort of*
Do not use these words to mean "rather" or "somewhat."

**60.** *kind of a, sort of a*
Do not use *a* following *kind of* or *sort of*.

**61.** *lay, lie*
*Lay* means "to set or put something down," and it is usually followed by a direct object. *Lie* means "to recline," and it is never followed by a direct object.

**62.** *learn, teach*
*Learn* refers to "gaining knowledge," whereas *teach* means "to give knowledge."

**63.** *leave, let*
*Leave* means "to allow to remain," and *let* means "to permit."

**64.** *like*
*Like* is a preposition and should not be used in place of *as*.

**65.** *loose, lose*
*Loose* is commonly an adjective. *Lose* is always a verb meaning "to miss from one's possession."

**66.** *mad*
When used in formal language, *mad* means "insane." When it is used in informal language, it means "angry."

**67.** *maybe, may be*
*Maybe* is an adverb that means "perhaps." *May be* is a verb.

**68.** *number, numeral*
Use *number* to mean quantity and *numeral* to mean the figure representing the number, that is, *the numeral that comes after 3 is 4.*

### Test-Taking Strategy

*If a word ends in* a *or* i, *be careful. It may be plural.*

## 98 COMMON USAGE PROBLEMS—*continued*

### Study Strategy

*You can remember the difference by thinking of "your princiPAL as your PAL."*

**69.** *of*
Do not use *of* after the verbs *should, would, could,* or *must.* Use *have* instead. Also eliminate *of* after the words *outside, inside, off,* and *atop.*

**70.** *OK, O.K., okay*
Do not use these words in formal writing.

**71.** *only*
Make sure to place *only* immediately preceding the word it logically modifies. *You only say you love me,* that is, you say it but you don't mean it; *You say you love only me,* that is, I am the only one you love.

**72.** *ought*
Do not use *have* or *had* with *ought. Ought* is used with an infinitive; for example, *ought to wash, ought not to cry.*

**73.** *outside of*
Do not use *outside of* to mean "besides" or "except."

**74.** *parameter*
Use *parameter* only in mathematical contexts to designate a variable.

**75.** *persecute, prosecute*
*Persecute* means "to subject to ill treatment," whereas *prosecute* means "to bring a lawsuit against."

**76.** *plurals that do not end in "s"*
Some nouns are made plural in the same way that they were in their original language. For example, *criteria* and *phenomena* are plural. Make sure that you treat them as plural, not singular, nouns.

**77.** *poorly*
Do not use *poorly* to mean "ill" in formal writing.

**78.** *precede, proceed*
*Precede* means "to go before," and *proceed* means "to go forward."

### Writing Strategy

*Careful writers still use* slow *only as an adjective.*

# 98 COMMON USAGE PROBLEMS—*continued*

## Writing Strategy

*To correct a sentence containing* them there, these here, this here, *or* that there, *delete* here *or* there *in these expressions.*

79. *principal, principle*
    *Principal* can be a noun or an adjective. As a noun, it means "a person who has controlling authority," and as an adjective, it means "most important." *Principle* is always a noun, and it means "a basic law."

80. *raise, rise*
    *Raise* normally takes a direct object, but *rise* never takes a direct object, as in "I *raised* the flag," but "I *rise* every morning at 6."

81. *real*
    Do not use *real* to mean "very" or "really" in formal language.

82. *says*
    Do not use *says* in place of *said*.

83. *seen*
    *Seen* requires a helping verb, as in "I was *seen* at the movies," not "I *seen* him at the movies."

84. *set, sit*
    *Set* is usually followed by a direct object and means "to put something in a specific place." *Sit* means "to be seated," and it is never followed by a direct object.

85. *shape*
    In formal language, do not use the word *shape* to mean "condition," as in *The boxer was in good shape.*

86. *since, because*
    Use *since* when time is involved and *because* when a reason is involved. *Since I last saw them, I read a book,* but *Because they came last Saturday, I did not finish the book I was reading.*

87. *slow, slowly*
    It is preferable to use *slow* as the adjective and *slowly* as the adverb.

88. *than, then*
    *Than* is a comparative and is not to be confused with *then,* which refers to time.

## 98 COMMON USAGE PROBLEMS—*continued*

**89.** *that, which, who*
These pronouns refer to the following: *that*—people and things, *which*—only things, and *who*—only people.

**90.** *their, there, they're*
*Their* is a possessive pronoun. *There* is an expletive or an adverb. *They're* is a contraction of *they are*.

**91.** *them, them there, these here, this here, that there*
Replace with *these* or *those* if an adjective is required.

**92.** *till, until*
These words are interchangeable, but they are often misspelled.

**93.** *to, too, two*
*To* is a preposition. *Too* is an adverb used to modify adjectives and adverbs. *Two* is a number.

**94.** *unique*
*Unique* means "one of a kind"; therefore, it should not be modified by words such as *very* or *most*.

**95.** *want in, want out*
These are nonstandard expressions and should be avoided.

**96.** *ways*
*Ways* is plural. Do not use the article *a* immediately preceding *ways*.

**97.** *when, where*
Do not use these words directly after a linking verb. Also, do not use *where* as a substitute for *that*.

**98.** *-wise*
Do not use this suffix to create new words.

**Be sure to use**
*but that*, not *but what*
*because of*, not *due to*
*because*, not *on account of*
*rarely* or *hardly ever*, not *rarely ever*
*kind* or *kind of a*, not *sort, sort of*

# Chapter 4

# A QUICK REVIEW OF LITERARY AND RHETORICAL TERMS

You will not find any questions on the test that ask you to define a literary or rhetorical term, but you may find questions that give you an example and ask you to identify what it is an example of. As you study for your AP test, review the terms in the following list. As you read your assignments in English class, find examples of the concepts that underlie these literary and rhetorical terms. When you write your critical essays for class, incorporate terms and concepts from the list, where appropriate, to make your essays more precise.

**allegory:** an extended narrative in prose or verse in which characters, events, and settings represent abstract qualities and in which the writer intends a second meaning to be read beneath the surface story; the underlying meaning may be moral, religious, political, social, or satiric

**alliteration:** the repetition of consonant sounds at the beginning of words that are close to one another; for example, "beautiful blossoms blooming between the bushes"

**allusion:** a reference to another work or famous figure that is assumed to be well-known enough to be recognized by the reader

**anachronism:** an event, object, custom, person, or thing that is out of order in time; some anachronisms are unintentional, such as when an actor performing Shakespeare forgets to take off his watch; others are deliberately used to achieve a humorous or satiric effect, such as the sustained anachronism of Mark Twain's *A Connecticut Yankee in King Arthur's Court*

**analogy:** a comparison of two similar but different things, usually to clarify an action or a relationship, such as comparing the work of a heart to that of a pump

**anaphora:** specific type of repetition; word, phrase, or clause repeated at the beginning of two or more sentences in a row

**anecdote:** a short, simple narrative of an incident; often used for humorous effect or to make a point

**aphorism:** a short, often witty statement of a principle or a truth about life

**apostrophe:** usually in poetry but sometimes in prose; the device of calling out to a imaginary, dead, or absent person or to a place, thing, or personified abstraction

**argumentation:** writing that attempts to prove the validity of a point of view or an idea by presenting reasoned arguments; *persuasive writing* is a form of argumentation

**assonance:** the repetition of vowel sounds between different consonants, such as in *neigh/fade*

**authority:** support for an argument that is based on recognized experts in the field

**burlesque:** broad parody; whereas a parody will imitate and exaggerate a specific work, such as *Romeo and Juliet*, a burlesque will take an entire style or form, such as myths, and exaggerate it into ridiculousness

**cacophony:** harsh, awkward, or dissonant sounds used deliberately in poetry or prose; the opposite of **euphony**

**caricature:** descriptive writing that greatly exaggerates a specific feature of a person's appearance or a facet of personality

**classicism:** the principles and styles admired in the classics of Greek and Roman literature, such as objectivity, sensibility, restraint, and formality

**colloquialism:** a word or phrase used in everyday conversation and informal writing but that is often inappropriate in formal writing

**coherence:** quality of a piece of writing in which all the parts contribute to the development of the central idea, theme, or organizing principle

**conceit:** an elaborate **figure of speech** in which two seemingly dissimilar things or situations are compared

**connotation:** implied or suggested meaning of a word because of its association in the reader's mind

**consonance:** the repetition of identical consonant sounds before and after different vowel sounds, as in *boost/best*; it can also be seen within several compound words, such as *fulfill* and *Ping-Pong*

**conundrum:** a riddle whose answer is or involves a pun; it may also be a paradox or difficult problem

**denotation:** literal meaning of a word as defined

**description:** the picturing in words of something or someone through detailed observation of color, motion, sound, taste, smell, and touch; one of the four **modes of discourse**

**diction:** word choice, an element of style; also called **syntax**

**discourse:** spoken or written language, including literary works; the four traditionally classified **modes of discourse** are **description, exposition, narration,** and **persuasion**

**dissonance:** harsh or grating sounds that do not go together

**epigram:** a concise, witty saying in poetry or prose that either stands alone or is part of a larger work; it may also refer to a short poem of this type

**euphony:** a succession of harmonious sounds used in poetry or prose; the opposite of **cacophony**

**exemplum:** a brief tale used in medieval times to illustrate a sermon or to teach a lesson

**exposition:** the immediate revelation to the audience of the setting and other background information necessary for understanding the plot; also, explanation; one of the **four modes of discourse**

**figurative language:** language that contains **figures of speech,** such as similes and metaphors, in order to create associations that are imaginative rather than literal

**figures of speech:** expressions, such as similes, metaphors, and personifications, that make imaginative, rather than literal, comparisons or associations

**folklore:** traditional stories, songs, dances, and customs that are preserved among a people; folklore usually precedes literature, being passed down orally from generation to generation until recorded by scholars

**foreshadowing:** the use of a hint or clue to suggest a larger event that occurs later in the work

**genre:** a type of literary work, such as a novel or poem; there are also subgenres, such as science fiction or sonnet, within the larger genres

**hubris:** the excessive pride or ambition that leads a tragic hero to disregard warnings of impending doom, eventually causing his or her downfall

**humor:** anything that causes laughter or amusement; up until the end of the Renaissance, humor meant a person's temperament

**hyperbole:** deliberate exaggeration in order to create **humor** or emphasis

**idyll:** a short descriptive narrative, usually a poem, about an idealized country life; also called a **pastoral**

**imagery:** words or phrases that use a collection of images to appeal to one or more of the five senses in order to create a mental picture

**interior monologue:** writing that records the conversation that occurs inside a character's head

**inversion:** reversing the customary order of elements in a sentence or phrase; it is used effectively in many cases, such as posing a question: "Are you going to the store?"; often, it is used ineffectively in poetry, making it sound artificial and stilted: "To the hounds she rode, with her flags behind her streaming"

**irony:** a situation or statement in which the actual outcome or meaning is opposite to what was expected

**loose sentence:** a sentence that is grammatically complete before its end, such as "Thalia played the violin with an intensity never before seen in a high school music class"; the sentence is grammatically complete after the word *violin*

**metaphor:** a **figure of speech** in which one thing is referred to as another; for example, "my love is a fragile flower"

**metonymy:** a **figure of speech** that uses the name of an object, person, or idea to represent something with which it is associated, such as using "the crown" to refer to a monarch

**mode:** the method or form of a literary work; the manner in which a work of literature is written

**mood:** similar to **tone**, mood is the primary emotional attitude of a work

**motif:** main theme or subject of a work that is elaborated on in the development of the piece; a repeated pattern or idea

**myth:** one story in a system of narratives set in a complete imaginary world that once served to explain the origin of life, religious beliefs, and the forces of nature as supernatural occurrences

**narration:** the telling of a story in fiction, nonfiction, poetry, or drama; one of the four **modes of discourse**

**naturalism:** a literary movement that grew out of realism in France, the United States, and England in the late-nineteenth and early-twentieth centuries; it portrays humans as having no free will, being driven by the natural forces of heredity, environment, and animalistic urges over which they have no control

**objectivity:** an impersonal presentation of events and characters

**onomatopoeia:** the use of words that sound like what they mean, such as *hiss* and *boom*

**oxymoron:** a **figure of speech** composed of contradictory words or phrases, such as "wise fool"

**parable:** a short tale that teaches a moral; similar to but shorter than an **allegory**

**paradox:** a statement that seems to contradict itself but that turns out to have a rational meaning, as in this quotation from Henry David Thoreau: "I never found the companion that was so companionable as solitude."

**parallelism:** the technique of arranging words, phrases, clauses, or larger structures by placing them side by side and making them similar in form

**parody:** a work that ridicules the style of another work by imitating and exaggerating its elements

**periodic sentence:** a sentence that is not grammatically complete until its last phrase, such as, "Despite Glenn's hatred of his sister's laziness and noisy eating habits, he still cared for her."

**persona:** a fictional voice that a writer adopts to tell a story, determined by subject matter and audience; e.g., Mark Twain

**personification:** the attribution of human qualities to a nonhuman or an inanimate object

**persuasion:** a form of argumentation, one of the four **modes of discourse;** language intended to convince through appeals to reason or emotion

**point of view:** the perspective from which a story is presented; common points of view include the following:

- **first person narrator:** a narrator, referred to as "I," who is a character in the story and relates the actions through his or her own perspective, also revealing his or her own thoughts

- **stream of consciousness narrator:** like a first person narrator, but instead placing the reader inside the character's head, making the reader privy to the continuous, chaotic flow of disconnected, half-formed thoughts and impressions in the character's mind

- **omniscient narrator:** a third person narrator, referred to as "he," "she," or "they," who is able to see into each character's mind and understands all the action

- **limited omniscient narrator:** a third person narrator who reports the thoughts of only one character and generally only what that one character sees

- **objective narrator:** a third person narrator who only reports what would be visible to a camera; thoughts and feelings are only revealed if a character speaks of them

**protagonist:** the main character of a literary work

**realism:** a nineteenth-century literary movement in Europe and the United States that stressed accuracy in the portrayal of life, focusing on characters with whom middle-class readers could easily identify; it is in direct contrast with **romanticism**

**regionalism:** an element in literature that conveys a realistic portrayal of a specific geographical locale, using the locale and its influences as a major part of the plot

**rhetoric:** the art of using language effectively; involves (1) writer's purpose, (2) his or her consideration of the audience, (3) the exploration of the subject, (4) arrangement and organization of the ideas, (5) style and tone of expression, and (6) form.

**rhetorical modes:** *exposition, description, narration, argumentation*

**romanticism:** a literary, artistic, and philosophical movement that began in the eighteenth century as a reaction to neoclassicism; the focal points of the movement are imagination, emotion, and freedom, stressing subjectivity, individuality, the love and worship of nature, and a fascination with the past

**sarcasm:** harsh, caustic personal remarks to or about someone; less subtle than **irony**

**simile:** a **figure of speech** that uses *like*, *as*, or *as if* to make a direct comparison between two essentially different objects, actions, or qualities; for example, "the sky looked like an artist's canvas"

**speaker:** the voice of a work; an author may speak as himself or herself or as a fictitious persona

**stereotype:** a character who represents a trait that is usually attributed to a particular social or racial group and who lacks individuality

**style:** an author's characteristic manner of expression

**subjectivity:** a personal presentation of events and characters, influenced by the author's feelings and opinions

**suspension of disbelief:** the demand made that the reader accept the incidents recounted in the literary work

**symbolism:** the use of symbols or anything that is meant to be taken both literally and as representative of a higher and more complex significance

**synecdoche:** a **figure of speech** in which a part of something is used to represent a whole, such as using "boards" to mean a stage or "wheels" to mean a car

**syntax:** word choice or **diction**

**theme:** the central idea or "message" of a literary work

**tone:** the characteristic emotion or attitude of an author toward the characters, subject, and audience

**unity:** quality of a piece of writing; see also **coherence**

**voice:** the way a written work conveys an author's attitude

# Practice Test 1

## AP ENGLISH LANGUAGE AND COMPOSITION

On the front page of your test booklet, you will find some information about the test. Because you have studied this book, none of it should be new to you, and much of it is similar to other standardized tests you have taken.

The page will tell you that the following exam will take 3 hours—1 hour for the multiple-choice section and 2 hours for the three essays—and that there are two booklets for this exam, one for the multiple-choice section and one for the essays.

The page will also say that SECTION I

- is 1 hour.

- has 50 questions (or some number from 50 to 60).

- counts for 45 percent of your total grade.

Then you will find a sentence in capital letters telling you not to open your exam booklet until the monitor tells you to open it.

Other instructions will tell you to be careful to fill in only ovals 1 through 50 (or whatever the number is) in Section I on your separate answer sheet. Fill in each oval completely. If you erase an answer, erase it completely. You will not receive any credit for work done in the test booklet, but you may use it for making notes.

You will also find a paragraph about the guessing penalty—a deduction of one-quarter point for every wrong answer—as well as words of advice about guessing if you know something about the question and can eliminate several of the answers.

The final paragraph will remind you to work effectively and to pace yourself. You are told that not everyone will be able to answer all the questions. The page does suggest that you skip questions that are difficult and come back to them if you have time—just what we have been telling you.

<table>
<tr><td>SECTION I</td><td>TIME 60 MINUTES</td><td>55 QUESTIONS</td></tr>
</table>

**Directions:** This section consists of selections of literature and questions on their content, style, and form. After you have read each passage, select the response that best answers the question and mark the corresponding space on the answer sheet.

**Questions 1 through 15** refer to the following passage. Read the passage carefully and then choose the answers to the questions.

## FROM THE "PREFACE" OF *MODERN AMERICAN POETRY, A CRITICAL ANTHOLOGY*

Line It may be difficult, if not impossible, to determine the boundaries as well as the beginnings of "modernism," but only a few appraisers will deny that American literature became modern as well as American with the advent of Mark Twain, Herman Melville, and Walt Whitman.
5 In the history of poetry the line may be drawn with a measure of certainty, and it is with the Civil War and the publication of the third edition of *Leaves of Grass* that modern American poetry is defined.

Aftermath of the Civil War

The Civil War inspired volumes of indignant, military, religious,
10 and patriotic verse without adding more than four or five memorable pieces to the anthologies; the conflict produced a vast quantity of poems but practically no important poetry. Its end marked the end of an epoch—political, social, and literary. The arts declined; the New England group began to disintegrate. The poets had overstrained and
15 outsung themselves; it was a time of surrender and swan-songs. Unable to respond to the new forces of political nationalism and industrial reconstruction, the Brahmins (that famous group of intellectuals who had dominated literary America) withdrew into their libraries. Such poets as Longfellow, Bryant, Taylor, turned their eyes
20 away from the native scene, or left creative writing altogether and occupied themselves with translations. "They had been borne into an era in which they had no part," writes Fred Lewis Pattee (*A History of American Literature Since 1870*), "and they contented themselves with reëchoings of the old music." For them poetry ceased to be a
25 reflection of actuality, "an extension of experience." Within a period of six years, from 1867 to 1872, there appeared Longfellow's *Divina*

*Commedia,* C. E. Norton's *Vita Nuova,* T. W. Parson's *Inferno,* William Cullen Bryant's *Iliad* and *Odyssey,* and Bayard Taylor's *Faust.*

30 Suddenly the break came. America developed a national consciousness; the West discovered itself, and the East discovered the West. Grudgingly at first, the aristocratic leaders made way for a new expression; crude, jangling, vigorously democratic. The old order was changing with a vengeance. All the preceding writers—poets like Emerson, Lowell, Longfellow, Holmes—were not only products of the
35 New England colleges, but typically "Boston gentlemen of the early Renaissance." To them, the new men must have seemed like a regiment recruited from the ranks of vulgarity. Walt Whitman, Mark Twain, Bret Harte, John Hay, Joaquin Miller, Joel Chandler Harris, James Whitcomb Riley—these were men who had graduated from the
40 farm, the frontier, the mine, the pilothouse, the printer's shop! For a while, the movement seemed of little consequence; the impact of Whitman and the Westerners was averted. The poets of the transition, with a deliberate art, ignored the surge of a spontaneous national expression. They were even successful in holding it back.
45 But it was a gathering force.

—Louis Untermeyer

1. What is the meaning of the expression, "overstrained and outsung themselves" (line 15)?

   (A) Tired out
   (B) Lost creativity
   (C) Worked too hard
   (D) Gone beyond their knowledge
   (E) Sought new insights

2. This selection is an example of which mode of writing?

   (A) Descriptive
   (B) Narrative
   (C) Persuasive
   (D) Expository
   (E) Argument

3. What is the best explanation of the expression, "an extension of experience" (line 25)?

   (A) A reference to existentialism in poetry
   (B) Poetry as a reflection of the real world
   (C) A definition of modern poetry
   (D) A reflection of the universal nature of poetry
   (E) Poetry as an art form

4. Which of the following is the thesis that the author explores?

    (A) The Civil War inspired volumes of indignant, military, religious, and patriotic verse without adding more than four or five memorable pieces to the anthologies.

    (B) It may be difficult, if not impossible, to determine the boundaries as well as the beginnings of "modernism."

    (C) Only a few appraisers will deny that American literature became modern as well as American with the advent of Mark Twain, Herman Melville, and Walt Whitman.

    (D) The conclusion of the Civil War marked the end of an epoch— political, social, and literary.

    (E) The Brahmins withdrew from the literary scene because they could not respond to the changes made by the Civil War.

5. Which of the following changed the role of the Brahmins?

    (A) The Civil War and Reconstruction
    (B) Religious freedom and politics
    (C) Political nationalism and industrial reconstruction
    (D) Industrial growth and the westward movement
    (E) Philosophical creativity and the scientific revolution

6. Longfellow's *Divina Commedia* is an example of the author's contention that

    (A) modernism began with the end of the Civil War.
    (B) the New England poets no longer created vibrant, original verse, but turned to translations.
    (C) modernism developed along political lines.
    (D) modern literature grew slowly in most areas.
    (E) The New England writers provided a more studied view of life.

7. What is meant by the expression, "reëchoings of old music" (line 24)?

    (A) Tired old songs
    (B) Rewriting old material
    (C) Hearing influences from the past
    (D) Metaphorical sounds of the past
    (E) Redone philosophical treatises

8. The author contends that the Brahmins viewed the new poets as

    (A) vulgar
    (B) intellectual
    (C) uneducated
    (D) simple
    (E) insightful

9. What does the author mean in the first lines of the final paragraph, "Suddenly the break came. America developed a national consciousness; the West discovered itself, and the East discovered the West"?

    (A) People in the East were moving west.
    (B) There was a break in thought between the East and West.
    (C) American modern poetry found itself.
    (D) The Brahmins and modern poets were in conflict.
    (E) Poetry from the West became the dominant verse.

10. Which of the following is the best characterization of the tone of this passage?

    (A) Harsh and scathing
    (B) Scholarly and informative
    (C) Condescending and irritating
    (D) Humorous and witty
    (E) Dry and pretentious

11. Which of the following best summarizes the thoughts of the author in this piece?

    (A) The Brahmins' poetry, although superior to modern poetry, was lost after the Civil War.
    (B) The more liberated modern American poetry outshone the older styles.
    (C) The Brahmins were essentially the creators of modern American poetry.
    (D) The Civil War marked the beginning of modern American poetry.
    (E) The experiences of the Civil War formed the basis of some of the Brahmins' work.

12. The author would agree with which of the following statements about the Civil War?

    (A) It produced a great number of poems, but little poetry.
    (B) It produced many poets.
    (C) It developed the skills of the Brahmins.
    (D) It created new advocates of poetry.
    (E) It produced a number of forums for poets.

13. What is the meaning of the sentence beginning "The poets of the transition, with a deliberate art" (line 43)?

    (A) The transitional poets were deliberate in their poetry.
    (B) The Brahmins worked to prevent changes in American poetry.
    (C) The Brahmins paid little attention to the changes in poetry.
    (D) The spontaneous growth of modern American poetry overwhelmed the Brahmins.
    (E) There was little support for the Brahmins' poetry.

14. The author characterizes the new poets as

    (A) brash and arrogant
    (B) spiritual and philosophical
    (C) malleable and whimsical
    (D) forceful and inventive
    (E) crude and cutting edge

15. The author characterizes the Brahmins as

    (A) educated and mercurial
    (B) stuffy and intransigent
    (C) light-hearted and introspective
    (D) serious but easygoing
    (E) brilliant and forgiving

**Questions 16 through 30** refer to the following selection. Read the passage carefully and then choose the answers to the questions. This piece was written in 1780 when Benjamin Franklin was restricted to his house during an attack of gout.

# FROM "DIALOGUE BETWEEN GOUT AND MR. FRANKLIN"

Line **Franklin.** How can you so cruelly sport with my torments?

**Gout.** Sport! I am very serious. I have here a list of offenses against your own health distinctly written and can justify every stroke inflicted on you.

5 **Franklin.** Read it, then.

**Gout.** It is too long a detail, but I will briefly mention some particulars.

**Franklin.** Proceed. I am all attention.

**Gout.** Do you remember how often you have promised

10 yourself, the following morning, a walk in the grove of Boulogne, in the garden de la Muette, or in your own garden, and have violated your promise, alleging, at one time, it was too cold, at another, too warm, too wind, too moist, or what else you pleased, when in truth it was

15 too nothing but your insuperable love of ease?

**Franklin.** That I confess may have happened occasionally, probably ten times in a year.

**Gout.** Your confession is very far short of the truth. The gross amount is one hundred and ninety-nine times.

20 **Franklin.** Is it possible?

**Gout.** So possible, that it is fact. You may rely on the accuracy of my statement. You know M. Brillon's gardens and what fine walks they contain, you know the handsome flight of a hundred steps which lead from the terrace

25 above to the lawn below. You have been in the practice of visiting this amiable family twice a week, after dinner, and it is a maxim of your own that "a man may take as much exercise in walking a mile up and down stairs as in ten on level ground." What an opportunity was here for

30 you to have had exercise in both these ways! Did you embrace it, and how often?

**Franklin.** I cannot immediately answer that question.

**Gout.** I will do it for you: not once.

**Franklin.** Not once?

35 **Gout.** Even so. During the summer you went there at six o'clock. You found the charming lady with her lovely children and friends eager to walk with you and entertain you with their agreeable conversation, and what has been

40

your choice? Why to sit on the terrace, satisfying yourself with the fine prospect and passing your eye over the beauties of the garden below, without taking one step to descend and walk about in them. On the contrary, you call for tea and the chessboard, and lo! You are occupied in your seat till nine o'clock, and that besides two hours'

45

play after dinner; and then, instead of walking home, which would have bestirred you a little, you step into your carriage. How absurd to suppose that all this carelessness can be reconcilable with health without my interposition!

50 **Franklin.** I am convinced now of the justness of poor Richard's remark that "Our debts and our sins are always greater than we think for."

**Gout.** So it is. You philosophers are sages in your maxims and fools in your conduct.

55 **Franklin.** But do you charge among my crimes that I return in a carriage from M. Brillon's?

**Gout.** Certainly, for, having been seated all the while, you cannot object the fatigue of the day and cannot want therefore the relief of a carriage.

60 **Franklin.** What then would you have me do with my carriage?

**Gout.** Burn it if you choose, you would at least get heat out of it once in this way; or, if you dislike that proposal, here's another for you: observe the poor peasants who work in the vineyard and grounds about the villages of Passy,

65

Auteuil, Chaillot, etc., you may find every day among these deserving creatures four or five old men and women bent and perhaps crippled by weight of years and too long and too great labor. After a most fatiguing day these people have to trudge a mile or two to their

70

smoky huts. Order your coachman to set them down. This is an act that will be good for your soul; and, at the same time, after your visit to the Brillons', if you return on foot, that will be good for your body.

**Franklin.** Ah! How tiresome you are!

75   **Gout.** Well, then, to my office, it should not be forgotten that I am your physician. There . . .

**Franklin.** Oh! Oh!—for Heaven's sake leave me! And I promise faithfully never more to play at chess but to take exercise daily and live temperately.

80   **Gout.** I know you too well. You promise fair, but, after a few months of good health, you will return to your old habits; your fine promises will be forgotten like the forms of last year's clouds. Let us then finish the account, and I will go. But I leave you with an assurance of visiting you

85   again at a proper time and place, for my object is your good, and you are sensible now that I am your *real friend.*

                           —Benjamin Franklin

16. Which of the following best summarizes the theme of this excerpt?

    (A) A statement on the health of wealthy individuals

    (B) A delineation of the reasons to exercise

    (C) A fanciful discussion between a man and his disease

    (D) A lamentation of a man who is hurting

    (E) A dialogue for a morality play

17. What is the literary process that gives Gout voice?

    (A) Alliteration

    (B) Metaphor

    (C) Allegory

    (D) Personification

    (E) Simile

18. What is the tone of the dialogue?

    (A) Clinical, scientific

    (B) Reasoned, yet humorous

    (C) Formal and structured

    (D) Silly and frivolous

    (E) Objective

19. When Franklin acknowledges the justness of the statement, "Our debts and our sins are always greater that we think for," (lines 51-52) which of the following is he confirming?

    (A) We believe that many of our debts are too great.

    (B) We believe that we should not have any debts.

    (C) We believe that our debts and our sins are always smaller than they turn out to be.

    (D) We believe that committing a sin should not create a debt that we must pay.

    (E) We believe that others do not have to pay as heavily for their sins.

20. What is the best definition for the word "interposition" (line 49)?

    (A) Intercession

    (B) Interdiction

    (C) Involvement

    (D) Absence

    (E) Interview

21. Which of the following is the best characterization of Gout's reaction to Franklin's statement that Gout is sporting with him (line 1)?

    (A) Indignation
    (B) Pleased
    (C) Chastised
    (D) Contrite
    (E) Oblivious

22. From this dialogue, what assumption can be made about what Franklin advocates?

    (A) Walking when in a foreign country
    (B) Helping the poor and less fortunate
    (C) Reasonable and responsible behavior on the part of the individual
    (D) Involvement in the health practices of others
    (E) Limiting time playing games

23. Gout's attitude towards Franklin is best described as

    (A) disgusted
    (B) conciliatory
    (C) superficial
    (D) stern
    (E) pedantic

24. Why does the author elect to express his ideas with a dialogue between Gout and Franklin?

    (A) It allows clarity between Gout's thoughts and Franklin's reaction.
    (B) It makes it easier for Franklin to dispute the misinterpretation of Gout.
    (C) The author's only purpose was to be light-hearted.
    (D) It challenges the reader to take the side of either Gout or Franklin.
    (E) It leaves ambiguity as to the motives of Gout and Franklin.

25. Which of the following statements most accurately characterizes the interests of Franklin?

    (A) He likes walking in the gardens.
    (B) He enjoys being with friends.
    (C) He likes to be outside in the sun.
    (D) He enjoys a sedentary lifestyle.
    (E) He puts his work second to pleasure.

26. What is the meaning of the word "object" (line 85)?

    (A) Feel
    (B) Dispute
    (C) Argue
    (D) Silence
    (E) Save

27. The sentence "You found the charming lady with her lovely children and friends eager to walk with you and entertain you with their agreeable conversation, and what has been your choice?" contains

    I. A participial phrase
    II. A compound verb in the past tense
    III. An infinitive

    (A) I only
    (B) II only
    (C) III only
    (D) I and III
    (E) I, II, and III

28. What does the sentence "I cannot immediately answer that question" (line 32) say about Franklin's state of mind?

    (A) He is argumentative.
    (B) He is forgetful.
    (C) He is feeling guilty.
    (D) He is not being serious.
    (E) He is tired of Gout.

29. How does the dialogue reflect the eighteenth century's interest in science?

    (A)  The mention of gardens

    (B)  Recognition that walking is important exercise

    (C)  Use of scientific reasons for medical conditions

    (D)  Use of scientific language

    (E)  Inclusion of quotations from an important scientific work

30. What is Franklin the author suggesting by Gout's statement, "So it is. You philosophers are sages in your maxims and fools in your conduct" (lines 53–54)?

    (A)  Philosophers are ignorant.

    (B)  Wise people are infallible.

    (C)  People can make wise statements and take unwise actions.

    (D)  Intelligent comments aren't always used.

    (E)  People can make ill-considered statements.

**Questions 31 through 42** refer to the following selection. Read the passage carefully and then choose the answers to the questions.

Line  The discovery of America, and that of a passage to the East Indies by the Cape of Good Hope, are the two greatest and most important events recorded in the history of mankind. Their consequences have already been very great: but, in the short period of between two and
5  three centuries which has elapsed since these discoveries were made, it is impossible that the whole extent of their consequences can have been seen. What benefits or what misfortunes to mankind may hereafter result from those great events, no human wisdom can foresee. By uniting, in some measure, the most distant parts of the
10  world, by enabling them to relieve one another's wants, to increase one another's enjoyments, and to encourage one another's industry, their general tendency would seem to be beneficial.

    In the mean time, one of the principal effects of those discoveries has been to raise the mercantile system to a degree of splendour
15  and glory which it could never otherwise have attained to. It is the object of that system to enrich a great nation rather by trade and manufactures than by the improvement and cultivation of land, rather by the industry of the towns than by that of the country. But, in consequence of those discoveries, the commercial towns of Europe,
20  instead of being the manufacturers and carriers for but a very small part of the world, (that part of Europe which is washed by the Atlantic ocean, and the countries which lie round the Baltic and Mediterranean seas), have now become the manufacturers for the numerous and thriving cultivators of America, and the carriers, and in
25  some respects the manufacturers too, for almost all the different nations of Asia, Africa, and America. Two new worlds have been opened to their industry, each of them much greater and more extensive than the old one, and the market of one of them growing still greater and greater every day.
30      The countries which possess the colonies of America, and which trade directly to the East Indies, enjoy, indeed, the whole show and splendour of this great commerce. Other countries, however, notwithstanding all the invidious restraints by which it is meant to exclude them, frequently enjoy a greater share of the real benefit of
35  it. The colonies of Spain and Portugal, for example, give more real encouragement to the industry of other countries than to that of Spain and Portugal. In the single article of linen alone the consumption of those colonies amounts, it is said, but I do not pretend to warrant the quantity, to be more than three million sterling a year.
40  But this great consumption is almost entirely supplied by France, Flanders, Holland, and Germany. Spain and Portugal furnish but a small part of it. The capital which supplies the colonies with this great quantity of linen is annually distributed among, and furnishes a revenue to, the inhabitants of those other countries.

31. The author's tone in the passage is best described as

   (A) objective
   (B) didactic
   (C) pedantic
   (D) persuasive
   (E) reasoned

32. Which of the following best describes the author's attitude toward expansionism?

   (A) Ambivalent
   (B) Sympathetic
   (C) Very positive
   (D) Conservative
   (E) Progressive

33. In the sentence beginning "Other countries, however, notwithstanding all the invidious restraints" (lines 32–33), the best meaning for the word "invidious" is

   (A) ensnaring
   (B) deceptive
   (C) treacherous
   (D) offensive
   (E) invincible.

34. This selection is an example of which of the following modes of discourse?

   (A) Narrative
   (B) Description
   (C) Exposition
   (D) Argument
   (E) Persuasion

35. The first sentence in the first paragraph, "The discovery of America, and that of a passage to the East Indies by the Cape of Good Hope, are the two greatest and most important events recorded in the history of mankind," presents the author's view of

   I. History
   II. Expansionism
   III. Economics

   (A) I only
   (B) II only
   (C) III only
   (D) I and II
   (E) I, II, and III

36. This passage reads most like which of the following?

   (A) A letter
   (B) A history lesson
   (C) A current events lesson
   (D) A statement of opinion
   (E) An essay supporting expansionism

37. In the first paragraph, the sentence beginning "By uniting, in some measure, the most distant parts of the world" (lines 9–10) contains which of the following elements?

   (A) A gerund phrase
   (B) An infinitive phrase
   (C) A prepositional phrase
   (D) An adverb phrase
   (E) All of the above

38. In the sentence beginning "In the mean time, one of the principal effects of those discoveries" (lines 13–14), the writer employs which of the following rhetorical devices?

   (A) Overstatement
   (B) Hyperbole
   (C) Conceit
   (D) Oversimplification
   (E) Imagery

39. This passage is primarily concerned with the writer's views on

    (A) the benefits of global commerce
    (B) the effects of colonialism on America and the East Indies
    (C) the effects of global commerce on colonies
    (D) the effects of laissez-faire economics
    (E) the effects of revenues on imperialist nations

40. According to this passage, what does the writer believe about European expansionism?

    I. It is impossible to evaluate fully.
    II. It represents exploitation of native populations.
    III. It creates global commerce, which is good for all.
    IV. It enriches countries other than those possessing the colonies.

    (A) I and II
    (B) I, II, and III
    (C) II and III
    (D) II, III, and IV
    (E) I, III, and IV

41. In the last paragraph, the writer employs which of the following stylistic devices to support his arguments?

    (A) Generalization
    (B) Causal relation
    (C) Analogy
    (D) Anecdote
    (E) Example

42. What is the antecedent of "their" in the following independent clause from the first paragraph?

    . . . but, in the short period of between two and three centuries which has elapsed since these discoveries were made, it is impossible that the whole extent of their consequences can have been seen.

    (A) The discovery of the Americas and the passage to the East Indies
    (B) The short period
    (C) These discoveries
    (D) Important events
    (E) Whole extent

43. Which of the following is the best rephrasing of this sentence from the final paragraph?

    In the single article of linen alone the consumption of those colonies amounts, it is said, but I do not pretend to warrant the quantity, to be more than three million sterling a year.

    (A) In the single article of linen alone the consumption of those colonies' amounts, it is said, but I do not pretend to warrant the quantity, to be more than three million sterling a year.
    (B) The consumption of those colonies' amounts of linen alone may be more than three million sterling a year, although I cannot warrant the quantity.
    (C) Regarding the consumption of linen alone, those colonies' amounts of that article, it is said, to be more than three million sterling a year, but I do not pretend to warrant the quantity.
    (D) Not pretending to warrant the quantity, in the single article of linen alone the consumption of those colonies amounts, I have heard said, to be more than three million sterling a year.
    (E) In the single article of linen alone the consumption of those colonies amounts being more than three million sterling a year, but I do not confirm that quantity.

**Questions 44 through 54** refer to the following selection. Read the passage carefully and then choose the answers to the questions. This passage from "Finding Pharaoh" by Bey Emil Brugsch, curator of the Bûlâq Museum, comes from the account of the discovery of the tomb of Ramses II in the late nineteenth century.

Line Plunging on ahead of my guide, I came to the chamber . . . , and there, standing against the walls or here lying on the floor, I found even a greater number of mummy-cases of stupendous size and weight.

5     Their gold coverings and their polished surfaces so plainly reflected my own excited visage that it seemed as though I was looking into the faces of my own ancestors. The gilt face on the coffin of the amiable Queen Nofretari* seemed to smile upon me like an old acquaintance.

10     I took in the situation quickly, with a gasp, and hurried to the open air lest I should be overcome and the glorious prize still unrevealed be lost to science.

    It was almost sunset then. Already the odor which arose from the tomb had cajoled a troupe of slinking jackals to the neighbor-
15 hood, and the howl of hyenas was heard not far distant. A long line of vultures sat upon the highest pinnacles of the cliffs near by, ready for their hateful work.

    The valley was as still as death. Nearly the whole of the night was occupied in hiring men to help remove the precious relics from
20 their hiding-place. There was but little sleep in Luxor that night. Early the next morning three hundred Arabs were employed under my direction . . . . One by one the coffins were hoisted to the surface, were securely sewed up in sail-cloth and matting, and then were carried across the plain of Thebes to the steamers awaiting them at
25 Luxor.

———————
\* The wife of Ramses II.

**44.** The phrase, "Plunging on ahead of my guide," (line 1)

(A) modifies the verb
(B) describes the physical setting
(C) is a noun phrase
(D) modifies the subject
(E) functions as an adverbial clause

**45.** In the sentence beginning "Their gold coverings and their polished surfaces" (line 5), what is the best meaning for the word "visage"?

(A) Face
(B) Expression
(C) Aspect
(D) Vision
(E) Facade

46. Which of the following stylistic devices does the writer employ to convey his excitement about his discovery?

   I. Diction and sentence length
   II. Vivid language and narrative pace
   III. Diction and hyperbole

   (A) I only
   (B) II only
   (C) III only
   (D) I and II
   (E) I and III

47. In the second paragraph, what does the writer use to enhance the description of his experience?

   I. Imagery
   II. Parallelism
   III. Personification

   (A) I only
   (B) II only
   (C) III only
   (D) I and II
   (E) II and III

48. Which of the following best characterizes the mode of discourse of this passage?

   (A) Description
   (B) Exposition
   (C) Persuasion
   (D) Argument
   (E) Narration

49. The phrase "lest I should be overcome" (line 11) implies that the writer may be stunned by

   (A) the beauty of the mummy cases
   (B) the lack of oxygen in the chamber
   (C) the stench of the air
   (D) his own excitement
   (E) the significance of his discovery

50. Which of the following phrases best defines the purpose of the fourth paragraph in relation to the passage as a whole?

   (A) To describe the scent of death
   (B) To describe the physical setting
   (C) To describe the emotional tone
   (D) To describe the local animals
   (E) To describe the sunset in Egypt

51. The passage reads most like which of the following?

   (A) A historical paper
   (B) A letter
   (C) A conversation
   (D) A magazine article
   (E) A lecture

52. The first sentence in the third paragraph, "I took in the situation quickly, with a gasp, and hurried to the open air lest I should be overcome and the glorious prize still unrevealed be lost to science," (lines 10–12) is an example of which of the following kinds of sentence structure?

   (A) Simple sentence
   (B) Compound sentence
   (C) Complex sentence
   (D) Compound-complex sentence
   (E) Sentence fragments

53. The second sentence in the last paragraph, "Nearly the whole of the night was occupied in hiring men to help remove the precious relics from their hiding-place," (lines 00–00) contains all of the following elements EXCEPT

   (A) a noun phrase
   (B) a gerund phrase
   (C) an infinitive phrase
   (D) an adverbial clause
   (E) an adjective phrase

**54.** What is the best meaning of the word "amiable" in the phrase "The gilt face on the coffin of the amiable Queen Nofretari" (lines 8-9)?

(A) Friendly
(B) Lovable
(C) Pleasant
(D) Kindly
(E) Genial

**55.** The phrase "the howl of hyenas" is an example of which of the following?

(A) Alliteration
(B) Simile
(C) Metaphor
(D) Allusion
(E) Conceit

 **END OF SECTION I**

| SECTION II | TIME 2 HOURS | 3 QUESTIONS |
|---|---|---|

**Question 1**
Suggested time—40 minutes.

> **Directions:** Read the passage below carefully. Write a well-developed essay analyzing how the author uses rhetoric and style to engage the reader. Pay special attention to such elements as diction, tone, style, and narrative pace.

Line The Publishers of the Standard Novels, in selecting *Frankenstein* for one of their series, expressed a wish that I should furnish them with some account of the origin of the story. I am the more willing to comply, because I shall thus give a general answer to the question, so

5 very frequently asked me: "How I, then a young girl, came to think of, and to dilate upon, so very hideous an idea?" It is true that I am very averse to bringing myself forward in print; but as my account will only appear as an appendage to a former production, and as it will be confined to such topics as have connection with my author-

10 ship alone, I can scarcely accuse myself of a personal intrusion. . . .

I busied myself *to think of a story*, a story to rival those which had excited us to this task. One which would speak to the mysterious fears of our nature and awaken thrilling horror—one to make the reader dread to look round, to curdle the blood, and quicken the

15 beatings of the heart. If I did not accomplish these things, my ghost story would be unworthy of its name. I thought and pondered—vainly. I felt that blank incapability of invention which is the greatest misery of authorship, when dull Nothing replies to our anxious invocations. *Have you thought of a story? I* was asked each morning,

20 and each morning I was forced to reply with a mortifying negative. . . .

Many and long were the conversations between Lord Byron and Shelley, to which I was a devout but nearly silent listener. During one of these, various philosophical doctrines were discussed, and among

25 others the nature of the principle of life and whether there was any probability of its ever being discovered and communicated. . . . Perhaps a corpse would be reanimated: galvanism had given token such things. Perhaps the component parts of a creature might be manufactured, brought together, and endured with vital warmth.

30 Night waned upon this talk, and even the witching hour had gone by, before we retired to rest. When I placed my head on my pillow, I did not sleep, nor could I be said to think. My imagination,

unbidden, possessed and guided me, gifting the successive images
that arose in my mind with a vividness far beyond the usual bounds
35  of reverie. I saw—with shut eyes but acute mental vision—I saw the
pale student of unhallowed arts kneeling beside the thing he had put
together. I saw the hideous phantasm of a man stretched out, and
then, on the working of some powerful engine, show signs of life and
stir with an uneasy, half vital motion. Frightful must it be, for
40  supremely frightful would be the effect of any human endeavor to
mock the stupendous mechanism of the Creator of the world. His
success would terrify the artist; he would rush away from his odious
handiwork, horror-stricken he would hope that, left to itself, the
slight spark of life which he had communicated would fade; that this
45  thing, which had received such imperfect animation, would subside
into dead matter; and he might sleep in the belief that the silence of
the grave would quench forever the transient existence of the
hideous corpse which he had looked upon as the cradle of life. He
sleeps; but he is awakened; he opens his eyes; behold the horrid
50  thing stands at his bedside, opening his curtains, and looking on him
with yellow, watery, but speculative eyes.

I opened mine in terror. The idea so possessed my mind, that a
thrill of fear ran through me, and I wished to exchange the ghastly
image of my fancy for the realities around. I see them still: the very
55  room, the dark parquet, the closed shutters, with the moonlight
struggling through, and the sense I had that the glassy lake and white
high Alps were beyond. I could not so easy get rid of my hideous
phantom: still it haunted me. I must try to think of something else. I
recurred to my ghost story—my tiresome unlucky ghost story! O! if I
60  could only contrive one which would frighten my reader as I myself
had been frightened that night!

Swift as light and as cheering was the idea that broke in upon
me. "I have found it! What terrified me will terrify others, and I need
only describe the specter which haunted my midnight pillow." On
65  the morrow I announced that I had *thought of a story.* I began that
day with the words, *It was on a dreary night of November,* making
only a transcript of the grim terrors of my waking dream.

—Mary Shelley

**Question 2**

Suggested time—40 minutes.

> **Directions:** Read carefully this passage from Ralph Waldo Emerson's speech, "The American Scholar," given as the Phi Beta Kappa address at Harvard in 1837. Write a well-organized, well-reasoned essay that critically analyzes how Emerson used the English language and conventions to promote his ideas.

Line    The theory of books is noble. The scholar of the first age received into him the world around: brooded thereon; gave it a new arrangement of his own mind, and uttered it again. . . . It can stand, and it can go. It now endures, it now flies, it now inspires. Precisely in

5      proportion to the depth of mind from which it issued, so high does it soar, so long does it sing.

Or, I might say, it depends on how far the process had gone, of transmuting life into truth. In proportion to the completeness of the distillation, so will the purity and imperishableness of the product be.

10      But none is quite perfect. . . . Each age, it is found, must write its own books; or rather, each generation for the next succeeding. The books of an older period will not fit this.

Yet hence arises a grave mischief. The sacredness which attaches to the act of creation, the act of thought, is instantly

15      transferred to the record. The poet chanting, was felt to be a divine man. Henceforth the chant is divine also. The writer was a just and wise spirit. Henceforward it is settled, the book is perfect; as love of the hero corrupts into worship of his statue. Instantly, the book becomes noxious. The guide is a tyrant. . . . The sluggish and

20      perverted mind of the multitude, always slow to open to the incursions of Reason, having once so opened, having one received this book, stands upon it, and makes an outcry, if it disparaged. Colleges are built on it. Books are written on it by thinkers, not by Man Thinking; by men of talent, that is, who start wrong, who set out

25      from accepted dogmas, not from their own sight of principles. Meek young men grow up in libraries, believing it their duty to accept the views which Cicero, which Locke, which Bacon, have given, forgetful that Cicero, Locke and Bacon were only young men in libraries when they wrote these books.

30      Hence, instead of man thinking, we have book worm. . . .
Books are the best of things, well used; abused, among the worst.

—Ralph Waldo Emerson

**Question 3**
Suggested time—40 minutes.

> **Directions:** Samuel Johnson, one of the most important literary figures of the English Enlightenment, created an anthology of William Shakespeare's works. In this passage from his "Preface," Johnson discusses some of Shakespeare's admirable qualities as a dramatist. Write a well-organized, well-reasoned essay that defends or challenges Johnson's assertions about Shakespeare's writing. Use evidence from your observations, experience, or reading to develop and support your position.

Line    Shakespeare is, above all writers, at least above all modern writers, the poet of nature; the poet that holds up to his readers a faithful mirror of manners and of life. His characters are not modified by the customs of particular places, unpracticed by the rest of the world; by
5    the peculiarities of studies or professions, which can operate but upon small numbers; or by the accidents of transient fashions or temporary opinions; they are the genuine progeny of common humanity, such as the world will always supply and observation will always find. His persons act and speak by the influence of those
10    general passions and principles by which all minds are agitated and the whole system of life is continued in motion. In the writings of other poets a character is too often an individual; in those of Shakespeare it is commonly a species.

      It is from this wide extension of design that so much instruction
15    is derived. It is this which fills the plays of Shakespeare with practical axioms and domestic wisdom. It was said of Euripides that every verse was a precept; and it may be said of Shakespeare that from his works may be collected a system of civil and economical prudence. Yet his real power is not shown in the splendor of particular pas-
20    sages, but by the progress of his fable and the tenor of his dialogue; and he that tries to recommend him by select quotations will succeed like the pedant in Hierocles, who, when he offered his house to sale, carried a brick in his pocket as a specimen. . . .

      Other dramatists can only gain attention by hyperbolical or
25    aggravated characters, by fabulous and unexampled excellence or depravity, as the writers of barbarous romances invigorated the reader by a giant and a dwarf; and he that should form his expecta-tions of human affairs from the play, or from the tale, would be equally deceived. Shakespeare has no heroes; his scenes are occupied
30    only by men who act and speak as the reader thinks that he should himself have spoken or acted on the same occasion. Even where the agency is supernatural, the dialogue is level with life. Other writers

35

40

disguise the most natural passions and most frequent incidents, so that he who contemplates them in the book will not know them in the world. Shakespeare approximates the remote, and familiarizes the wonderful; the event which he represents will not happen, but if it were possible, its effects would be probably such as he has assigned; and it may be said that he has not only shown human nature as it acts in real exigences, but as it would be found in trials to which it cannot be exposed.

45

This therefore is the praise of Shakespeare, that his drama is the mirror of life; that he who has mazed his imagination in following the phantoms which other writers raise up before him may here be cured of his delirious ecstasies by reading human sentiments in human language, by scenes from which a hermit may estimate the transactions of the world, and a confessor predict the progress of the passions.

—Samuel Johnson

 END OF SECTION II

# ANSWERS AND EXPLANATIONS

## Quick-Score Answers

| | | | | |
|---|---|---|---|---|
| 1. B | 12. A | 23. D | 34. E | 45. A |
| 2. D | 13. B | 24. A | 35. A | 46. B |
| 3. B | 14. E | 25. D | 36. E | 47. A |
| 4. C | 15. B | 26. C | 37. E | 48. E |
| 5. A | 16. C | 27. C | 38. A | 49. E |
| 6. B | 17. D | 28. C | 39. A | 50. B |
| 7. B | 18. B | 29. C | 40. E | 51. D |
| 8. A | 19. C | 30. C | 41. E | 52. C |
| 9. C | 20. B | 31. D | 42. C | 53. D |
| 10. B | 21. A | 32. C | 43. B | 54. A |
| 11. D | 22. C | 33. D | 44. D | 55. A |

# PRACTICE TEST 1

## Review Strategy

*See the "Quick Review of Literary and Rhetorical Terms," p. 173.*

1. **The correct answer is (B).** The context is that the New England group was beginning to fall apart. As poets, this means that they were beginning to lose their creativity. Although choices (A), (C), (D), and (E) may express some of the feelings and experiences of the New England group, none addresses the core problem of these poets in the manner that choice (B) does.

2. **The correct answer is (D).** This selection is not descriptive, so the mode can not be description, choice (A). It does not attempt to argue or persuade, so it cannot be persuasive, choice (C), or argumentative, choice (E), writing. Nor does it tell a story; therefore, it is not a narrative, choice (B). It simply presents the facts—exposition, choice (D).

3. **The correct answer is (B).** The sentence cited contains the statement, "a reflection of actuality, 'an extension of experience.'" Choice (B) closely matches that thought. There is no development of an existential subject, choice (A). Modern poetry is not defined, choice (C). Choices (D) and (E) are similarly not discussed in the excerpt.

4. **The correct answer is (C).** All of these statements are true. The trick here is to figure out which gives the author's main idea. The writer is discussing the beginning of modern American writing. That is what choice (C) is presenting. The other choices, (A), (B), (D), and (E), are facts that support and illuminate the writer's thesis.

5. **The correct answer is (A).** The correct answer is developed in the first paragraph with the observation that the Civil War marked the start of modern poetry. In the second paragraph, a link is shown between the close of the Civil War and the decline of the New England group, also known as the Brahmins. Religious freedom and politics, choice (B), were never shown to be an issue. Political nationalism, industrial growth, and philosophical creativity were also never developed as an influence on the Brahmins, choices (C), (D), and (E).

6. **The correct answer is (B).** In the second paragraph, Louis Untermeyer states that some of the Brahmins "occupied themselves with translations." *Divina Commedia* is such a translation. This makes choice (B) the correct answer. Choice (A) is true, but incorrect because it is not relevant to the question. Choices (C), (D), and (E) are not related to the question, and the author does not explore them.

7. **The correct answer is (B).** The context of this expression is another way that Untermeyer shows that the creativity of the Brahmins had been lost. In this case, he is saying that the Brahmins were satisfied with the sounds of old music, an allusion to their focus on translations of old writings. The author is not speaking of sounds per se—that eliminates choices (A), (C), and (D). The author is not speaking of philosophical concepts, choice (E).

8. **The correct answer is (A).** This question is from the point of view of the Brahmins, not the author. It probably does not reflect the thoughts of the author. In the third paragraph, Untermeyer writes, "To them [the Brahmins], the new men must have seemed like a regiment recruited from the ranks of vulgarity." This passage is a direct response to the question and is represented by choice (A). Choices (B), (C), (D), and (E) do not express the point of view of the New England poets.

9. **The correct answer is (C).** The passage from the final paragraph is the identification by the author of the change from the Brahmin-influenced era to modern American poetry. This can be most readily seen by Untermeyer's comment that "America developed a national conscience." Choices (A) and (D) are true but do not reflect the writer's thoughts in this passage. Choices (B) and (E) are neither true nor relevant.

10. **The correct answer is (B).** Although the Brahmins might have been harsh and scathing in their commentary about modern American poets, the passage itself does not have that tone; therefore, choice (A) is incorrect. There is no wit or humor contained in the excerpt, making choice (D) incorrect. The remaining three answers have some elements that may seem to be true. A reader may see the article as dry or even irritating, but not condescending, choice (C), or pretentious, choice (E). Only one of these three answer choices has both elements that are true. Choice (B), scholarly and informative, correctly answers the question.

11. **The correct answer is (D).** The author never made a judgment about which type of poetry was superior, so choice (A) is incorrect. The same can be said of choice (B). The Brahmins were not identified as the creators of modern American poetry, choice (C). The author specifically said that the Civil War produced little quality poetry, eliminating choice (E). The author develops the Civil War as the starting point of modern American poetry in the first two paragraphs, choice (D).

12. **The correct answer is (A).** The author says in the first sentence of the second paragraph "the Civil War . . . produced a vast quantity of poems but practically no important poetry." Choice (A) mirrors Untermeyer's commentary. If Untermeyer says that no poetry was produced, that implies that no poets were produced, so choice (B) cannot be correct. Choices (C), (D), and (E) do not accurately reflect this passage.

13. **The correct answer is (B).** The sentence taken from the end of the concluding paragraph is a reference to the Brahmins' attempt to keep their style of poetry the dominant form. Untermeyer does not suggest that the poets of transition were deliberate in the execution of their art as indicated in choice (A). The author proposes that the poets of transition resisted the change; therefore, they were aware of it, making choice (C) incorrect. The author states neither of the meanings described in choices (D) and (E).

14. **The correct answer is (E).** In the third sentence of the final paragraph, Untermeyer identifies the new poetic expression as "crude, jangling, and vigorously democratic." Choice (E) repeats the description as crude, and it relies on the reader to recognize that a democratic form of poetry is cutting edge. The descriptions of the poets in choices (A), (B), (C), or (D) are not consistent with the description or even mentioned by the author.

15. **The correct answer is (B).** Untermeyer describes the Brahmins as educated, but he does not contend that they are mercurial, choice (A). The author leaves the reader with the impression that the Brahmins are anything but lighthearted or easygoing, choices (C) and (D). They are portrayed as brilliant but not forgiving; thus, choice (E) is incorrect. This leaves (B) as the correct answer. Untermeyer does give the impression that the Brahmins were stuffy and intransigent.

16. **The correct answer is (C).** Each of the choices has a small element of correctness. The characters do make comments about health, choice (A), and some discussion about exercise takes place, choice (B). Franklin does mention the pain of the gout attack, choice (D). Dialogue occurs, although not suited for a morality play, choice (E). However, because the question asks for the theme of the passage, only choice (C) is correct.

**Review Strategy**

*See the "Quick Review of Literary and Rhetorical Terms," p. 173.*

17. **The correct answer is (D).** An alliteration is the repetition of initial consonant sound, choice (A). A metaphor is a figure of speech in which one thing is spoken of as though it were something else, choice (B). An allegory is a literary work with two or more levels of meaning; one of which is literal and others symbolic, choice (C). A simile is a figure of speech that compares two unlike things by using words such as *like* or *as,* choice (E). None of these apply to the selection. Allowing the disease to speak is personification, the giving of human characteristics to nonhuman things, choice (D).

18. **The correct answer is (B).** Choices (A), (C), and (E), but not choice (D), seem reasonable. However, only choice (B) includes both elements of the tone—the humor and the reasoned presentation of the medical information given.

19. **The correct answer is (C).** Franklin is lamenting the thought that people's debts and sins are always greater than people imagine them to be. Choice (A) restates part of the maxim, while choices (B), (D), and (E) are not accurate restatements.

20. **The correct answer is (B).** If you did not know what *interposition* means, you could try your knowledge of prefixes to determine that it means to be placed between; it's the noun form of the verb *interpose.* Choice (A) means an intervention between parties with a view to reconciling differences; this does not fit Gout's role in the piece. Choice (B) means the act of prohibiting or restraining someone from doing something; it is much stronger than choice (C), involvement. Gout is very much in evidence, so choice (D), absence, is illogical. Based on the context—Gout has just recited a list of Franklin's transgressions—choice (E), interview, seems too mild a meaning. Choice (B) is the strongest word and seems to best match Gout's tone.

**Test-Taking Strategy**

*The answer to this question should reassure you about question 20. Look for consistency among the answers you choose for passages.*

21. **The correct answer is (A).** (The character of Gout is female in the dialogue.) Gout states that she is very serious and she can justify every action (lines 2–4). She is indignant, or righteously angry, choice (A), and is not pleased, choice (B), or feeling chastised, choice (C), or contrite, choice (D). Gout certainly is not oblivious, choice (E), but very concerned about Franklin's health.

22. **The correct answer is (C).** On the surface, all these choices seem correct because each is mentioned in the selection. However, choices (A), (B), (D), and (E) are specific details of Franklin's point that reasonable and responsible behavior cures the gout, choice (C).

23. **The correct answer is (D).** The challenge of determining the correct answer is between choices (D) and (E) because the other choices do not express the tone of Gout's comments. If Gout were disgusted, choice (A), she would not bother trying to reason with Franklin. There is no conciliation in her tone, choice (B), nor are her arguments superficial, choice (C). Gout is not dealing with trivial ideas in a narrow bookish manner, so choice (D) is the correct description.

24. **The correct answer is (A).** Choice (B) is incorrect because Gout is not misinterpreting Franklin the character's actions; Franklin agrees with Gout. The topic is serious—Franklin the character agrees with Gout—so Franklin the author's purpose is more than to write some lighthearted prose, choice (C). The theme is developed in such a way as to make Gout's argument more persuasive, thus eliminating choice (D) as untrue. Choice (E) is inaccurate because the motives are clearly developed. Choice (A) is the best answer in that the use of dialogue permits Franklin the writer to focus on Gout's comments and easily refute Franklin the character's defense.

**25. The correct answer is (D).** The key here is to notice that the word *interests* is plural. Franklin does enjoy being with friends, choice (B), but that is only one interest. He says he likes walking in the gardens, choice (A), but does not act as if he does. There is no information in the selection to support choice (C). Knowing Franklin as a historical figure would help you see that choice (E) is incorrect. Therefore, the statement that best characterizes what we do know about Franklin from the selection is that he enjoys those interests that do not require him to do anything more than sit, choice (D).

**26. The correct answer is (C).** First, read the sentence. While *object* may be a noun or a verb, it is used as a verb in this sentence. The answer choices are either verbs or may be used as verbs (*dispute* and *silence*) so you can't eliminate any choices immediately. Next, substitute each answer choice in the sentence to see which best fits the context. If you realize the sentence means that Franklin cannot use the fatigue of the day as an excuse (argument) for needing a carriage, choice (C) is clearly the answer. While *object* can mean *dispute*, choice (B), it does not have that meaning in this passage. Choices (A), (D), and (E) make little or no sense in context.

**Review Strategy**

*Study the grammar review beginning on page 143 to help you review the conventions of English.*

**27. The correct answer is (C).** First, you need to determine which points are true about the sentence. The sentence has neither a participial phrase (I) nor a compound verb in the past tense, so points I and II are incorrect. There is an infinitive (III). Then determine which answer choice has only III—choice (C).

**28. The correct answer is (C).** Franklin will not answer because he knows he did not follow his own advice. At this point in the dialogue, he is not arguing with Gout nor is there any sign that he has tired of the conversation, so choices (A) and (E) are incorrect. Franklin has not shown himself to be forgetful, thus eliminating choice (B). While the tone of the passage is amusing, the Franklin of the dialogue is serious, thus eliminating choice (D).

**29. The correct answer is (C).** Use of scientific reasoning, rather than superstitions or religious beliefs, for medical conditions was a discovery of the eighteenth century. Neither choice (D) nor choice (E) is true of the selection. Choice (A) is irrelevant, and although choice (B) is true, choice (C) is a better overall statement.

**30. The correct answer is (C).** The statement in question contrasts two sets of circumstances. The correct answer must then have two sets of answers as well. Only choice (C) fulfills the requirement (sages/fools; wise statements/unwise actions). Choices (A), (B), (D), and (E) all deal with single concepts.

**31. The correct answer is (D).** The passage is not objective, but strongly one-sided, so choice (A) is incorrect. The author is not attempting to teach you about his position; therefore, choices (B) and (C) are incorrect. The passage is reasoned, but the writer presents his arguments to convince the reader of his position. This makes the better choice (D) rather than choice (E).

**32. The correct answer is (C).** A review of the first sentence of the last paragraph of the passage contains the phrase "the whole show and splendour of this great commerce." The wording clearly indicates that the author is "very positive," choice (C), about commerce and expansionism. The essay's purpose is to persuade you of the greatness of expansionism. Choice (B) has the right sentiment but is not strong enough. Choice (A) is contrary to the tone of the selection, as is choice (D). Choice (E) is a distracter.

**33. The correct answer is (D).** The word *invidious* means "to create ill will or envy" or " to give offense." If you did not know that, you could use the context to realize that choice (E) makes no sense. While the author is obviously expressing the opinion that the restraints are negative, he does not imply that they are entrapping, deceitful, or untrustworthy, choices (A), (B) and (C), respectively.

**34. The correct answer is (E).** This question is similar to, but not the same as, question 31. The author is not relating a story, so choice (A) is incorrect. He is not merely describing an event or place, so choice (B) is incorrect. Choice (C) is incorrect because the author is not simply explaining a topic. Argument, choice (D), is writing that attempts to prove a point with a well-reasoned discussion. The writer of this passage is doing more than that; he is attempting to persuade the reader to accept his position, choice (E).

**35. The correct answer is (A).** The opening sentence of the first paragraph identifies what the writer believes to be the most important events in history (I). The sentence does not mention expansionism (II) or economics (III), so choices (B), (C), (D), and (E) are incorrect. The only answer that identifies only the element of history is choice (A).

**36.** **The correct answer is (E).** With no salutation, direct address, or closing, the selection gives no evidence of correspondence, eliminating choice (A). Since the selection discusses history, choice (C) is unlikely. Choices (B), (D), and (E) all apply to the passage, but the correct answer is the most precise, choice (E).

**37.** **The correct answer is (E).** You could determine the answer to this question even if you could not remember what all the grammatical terms mean. Once you recognized two of the grammatical elements, perhaps an infinitive, choice (B), and a prepositional phrase, choice (C), you know that the answer must be choice (E), since only choice (E) allows for multiple answers.

**Test-Taking Strategy**

*When you know something about an answer but aren't sure, use the strategies of educated guessing to eliminate more answer choices.*

**38.** **The correct answer is (A).** Although you may not recognize overstatement, choice (A), as a rhetorical device, you could establish that it is the correct answer through the process of elimination. Choice (B) may seem to apply, but hyperbole is not intended to be taken literally, so choice (B) cannot be correct. Likewise, a conceit may seem to be correct, but it is an analogy and there is none in the sentence, thus making choice (C) incorrect. The sentence certainly is not an oversimplification nor is there any imagery, so choices (D) and (E) do not apply.

**39.** **The correct answer is (A).** At first glance, all the choices may seem to pertain to the passage, so you must decide which most accurately applies to the entire essay. The passage deals more with the effects of the colonial production than the effects of colonialism on the colonies, so choices (B) and (C) are not the best alternatives. Choices (D) and (E) are distracters.

**40.** **The correct answer is (E).** The passage does not recognize the exploitation involved in colonization (II), so any answer that includes II should be eliminated—choices (A), (B), (C), and (D).

**41.** **The correct answer is (E).** The writer uses the example of linen production to support his point, making choice (E) correct. The use of examples to support his argument makes the piece specific, so choice (A) is incorrect. There is no comparison or story, eliminating choices (C) and (D). You might have thought that the writer employs causal relation by arguing that expansionism results in economic wealth for noncolonial nations, choice (B), but that is an organizational technique, not a method of support.

42. **The correct answer is (C).** An antecedent is the noun or noun phrase to which a pronoun refers. Only choices (A) and (C) make sense in the context of the clause. You need to pick the alternative that exactly reflects the words of the sentence, which would eliminate choice (A). The other possibilities, choices (B), (D), and (E), are distracters.

43. **The correct answer is (B).** Choice (A) corrects the possessive, *colonies',* but otherwise is identical to the convoluted original. Choice (C) moves one clause but does little else to clarify the sentence's meaning. Choice (D) is grammatically incorrect. Choice (E) is a lengthy but incomplete sentence.

44. **The correct answer is (D).** The phrase is a participial phrase that functions as an adjective, in this case modifying the subject *I.* Since it is a participial phrase, choices (A), (C), and (E) are incorrect. Choice (B) is a distracter that is not relevant to the question.

45. **The correct answer is (A).** The word *visage* means face. If you did not know that, you could figure out the meaning by recognizing that a reflection that is a face would mirror a face. Choice (D), vision, may mean something seen in a dream, so it is not an accurate choice to refer to one's reflection. People rarely use words such as *aspect* and *facade* to refer to their reflections, so choices (C) and (E) make little sense in context.

**Test-Taking Strategy**

*Be sure all parts of an answer are correct. A partially correct answer is a partially incorrect answer— and a quarter-point deduction.*

46. **The correct answer is (B).** This question requires an understanding of rhetorical terms. Diction, or word choice, presented in points I and III, is very broad. Any writer uses diction to convey meaning, so you must look at the other elements of the answer choices. The lengths of sentences vary (I) but do little to produce a feeling of excitement, and although the author is very descriptive, none of the descriptions are extravagantly exaggerated (III). If you were not aware of the definition of diction, you could still recognize that the author's effective choice of vivid, precise words (such as *stupendous, slinking,* and *pinnacles*) and the rapid pace of the passage convey excitement (II). This eliminates all choices except choice (B).

**Study Strategy**

*See "A Quick Review of Literary and Rhetorical Terms," p.173.*

47. **The correct answer is (A).** This question also requires a knowledge of rhetoric. Imagery, or making pictures through words, is a dominant device in the selection, so the correct answer must include item I. However, there is no parallelism (II) and little personification (III), so any response that includes items II or III is inaccurate. This eliminates choices (B), (C), (D), and (E).

**48. The correct answer is (E).** The writer is writing about his personal experience discovering an ancient Egyptian tomb. While the author is very descriptive, he uses description to make his story come alive, so choice (A) is not the best choice. There is some explanation, but the author's purpose is not to teach or explain, so choice (B) is incorrect. He does not argue or attempt to convince readers, eliminating choices (C) and (D).

**49. The correct answer is (E).** First, eliminate alternatives that are obviously wrong, choices (B) and (C), because there has been no mention of air, smelly or lacking. To figure out the correct answer, think of a causal relationship. The beauty of the mummy cases, choice (A), caused the writer's excitement, choice (D), but more importantly, his recognition of what the mummy cases were made him realize the significance of his discovery, choice (E).

**Test-Taking Strategy**

*This is a main idea question in disguise. For this type of question, always look for the most inclusive or broadest answer.*

**50. The correct answer is (B).** The paragraph mentions the scent of death, but the phrase is used to describe the desert environment, so choice (A) in inaccurate. The entire passage has an emotional element, but the paragraph does not describe it, excluding choice (C). Mention of local animals adds to the description of the setting, but they are not described, so choice (D) cannot be correct. Sunset sets the time, another element of the physical setting, so choice (E) is not the answer. Choices (D) and (E) are details that actually support choice (B).

**51. The correct answer is (D).** The key to this question is recognition of the tone and purpose. The selection is an engaging, informative narrative of one archaeologist's discovery. It is most like a magazine article, which in fact it is. The passage is too personal and informal for a historical paper, choice (A). The passage is missing the greeting and closing of a letter and does not address the reader directly as a letter would, so choice (B) cannot be correct. A conversation involves more than one person's input, so choice (C) is incorrect. This passage would have been an exciting talk, but a lecture implies a more academic purpose, eliminating choice (E).

**Review Strategy**

*Check the review of grammar and sentence structure in Chapter 3.*

**52. The correct answer is (C).** The sentence has two clauses, so choice (A) can be eliminated. There is a coordinating conjunction, but it joins two verbs, not two independent clauses, so the sentence is neither compound nor compound-complex, eliminating choices (B) and (D). The sentence expresses a complete thought, so choice (E) is incorrect.

53. **The correct answer is (D).** The noun phrase "the whole of the night" eliminates choice (A). The gerund "in hiring men" eliminates choice (B). "To help remove the precious relics" is an infinitive phrase, so choice (C) cannot be the answer. "Of the night" is a prepositional phrase modifying the subject, so choice (E) is excluded. While there is an adverb and an adverbial phrase, there is no adverbial clause, making choice (D) wrong about the sentence but the correct answer.

54. **The correct answer is (A).** All the answers seem to make sense in the context of this sentence, so you must use your knowledge from other areas. If you know the French word *ami* or the Spanish word *amigo,* both of which mean friend, you have a strong clue to the meaning of the word in question. Another clue that can help uncover the meaning is the phrase "like an old acquaintance." Only choice (A) defines the word correctly.

55. **The correct answer is (A).** An alliteration is a repetition of consonant sounds at the beginning or within words. A simile, a metaphor, and a conceit are figures of speech that are used to compare two unlike things, so choices (B), (C), and (E) are illogical answers. An allusion is a reference to a classical work, so choice (D) is incorrect.

# SUGGESTIONS FOR ESSAY QUESTION 1

You might have chosen the following points to include in your essay on Mary Shelley's *Introduction to Frankenstein*. Consider them as you complete your self-evaluation. Revise your essay using points from the list to strengthen it.

## Form or Mode

- Prose; an introduction to the third edition of *Frankenstein*
- Narrative

## Theme

- Origins of the horror novel
- Aspects of writing a horror novel

## Characters/Individuals

- Mary Shelley, the speaker
- Percy Bysshe Shelley
- Lord Byron
- Audience, readers of the novel

## Conflict/Issue/Challenge

- Challenge from without: to write a horror story equal to those previously written
- Challenge from within: to think of a story

## Content/Important Points

- Challenge among friends
- Inspired by conversations with Byron and Shelley
- Vivid dreams
- Gothic tradition
- Dangers of technology/science in the wrong hands

## Development

- Chronological
- Slowly builds pace

## Literary Conventions

- Point of View: first person
- Setting: Switzerland during a rainy summer; confined to the house
- Tone: emotional, personal, somewhat dark

## Diction/Syntax/Style

- Use of both internal and external dialogue
- Vivid language
- Specific details
- Figurative language
- Complex sentence structure
- Chronological development; musical
- Word choice: sophisticated but comprehensible

# Suggestions for Essay Question 2

You might have chosen the following points to include in your essay analyzing Emerson's speech on books. Consider them as you complete your self-evaluation. Revise your essay using points from the list to strengthen it.

### Form or Mode

- Speech
- Persuasive/argument

### Theme

- Books can be the best of things or the worst of things

### Conflict/Issue/Challenge

- To overcome rigid reverence of great books
- To prevent transferring of respect for acts of creation (thought) to an imperfect outcome of that thought

### Content/Important Points

- Indictment of bookworms
- Greatest thinkers were once students
- Should not worship profound works to the extent that their creators are forgotten
- Respect books in moderation
- Individual thought paramount (an argument misused to deny the importance of the past)
- Write books of own truths
- Undertake own acts of creation
- Implies ideas are not great in and of themselves

### Literary Conventions

- Point of view: first person
- Audience: students
- Setting: university campus
- Tone: strident, argumentative

## Diction/Syntax/Style

- Sentences fairly short and not extremely complex; straightforward
- Language overstated; "tyrant," "sluggish," "perverted," "Meek men grow up in libraries"
- Use of active and passive voice
- Sentence variety
- Some parallel structure: "Colleges are built on it. Books are written on it. . . ."

# SUGGESTIONS FOR ESSAY QUESTION 3

You might have chosen to include the following points in your critical essay on Johnson's thoughts about Shakespeare. Consider them as you complete your self-evaluation. Revise your essay using points from the list to strengthen it.

## Form

- Introduction
- From *Preface to Shakespeare*

## Mode

- Exposition
- Informative

## Subject

- The genius of Shakespeare's work

## Literary Conventions

- Tone: laudatory, learned
- Setting/Time Period: mid-1700s, Enlightenment
- Point of View/Speaker: third person; the writer, Samuel Johnson

## Diction

- Formal, precise, clear interpretations and explanations
- Academic

## Style

- Sentence structure: varied, many complex and compound-complex structures; lengthy constructions
- Organization and Development: analysis, compare and contrast Shakespeare with other writers, developmental
- Accessible
- Alludes to classical Greek dramatists and scholars
- Colored by undisguised admiration of Shakespeare
- Elaborate and balanced
- Polysyllabic words
- Writing reflects a subtle and deep intellect

## Points

- Shakespeare's work timeless
- Rich knowledge of literature in general
- Realistic characters, not fantastic heroes
- Characters are "everyman."

- "Approximates the remote and familiarizes the wonderful"
- Shakespeare a student of human nature
- Plays mirror life.
- Shakespeare's dramatic style poetic
- Good that Shakespeare flouts convention; it is from this wide extension of design that so much instruction is derived
- Exchanges hyperbole for reality

# SELF-EVALUATION RUBRIC FOR THE ADVANCED PLACEMENT ESSAYS

| | 8–9 | 6–7 | 5 | 3–4 | 1–2 | 0 |
|---|---|---|---|---|---|---|
| **Overall Impression** | Demonstrates excellent control of the literature and outstanding writing competence; thorough and effective; incisive | Demonstrates good control of the literature and good writing competence; less thorough and incisive than the highest papers | Reveals simplistic thinking and/or immature writing; adequate skills | Incomplete thinking; fails to respond adequately to part or parts of the question; may paraphrase rather than analyze | Unacceptably brief; fails to respond to the question; little clarity | Lacking skill and competence |
| **Understanding of the Text** | Excellent understanding of the text; exhibits perception and clarity; original or unique approach; includes apt and specific references | Good understanding of the text; exhibits perception and clarity; includes specific references | Superficial understanding of the text; elements of literature vague, mechanical, overgeneralized | Misreadings and lack of persuasive evidence from the text; meager and unconvincing treatment of literary elements | Serious misreadings and little supporting evidence from the text; erroneous treatment of literary elements | A response with no more than a reference to the literature; blank response, or one completely off the topic |
| **Organization and Development** | Meticulously organized and thoroughly developed; coherent and unified | Well organized and developed; coherent and unified | Reasonably organized and developed; mostly coherent and unified | Somewhat organized and developed; some incoherence and lack of unity | Little or no organization and development; incoherent and void of unity | No apparent organization or development; incoherent |
| **Use of Sentences** | Effectively varied and engaging; virtually error free | Varied and interesting; a few errors | Adequately varied; some errors | Somewhat varied and marginally interesting; one or more major errors | Little or no variation; dull and uninteresting; some major errors | Numerous major errors |
| **Word Choice** | Interesting and effective; virtually error free | Generally interesting and effective; a few errors | Occasionally interesting and effective; several errors | Somewhat dull and ordinary; some errors in diction | Mostly dull and conventional; numerous errors | Numerous major errors; extremely immature |
| **Grammar and Usage** | Virtually error free | Occasional minor errors | Several minor errors | Some major errors | Severely flawed; frequent major errors | Extremely flawed |

Using the rubric on the previous page, rate yourself in each of the categories below for each essay on the test. Enter on the lines below the number from the rubric that most accurately reflects your performance in each category. Then calculate the average of the six numbers to determine your final score. It is difficult to score yourself objectively, so you may wish to ask a respected friend or teacher to assess your writing for a more accurate reflection of its strengths and weaknesses. On the AP test itself, a reader will rate your essay on a scale of 1 to 9, with 9 being the highest.

Rate each category from 9 (high) to 0 (low).

# QUESTION 1

**SELF-EVALUATION**

| | |
|---|---|
| **Overall Impression** | _____ |
| **Understanding of the Text** | _____ |
| **Organization and Development** | _____ |
| **Use of Sentences** | _____ |
| **Word Choice (Diction)** | _____ |
| **Grammar and Usage** | _____ |
| **TOTAL** | _____ |
| Divide by 6 for final score | _____ |

**OBJECTIVE EVALUATION**

| | |
|---|---|
| **Overall Impression** | _____ |
| **Understanding of the Text** | _____ |
| **Organization and Development** | _____ |
| **Use of Sentences** | _____ |
| **Word Choice (Diction)** | _____ |
| **Grammar and Usage** | _____ |
| **TOTAL** | _____ |
| Divide by 6 for final score | _____ |

# QUESTION 2

**SELF-EVALUATION**

| | |
|---|---|
| **Overall Impression** | _____ |
| **Understanding of the Text** | _____ |
| **Organization and Development** | _____ |
| **Use of Sentences** | _____ |
| **Word Choice (Diction)** | _____ |
| **Grammar and Usage** | _____ |
| **TOTAL** | _____ |
| Divide by 6 for final score | _____ |

**OBJECTIVE EVALUATION**

| | |
|---|---|
| **Overall Impression** | _____ |
| **Understanding of the Text** | _____ |
| **Organization and Development** | _____ |
| **Use of Sentences** | _____ |
| **Word Choice (Diction)** | _____ |
| **Grammar and Usage** | _____ |
| **TOTAL** | _____ |
| Divide by 6 for final score | _____ |

# QUESTION 3

**SELF-EVALUATION**

| | |
|---|---|
| **Overall Impression** | _____ |
| **Understanding of the Text** | _____ |
| **Organization and Development** | _____ |
| **Use of Sentences** | _____ |
| **Word Choice (Diction)** | _____ |
| **Grammar and Usage** | _____ |
| **TOTAL** | _____ |
| Divide by 6 for final score | _____ |

**OBJECTIVE EVALUATION**

| | |
|---|---|
| **Overall Impression** | _____ |
| **Understanding of the Text** | _____ |
| **Organization and Development** | _____ |
| **Use of Sentences** | _____ |
| **Word Choice (Diction)** | _____ |
| **Grammar and Usage** | _____ |
| **TOTAL** | _____ |
| Divide by 6 for final score | _____ |

# Practice Test 2

## AP ENGLISH LANGUAGE AND COMPOSITION

On the front page of your test booklet, you will find some information about the test. Because you have studied this book, none of it should be new to you, and much of it is similar to other standardized tests you have taken.

The page will tell you that the following exam will take 3 hours—1 hour for the multiple-choice section and 2 hours for the three essays—and that there are two booklets for this exam, one for the multiple-choice section and one for the essays.

The page will also say that SECTION I

- is 1 hour.

- has 50 questions (or some number from 50 to 60).

- counts for 45 percent of your total grade.

Then you will find a sentence in capital letters telling you not to open your exam booklet until the monitor tells you to open it.

Other instructions will tell you to be careful to fill in only ovals 1 through 50 (or whatever the number is) in Section I on your separate answer sheet. Fill in each oval completely. If you erase an answer, erase it completely. You will not receive any credit for work done in the test booklet, but you may use it for making notes.

You will also find a paragraph about the guessing penalty—deduction of one-quarter point for every wrong answer—as well as words of advice about guessing if you know something about the question and can eliminate several of the answers.

The final paragraph will remind you to work effectively and to pace yourself. You are told that not everyone will be able to answer all the questions. The page does suggest that you skip questions that are difficult and come back to them if you have time—just what we have been telling you.

| SECTION 1 | TIME—60 MINUTES |
|-----------|------------------|

> **Directions:** This section consists of selections of literature and questions on their content, style, and form. After you have read each passage, select the response that best answers the question and mark the corresponding space on the answer sheet.

**Questions 1 through 13** refer to the following selection—a speech by Queen Elizabeth I to Parliament. Read the passage carefully and then choose the answers to the questions.

Line To be a King, and wear a Crown, is a thing more glorious to them that see it, than it is pleasant to them that bear it: for my self, I never was so much inticed with the glorious name of a King, or the royal authority of a Queen, as delighted that God hath made me His
5 Instrument to maintain His Truth and Glory, and to defend this kingdom from dishonor, damage, tyranny, and oppression. But should I ascribe any of these things unto my self, or my sexly weakness, I were not worthy to live, and of all most unworthy of the mercies I have received at God's hands, but to God only and wholly all is given
10 and ascribed.

The cares and troubles of a Crown I cannot more fitly resemble than to the drugs of a learned physician, perfumed with some aromatical savour, or to bitter pills gilded over, by which they are made more acceptable or less offensive, which indeed are bitter and
15 unpleasant to take, and for my own part, were it not for conscience sake to discharge the duty that God hath laid upon me, and to maintain His glory and keep you in safety, in mine own disposition I should be willing to resign the place I hold to any other, and glad to be freed of the glory with the labors, for it is not my desire to live
20 nor to reign longer than my life and reign shall be for your good. And though you have had and may have many mightier and wiser Princes sitting in this Seat, yet you never had nor shall have any that will love you better.

Thus Mr. Speaker, I commend me to your loyal loves, and yours
25 to my best care and your further councels, and I pray you Mr. Controller, and Mr. Secretary, and you of my Councell, that before these Gentlemen depart unto their countries, you bring them all to kiss my hand.

1. It can be inferred from her use of the words "my sexly weakness" (line 7) that Elizabeth believes

   (A) she herself is weak
   (B) she is unworthy of God's mercies
   (C) she is too emotional
   (D) women are the weaker sex
   (E) kings make better monarchs

2. The passage as a whole can best be described as which of the following modes of discourse?

   (A) Narrative
   (B) Argument
   (C) Exposition
   (D) Description
   (E) Persuasion

3. Elizabeth's use of the phrase "pills . . . that are bitter and unpleasant to take" (lines 13-15) is an example of which of the following figures of speech?

   (A) Simile
   (B) Metaphor
   (C) Imagery
   (D) Personification
   (E) Hyperbole

4. Which of the following best describes the tone of this passage?

   (A) Religious
   (B) Regal
   (C) Persuasive
   (D) Powerful
   (E) Benevolent

5. In the second paragraph, Elizabeth says ". . . in mine own disposition I should be willing to resign the place I hold to any other" (lines 17-18) in order to

   I. give credence to the idea that she rules because of Divine Will
   II. confide that she is tired of the responsibilities of the monarchy
   III. suggest that she is willing to resign and let another ruler take over

   (A) I only
   (B) II only
   (C) III only
   (D) I and II
   (E) II and III

6. What does Elizabeth imply when she says "To be a King, and wear a Crown, is a thing more glorious to them that see it, than it is pleasant to them that bear it" (lines 1-2)?

   (A) The monarchy is a glorious thing to behold.
   (B) The responsibilities of a ruler are a heavy burden.
   (C) It is sometimes pleasant to be queen.
   (D) Do not challenge my royal authority.
   (E) The Crown brings with it both good things and bad.

7. Which of the following definitions best suits the words "fitly resemble" (line 11) in the context?

   (A) Closely approximate
   (B) Aptly describe
   (C) Accurately compare
   (D) Perfectly mirror
   (E) Closely relate to

8. In the first paragraph, by choosing the word "Instrument" Elizabeth wishes to emphasize specifically

   (A) the nature of her political power
   (B) an almost musical delight with being the Queen
   (C) her promise to God that she will rule fairly
   (D) her obedience to God's will
   (E) that her authority comes from the line of succession

9. In this address, what does Elizabeth say are her duties as monarch?

   (A) To reign with truth and glory
   (B) To overcome her sexly weakness
   (C) To love her subjects better than her predecessors did
   (D) To take her medicine dutifully
   (E) To defend England from tyranny and oppression

10. Rhetorically, the last sentence in the second paragraph (lines 20–23) is best described as

    (A) an extended metaphor supporting the antecedent metaphor
    (B) reductio ad absurdem
    (C) a promise to care for her subjects
    (D) argumentum ad hominem
    (E) an attempt to balance possible weakness with a greater virtue

11. In the context of her speech, what does Elizabeth mean when she says "Thus . . . I commend me to your loyal loves"(line 24)?

    (A) I want you to remember me to your families.
    (B) I continue to be devoted to you.
    (C) I demand your continued allegiance.
    (D) I ask for your continued affection.
    (E) I will love those of you who are loyal to me.

12. Given the speaker's rhetoric, what can one infer is the primary purpose of Elizabeth's address?

    (A) To curry favor with her subjects by expressing her affection
    (B) To elicit compassion for herself as a woman
    (C) To explain that she rules by divine will
    (D) To convince parliament that her motives are purely altruistic
    (E) To dispel any ill will that may exist

13. The metaphor that Elizabeth develops in the second paragraph is an attempt to inform Parliament that

    (A) the burdens of being queen have made her ill
    (B) she is no longer willing to accept the yoke of power
    (C) monarchs who rule irresponsibly are an offense to God
    (D) the privileges of power do not compensate for its burdens
    (E) she rules only from her conscience and her duty to God

**Questions 14 through 26** refer to the following selection. Read the passage carefully and then choose the answers to the questions.

White's Chocolate House, June 6

Line A letter from a young lady, written in the most passionate terms, wherein she laments the misfortune of a gentleman, her lover, who was lately wounded in a duel, has turned my thoughts to that subject and inclined me to examine into the causes which precipitate men
5  into so fatal a folly. And as it has been proposed to treat of subjects of gallantry in the article from hence, and no one point in nature is more proper to be considered by the company who frequent this place than that of duels, it is worth our consideration to examine into this chimerical groundless humor, and to lay every other thought
10  aside, until we have stripped it of all its false pretenses to credit and reputation amongst men.

But I must confess, when I consider what I am going about and run over in my imagination all the endless crowd of men of honor who will be offended at such a discourse, I am undertaking, me-
15  thinks, a work worthy an invulnerable hero in romance, rather than a private gentleman with a single rapier; but as I am pretty well acquainted by great opportunities with the nature of man, and know of a truth that all men fight against their will, the danger vanishes, and resolution rises upon this subject. For this reason, I shall talk very
20  freely on a custom which all men wish exploded, though no man has courage enough to resist it.

But there is one unintelligible word, which I fear will extremely perplex my dissertation, and I confess to you I find very hard to explain, which is the term "satisfaction." An honest country gentle-
25  man had the misfortune to fall into company with two or three modern men of honor, where he happened to be very ill treated, and one of the company, being conscious of his offense, sends a note to him in the morning, and tells him he was ready to give him satisfac-tion. "This is fine doing," says the plain fellow; "last night he sent me
30  away cursedly out of humor, and this morning he fancies it would be a satisfaction to be run through the body."

As the matter at present stands, it is not to do handsome actions that denominates a man of honor; it is enough if he dares to defend ill ones. Thus you often see a common sharper in competition with a
35  gentleman of the first rank; though all mankind is convinced that a fighting gamester is only a pickpocket with the courage of an highwayman. One cannot with any patience reflect on the unaccount-able jumble of persons and things in this town and nation, which occasions very frequently that a brave man falls by a hand below that
40  of a common hangman, and yet his executioner escapes the clutches

of the hangman for doing it. I shall therefore hereafter consider how the bravest men in other ages and nations have behaved themselves upon such incidents as we decide by combat; and show, from their practice, that this resentment neither has its foundation from true
45 reason or solid fame: but is an imposture, made of cowardice, falsehood, and want of understanding. For this work, a good history of quarrels would be very edifying to the public, and I apply myself to the town for particulars and circumstances within their knowl-edge, which may serve to embellish the dissertation with proper cuts.
50 Most of the quarrels I have ever known have proceeded from some valiant coxcomb's persisting in the wrong, to defend some prevailing folly, and preserve himself from the ingenuity of owning a mistake.

By this means it is called "giving a man satisfaction" to urge your offense against him with your sword; which puts me in mind of
55 Peter's order to the keeper, in *The Tale of a Tub*. "If you neglect to do all this, damn you and your generation forever: and so we bid you heartily farewell." If the contradiction in the very terms of one of our challenges were as well explained and turned into downright English, would it not run after this manner?

60    Sir,

Your extraordinary behavior last night and the liberty you were pleased to take with me makes me this morning give you this, to tell you, because you are an ill-bred puppy, I will meet you in Hyde Park an hour hence; and because you want both breeding
65 and humanity, I desire you would come with a pistol in your hand, on horseback, and endeavor to shoot me through the head to teach you more manners. If you fail of doing me this pleasure, I shall say you are a rascal, on every post in town: and so, sir, if you will not injure me more, I shall never forgive what you have
70 done already. Pray, sir, do not fail of getting everything ready; and you will infinitely oblige, sir, your most obedient humble servant, etc. . . .

**14.** In the second sentence of the first para-graph, what is the best meaning for the word "chimerical"?

(A) Meritless
(B) Imaginary
(C) Monstrous
(D) Unjustified
(E) Musical

**15.** The passage as a whole is an example of which of the following modes of dis-course?

(A) Description
(B) Exposition
(C) Narration
(D) Argument
(E) Persuasion

**16.** What does the writer say is the purpose of his essay?

(A) To educate his readers about dueling
(B) To offer alternatives to dueling
(C) To write amusing essays for his readers
(D) To discredit the practice of dueling
(E) To change a barbaric custom

**17.** What is meant by the phrase "giving a man satisfaction" (line 53)?

(A) To kill or wound another man
(B) To repay a debt
(C) To offer the opportunity to restore one's honor
(D) To challenge a man with swords
(E) To discredit an enemy

**18.** In the fourth paragraph, what does the author mean when he says "A brave man falls by a hand below that of a common hangman" (lines 39–40)?

  I. Dueling is a crime punishable by hanging.
  II. Gentlemen and commoners alike die by dueling.
  III. A gentleman could be killed by a person of a lower class.

(A) I only
(B) II only
(C) III only
(D) I and II
(E) II and III

**19.** What literary device does the writer employ in the third paragraph to attack the practice of dueling?

(A) Anecdote
(B) Satire
(C) Imagery
(D) Allegory
(E) Parable

**20.** According to this passage, what does the writer believe about the practice of dueling?

(A) It is a time-honored custom.
(B) It is against the nature of man.
(C) Men of honor have no alternative.
(D) Men of honor must defend their reputation.
(E) It is understandable in certain circumstances.

**21.** Which of the following best describes the writer's style?

(A) Formal diction, compound-complex sentences
(B) Idiomatic vocabulary, sentence fragments
(C) Colloquial diction, simple declarative sentences
(D) Colloquial diction, rambling sentences
(E) Idiomatic vocabulary, idiomatic punctuation

**22.** Which of the following best characterizes the tone of this selection?

(A) Persuasive, reasonable
(B) Serious, introspective
(C) Satirical, witty
(D) Impassioned, ardent
(E) Educated, scholarly

**23.** What is the rhetorical function of the first paragraph?

  I. To present the main purpose of the article
  II. To tell readers the genesis of the article
  III. To explain why the author has chosen this subject

(A) I only
(B) II only
(C) III only
(D) I and II
(E) I, II, and III

24. The first sentence of the first paragraph beginning "A letter from a young lady, written in the most passionate terms" (line 1) contains all of the following elements EXCEPT

(A) an adjectival phrase
(B) a gerund phrase
(C) an adverbial phrase
(D) a prepositional phrase
(E) a participial phrase

25. In the first sentence of the last paragraph, the phrase "you are an ill-bred puppy" (line 63) is an example of

(A) a simile
(B) a metaphor
(C) a personification
(D) an analogy
(E) an overstatement

26. What is the rhetorical function of the last paragraph?

I. It illustrates the contradictory nature of giving "satisfaction."
II. It paraphrases a challenge to a duel.
III. It pokes fun at the custom of dueling.

(A) I only
(B) II only
(C) III only
(D) I and II
(E) I, II, and III

228

*Peterson's AP Success:
English Language & Composition*

**Questions 27 through 39** refer to the following selection from an article entitled "The American Game of Football" written by Alexander Johnston and published in a popular magazine in May 1887. Read the passage carefully and then choose the answers to the questions.

Line  However odd the title of this article may seem, its implications are correct and legitimate. The undergraduates of American colleges, taking the so-called Rugby game of foot-ball, have developed it into a game differing in many of its phases from any of its English proto-
5  types. There were already differences in its primitive home. Kicking the ball was, of course, common to all; but there was, further, the so-called Rugby game, whose leading feature, speaking roughly, was that the player might run with the ball; there was the Association game, in which, speaking as roughly, the player might "charge," that
10  is, run against an opponent and might not run with the ball; and there were a dozen other variants of the game. The peculiar feature of the Rugby game was the "scrimmage," . . . and American players, working out the scrimmage into a new form, have changed the possibilities of the game very greatly, and have made it, in addition to
15  its individual opportunities for the exhibition of skill, one of the most scientific of outdoor games in its "team-playing," or management of the entire side as one body. . . .

The game has found little favor in the South, but almost every Northern college now plays it more or less. The Intercollegiate Foot
20  Ball Association, founded in 1876, consists of the three colleges named above [Yale, Harvard, and Princeton], Wesleyan University, and the University of Pennsylvania. Each team plays one game with each of the other four teams during the season, the last game falling to the two teams which stood highest during the previous season.
25  For the past few years these two teams have regularly been those of Yale and Princeton; and those two are to be the contestants this year. This is always the great game of the year; the two teams come to it, usually, with an unbroken record of victories over all their other opponents; and the result of the game is to decide the championship
30  for the coming year. . . .

It would be far easier to write a "vivid" description of this final game than of all the boat-races that were rowed; the excitement is more prolonged; the ups and downs of the game are constant and never to be foreseen; and the points of individual and team playing
35  vastly more numerous, more perceptible and more easily apprehended. The enormous crowd, the coaches filled with men and horns, the masses and shades of color among the spectators, the perpetual roar of cheers, including the peculiar slogans of almost all the Eastern colleges, combine to make up a spectacle such as no

40  other intercollegiate game can offer; while the instant response of the
spectators to every shifting phase of the play shows that a very large
number of them have enjoyed the advantage of a good foot-ball
training in the past. But, to him who really likes the game, and who
understands its possible influence on the development of Americans,
45  the excitement, the cheers, the blowing of horns, and the ebb and
flow of the game, count for little. There is, instead of them, a feeling
of thankfulness for the antecedent process of which all this is only a
symptom, and a moving force for the coming year; a satisfaction in
knowing that this outdoor game is doing for our college-bred men, in
50  a more peaceful way, what the experiences of war did for so many of
their predecessors in 1861–65, in its inculcation of the lesson that
bad temper is an element quite foreign to open, manly contest.

**27.** The overall style of this selection could best be characterized as

(A) pedantic and brusque
(B) colloquial and unrefined
(C) pretentious and ornamental
(D) instructive and spirited
(E) nostalgic and reflective

**28.** Which of the following best describes the mode of discourse of this article?

(A) Exposition
(B) Narrative
(C) Argument
(D) Description
(E) Persuasion

**29.** The phrase "primitive home" (line 5) refers to which of the following?

(A) American universities
(B) The football field
(C) The Civil War period
(D) England
(E) Australia

**30.** The sentence beginning "It would be far easier to write a 'vivid' description of this final game" (lines 31–32) draws its unity from the speaker's use of

(A) parallelism
(B) alliteration
(C) irony
(D) understatement
(E) allusion

**31.** From the selection, you could infer that

(A) the author is a fan of football
(B) many academics disapprove of football
(C) English football and American football are similar
(D) the speaker favors stricter regulations for fans
(E) the writer wishes more Southern colleges would field teams

**32.** The overall tone of the passage is best described as

   (A) ironic and wry

   (B) fervent and enthusiastic

   (C) objective and distant

   (D) academic and didactic

   (E) zealous and biased

**33.** Which of the following best characterizes the main point of the final paragraph?

   (A) Championship football is more exciting than rowing.

   (B) The noise of cheering and the cheers create an atmosphere of frenzy.

   (C) Football is more than a sport; it teaches a life lesson.

   (D) The excitement surrounding the championship football game counts for little.

   (E) War and football are similar.

**34.** What is the subject of the following sentence?

> But, to him who really likes the game, and who understands its possible influence on the development of Americans, the excitement, the cheers, the blowing of horns, and the ebb and flow of the game, count for little.

   I. Excitement; cheers

   II. Americans; influence

   III. Blowing; ebb and flow

   (A) I only

   (B) II only

   (C) III only

   (D) I and III

   (E) I, II, and III

**35.** The presentation of material in the final paragraph is characterized primarily by

   (A) generalization and vivid details

   (B) facts followed by wide-ranging analysis

   (C) interpretation and personal opinion

   (D) two of these

   (E) all of these

**36.** Which of the following best describes the writer's purpose in this selection?

   (A) To describe scoring in American football

   (B) To persuade his readers to watch American football

   (C) To tell his readers how football is played in the United States

   (D) To explain the game of football to his readers

   (E) To share his feelings about American football

**37.** With which of the following would the writer be least likely to agree?

   (A) Football requires more mental skill than rugby.

   (B) Football is one of the many variations of rugby.

   (C) Southern universities should field more football teams.

   (D) Football is as exciting as other college sports, such as rowing.

   (E) Football, like war, teaches courage and self control.

38. Why might the author tell his readers that the title of the article may seem "odd" to them?

    I.   His readers think Americans in general are odd.
    II.  The American type of football is quite different from the English.
    III. The title is odd given the content of the article.

    (A) I only
    (B) II only
    (C) III only
    (D) I and II
    (E) II and III

39. In the final paragraph, which of the following techniques does the writer use to develop coherence?

    (A) Chronological order
    (B) Spatial order
    (C) Order of importance
    (D) Developmental order
    (E) Comparison and contrast

**Questions 40 through 52** refer to the following selection. In this excerpt from *My Bondage and My Freedom* by Frederick Douglass, the author speaks about his youth as a slave. Read the passage carefully and then choose the answers to the questions.

Line When I was about thirteen years old and had succeeded in learning to read, every increase of knowledge, especially respecting the free states, added something to the almost intolerable burden of the thought—"I am a slave for life." To my bondage I saw no end, it was
5 a terrible reality, and I shall never be able to tell how sadly that thought chafed my young spirit. Fortunately, or unfortunately, about this time in my life, I had made enough money to buy what was then a very popular schoolbook, the *Columbian Orator*. I bought this addition to my library, of Mr. Knight, on Thames street Fell's Point,
10 Baltimore, and paid him fifty cents for it. I was first led to buy this book, by hearing some little boys say they were going to learn some little pieces out of it for the Exhibition. This volume was, indeed, a rich treasure, and every opportunity afforded me, for a time, was spent in diligently perusing it. . . . The dialogue and the speeches
15 were all redolent of the principles of liberty and poured floods of light on the nature and character of slavery. As I read, behold! The very discontent so graphically predicted by Master Hugh had already come upon me. I was no longer the light-hearted, gleesome boy, full of mirth and play, as when I landed first at Baltimore. Knowledge had
20 come. . . . This knowledge opened my eyes to the horrible pit and revealed the teeth of the frightful dragon that was ready to pounce upon me, but it opened no way for my escape. I have often wished myself a beast, or a bird—anything, rather than a slave. I was wretched and gloomy. Beyond my ability to describe. I was too
25 thoughtful to be happy. It was this everlasting thinking which distressed and tormented me; and yet there was no getting rid of the subject of my thoughts. All nature was redolent of it. Once awakened by the silver trump* of knowledge, my spirit was roused to eternal wakefulness. Liberty! The inestimable birthright of every man, had,
30 for me, converted every object into an asserter of this great right. It was heard in every sound, and beheld in every object. It was ever present, to torment me with a sense of my wretched condition. The more beautiful and charming were the smiles of nature, the more horrible and desolate was my condition. I saw nothing without seeing
35 it. I do not exaggerate, when I say, that it looked from every star, smiled in every clam, breathed in every wind, and moved in every storm.

—Frederick Douglass

---

\* trumpet

**40.** This passage is primarily concerned with

(A) the importance of reading for Frederick Douglass

(B) Douglass's conclusion that slavery is intolerable

(C) the author's experiences at the hands of white boys

(D) the writer's knowledge of the constitution of the United States

(E) reasons why he was no longer a happy youngster

**41.** Which of the following describes the tone of the passage?

(A) Light and humorous

(B) Ironic

(C) Academic

(D) Sincere and powerful

(E) Angry and violent

**42.** This passage is an example of

(A) a slave narrative

(B) a picaresque novel

(C) a biography

(D) a historical text

(E) a secondary source

**43.** The style of this excerpt can best be described as

(A) elaborate, complex, and circumspect

(B) poetic

(C) plain, forceful, and direct

(D) obscure and difficult

(E) Elizabethan

**44.** According to the author, why is education incompatible with slavery?

(A) The system keeps slaves from living in harmony with their souls.

(B) Education makes slaves dissatisfied with their position.

(C) Slaves learn about the Constitution and the Bill of Rights.

(D) Education makes slaves dangerous to their masters.

(E) Owners do not want slaves wasting work time by reading and learning.

**45.** What effect does reading the *Columbian Orator* have upon young Douglass?

(A) He decides to buy the book for fifty cents.

(B) Douglass decides to enter the Exhibition and compete against white boys.

(C) The book increases his longing for freedom.

(D) He discovers that he is a victim of an oppressive system.

(E) He develops a plan to escape north.

**46.** Which of the following is not an accurate analysis of this passage?

(A) Douglass's descriptions are straightforward.

(B) The author offers little interpretation of the significance of events.

(C) The passage is factual.

(D) The author employs many literary allusions.

(E) Douglass allows readers to draw their own conclusions.

47. When Douglass writes "This knowledge opened my eyes to the horrible pit, and revealed the teeth of the frightful dragon that was ready to pounce upon me," (lines 20-22) he was referring

   (A) to Mr. Hugh, his owner
   (B) to the effects of education
   (C) to the *Columbian Orator*
   (D) to the institution of slavery
   (E) to events that had happened to him

48. What structure does Douglass employ in the sentence "The more beautiful and charming were the smiles of nature, the more horrible and desolate was my condition" (lines 32-34)?

   (A) Metaphors
   (B) Parallelism
   (C) Exaggeration
   (D) Eloquence
   (E) Cacophony

49. In the sentence "It was this everlasting thinking which distressed and tormented me; and yet there was no getting rid of the subject of my thoughts" (lines 25-27), the word "thinking" is which of the following?

   (A) Participle
   (B) Verb
   (C) Infinitive
   (D) Adverbial phrase
   (E) Gerund

50. What significant change does Douglass describe in the lines "As I read, behold! The very discontent so graphically predicted by Master Hugh, had already come upon me" (lines 16-18)?

   (A) The young Douglass came to the conclusion that slavery was wrong.
   (B) Douglass decided he would pursue a higher education.
   (C) The writer decided he would act light-hearted and mirthful while planning his escape.
   (D) His spirit awakened.
   (E) Douglass found his soul.

51. Douglass uses the word "redolent" twice (line 15 and line 27). What does the word mean?

   (A) Filled with
   (B) Sweet-smelling
   (C) Evocative
   (D) Excessive
   (E) Exuding

52. Which of the following best describes the mode of discourse of this article?

   (A) Exposition
   (B) Narrative
   (C) Argument
   (D) Description
   (E) Persuasion

 **END OF SECTION I**

| SECTION II | TIME—2 HOURS |
| --- | --- |

**Question 1**
Suggested time—40 minutes.

> **Directions:** Read the following passage carefully. Write a
> well-organized essay in which you explain how Thoreau
> developed and supported his core theme, or argument. Be sure
> to consider rhetorical and stylistic devices such as diction,
> imagery, tone, theme, and mode of discourse.

# FROM *CIVIL DISOBEDIENCE*

Line     I heartily accept the motto, "That government is best which governs
least"; and I should like to see it acted up to more rapidly and
systematically. Carried out, it finally amounts to this, which also I
believe: "That government is best which governs not at all"; and
5     when men are prepared for it, that will be the kind of government
which they will have. Government is at best but an expedient; but
most governments are usually, and all governments are sometimes,
inexpedient. The objections which have been brought against a
standing army, and they are many and weighty, and deserve to
10     prevail, may also at last be brought against a standing government.
The standing army is only an arm of the standing government. The
government itself, which is only the mode which the people have
chosen to execute their will, is equally liable to be abused and
perverted before the people can act through it. Witness the present
15     Mexican war, the work of comparatively a few individuals using the
standing government as their tool; for in the outset, the people would
not have consented to this measure.

      This American government—what is it but a tradition, though a
recent one, endeavoring to transmit itself unimpaired to posterity, but
20     each instant losing some of its integrity? It has not the vitality and
force of a single living man; for a single man can bend it to his will. It
is a sort of wooden gun to the people themselves; and, if ever they
should use it in earnest as a real one against each other, it will surely
split. But it is not the less necessary for this; for the people must have
25     some complicated machinery or other, and hear its din, to satisfy that
idea of government which they have. Governments show thus how
successfully men can be imposed on, even impose on themselves, for
their own advantage. It is excellent, we must all allow; yet this
government never of itself furthered any enterprise, but by the

30    alacrity with which it got out of its way. It does not keep the country free. It does not settle the West. It does not educate. The character inherent in the American people has done all that has been accomplished; and it would have done somewhat more, if the government had not sometimes got in its way. For government is an expedient by

35    which men would fain succeed in letting one another alone; and, as has been said, when it is most expedient, the governed are most let alone by it. Trade and commerce, if they were not made of India rubber, would never manage to bounce over the obstacles which legislators are continually putting in their way; and, if one were to

40    judge these men wholly by the effects of their actions, and not partly by their intentions, they would deserve to be classed and punished with those mischievous persons who put obstructions on the railroads.

       But, to speak practically and as a citizen, unlike those who call

45    themselves no-government men, I ask for, not at once no government, but *at once* a better government. Let every man make known what kind of government would command his respect, and that will be one step toward obtaining it. . . .

**Question 2**

Suggested time—40 minutes.

> **Directions:** Read the passage below carefully. Write a well-organized essay in which you analyze how Mrs. Keckley uses language and style to describe both the moment in history and her own state of mind. Include a discussion of how Mrs. Keckley uses language to make the reader feel the impact of President Lincoln's assassination. Pay specific attention to elements such as diction, sentence structure, description, point of view, punctuation, and narrative pace.

Line

"Who wants her?" I asked.

"I come from Mrs. Lincoln. If you are Mrs. Keckley, come with me immediately to the White House."

I hastily put on my shawl and bonnet, and was driven at a rapid
5 rate to the White House. Everything about the building was sad and solemn. I was quickly shown to Mrs. Lincoln's room, and on entering, saw Mrs. L. tossing uneasily about upon a bed. The room was darkened, and the only person in it besides the widow of the President was Mrs. Secretary Welles, who had spent the night with
10 her. Bowing to Mrs. Welles, I went to the bedside.

"Why did you not come to me last night, Elizabeth—I sent for you?" Mrs. Lincoln asked in a low whisper.

"I did try to come to you, but I could not find you," I answered, as I laid my hand upon her hot brow.

15 I afterwards learned, that when she had partially recovered from the first shock of the terrible tragedy in the theater, Mrs. Welles asked:

"Is there no one, Mrs. Lincoln, that you desire to have with you in this terrible affliction?"

20 "Yes, send for Elizabeth Keckley. I want her just as soon as she can be brought here."

Three messengers, it appears, were successively despatched for me, but all of them mistook the number and failed to find me.

Shortly after entering the room on Saturday morning, Mrs.
25 Welles excused herself, as she said she must go to her own family, and I was left alone with Mrs. Lincoln.

She was nearly exhausted with grief, and when she became a little quiet, I asked and received permission to go into the Guests' Room, where the body of the President lay in state. When I crossed
30 the threshold of the room, I could not help recalling the day on which I had seen little Willie lying in his coffin where the body of his father now lay. I remembered how the President had wept over the

pale beautiful face of his gifted boy, and now the President himself
was dead. The last time I saw him he spoke kindly to me, but alas!
35 the lips would never move again. The light had faded from his eyes,
and when the light went out the soul went with it. What a noble soul
was his—noble in all the noble attributes of God! Never did I enter
the solemn chamber of death with such palpitating heart and
trembling footsteps as I entered it that day. No common mortal had
40 died. The Moses of my people had fallen in the hour of his triumph.
Fame had woven her choicest chaplet for his brow. Though the brow
was cold and pale in death, the chaplet should not fade, for God had
studded it with the glory of the eternal stars.

**Question 3**
Suggested time—40 minutes.

> **Directions:** Read the passage below carefully. Write a well-organized essay presenting a logical argument for or against Woodrow Wilson's Appeal for Neutrality. Address your personal position regarding U.S. involvement in foreign conflict. Include evidence from your own observation, experience, or reading to support your position.

Line The people of the United States are drawn from many nations, and
chiefly from the nations now at war. It is natural and inevitable that
there should be the utmost variety of sympathy and desire among
them with regard to the issues and circumstances of the conflict.

5 Some will wish one nation, others another, to succeed in the momentous struggle. It will be easy to excite passion and difficult to allay it.
Those responsible for exciting it will assume a heavy responsibility,
responsibility for no less a thing than that the people of the United
States, whose love of their country and whose loyalty to its Govern-

10 ment should unite them as Americans all, bound in honor and
affection to think first of her and her interests, may be divided in
camps of hostile opinion, hot against each other, involved in the war
itself in impulse and opinion if not in action.

Such divisions amongst us would be fatal to our peace of mind

15 and might seriously stand in the way of the proper performance of
our duty as the one great nation at peace, the one people holding
itself ready to play a part of impartial mediation and speak the
counsels of peace and accommodation, not as a partisan, but as a
friend.

 **END OF SECTION II**

# ANSWERS AND EXPLANATIONS

## Quick-Score Answers

| | | | | |
|---|---|---|---|---|
| 1. D | 12. D | 23. E | 34. D | 45. C |
| 2. E | 13. D | 24. B | 35. D | 46. D |
| 3. B | 14. B | 25. B | 36. D | 47. D |
| 4. C | 15. E | 26. E | 37. D | 48. B |
| 5. A | 16. D | 27. D | 38. B | 49. E |
| 6. B | 17. C | 28. A | 39. E | 50. A |
| 7. C | 18. C | 29. D | 40. B | 51. C |
| 8. D | 19. A | 30. A | 41. D | 52. B |
| 9. E | 20. B | 31. A | 42. A | |
| 10. E | 21. A | 32. B | 43. C | |
| 11. A | 22. A | 33. C | 44. B | |

## PRACTICE TEST 2

### Test-Taking Strategy

*Use a watch, clock, or timer to pace yourself as you take the practice tests. This will help you work out your pacing when you take the real AP exam.*

1. **The correct answer is (D).** Whenever a series of answer choices include broad statements or generalizations, check to see if the generalization may be the best response. In this case, choices (D) and (E) refer to concepts rather than to specific instances. Choice (D) relates directly to the phrase Elizabeth uses in her speech, whereas choice (E) does not relate to the content of the paragraph. Eliminate choice (E). A careful rereading of the sentence, in the context of the paragraph, will tell you that choices (A), (B), and (C) can be eliminated. Elizabeth does not say she is weak, choice (A), nor too emotional, choice (C). She would consider herself unworthy of God's mercies only if she believed that she ruled based on her own right rather than through God's will. Because she does not believe this, choice (B) is incorrect. Choice (D), the notion of women as the weaker sex, a belief widely held at the time, is the best answer.

2. **The correct answer is (E).** If you did not know immediately that this is a persuasive speech, using the process of elimination would tell you. You could rule out choice (A), because Elizabeth is not telling a story. Elizabeth is not presenting a well-reasoned argument, so cross off choice (B). Choice (C) is not correct because Elizabeth is not explaining something, and choice (D) can be eliminated because Elizabeth is not describing something to her audience. Choice (E) is the best answer because judging from her tone, diction, and content, Elizabeth is attempting to persuade her audience of something, to convince them of her position or point of view.

3. **The correct answer is (B).** This question asks you to identify a figure of speech. Elizabeth is comparing "pills" to the "cares and troubles of a Crown," so that rules out choices (C), (D), and (E), that have nothing to do with comparison. A simile must use *like* or *as*, which eliminates choice (A). That leaves choice (B), a metaphor.

4. **The correct answer is (C).** Although the passage has a bit of each of the choices, overall, given the speaker's rhetoric and purpose, the best answer is choice (C), persuasive.

5. **The correct answer is (A).** Elizabeth's purpose in this paragraph is to reinforce the premise that she rules by virtue of divine will (I), not by her own will. Elizabeth may indeed be tired of the burden of ruling (II), but that is not stated or implied here. She is saying that she *cannot* resign because God has given this burden to her, so item III is incorrect. Only item I is correct, and only choice (A) has item I.

**Review Strategy**

*To review strategies for answering the types of questions you will find on the AP exam, see Chapter 1.*

6. **The correct answer is (B).** This is an inference question. If you don't know the answer right away, then try educated guessing. It is easy to rule out choices (D) and (E), because they are obviously wrong. Do not be distracted by choices (A) and (C) simply because they contain words that you see in the sentence. Choice (B) is the best inference from the sentence.

7. **The correct answer is (C).** Remember that you are dealing with definition and context. Remember also that Elizabeth is making a comparison. Always substitute the answer choices in the sentence to see which one makes the most sense. Choices (B), (C), and (E) seem likely possibilities, but choices (A) and (D) don't make sense. Elizabeth cannot approximate nor mirror "the cares and burdens of a Crown . . . than to the drugs of a learned physician." Because of the words *than to*, choice (C), *accurately compare*, fits within the construction as well as makes sense.

8.  **The correct answer is (D).** Go back to the passage and read the entire sentence. The clue is in the clause "that God hath made me His Instrument to maintain His Truth and Glory." Choice (D) states the general idea that being God's instrument is synonymous with being obedient to God. Choice (B) has nothing to do with the passage. Choices (A) and (C) relate to Elizabeth's actions, whereas choice (D) restates God's action and is a truer statement of the clause. Choice (E) is the direct opposite of the clause.

**Test-Taking Strategy**

*This is another question with the potential to trip you up on a cursory reading of the passage. Each answer choice has some word or words that are repeated from the passage.*

9.  **The correct answer is (E).** This is a recall question, that is, the answer is stated directly in the first paragraph of the passage. Of the answer choices, only choice (E) is contained there. The other choices are not.

10. **The correct answer is (E).** If you don't know the Latin terms, skip them and try to find the answer in another way. If you do know the Latin terms, you know that they are incorrect and do not apply here. Reductio ad absurdem, choice (B), is a proposition that proves to be absurd when carried to its logical conclusion. Argumentum ad hominem, choice (D), is an argument that appeals to the emotions rather than the intellect (a secondary meaning of ad hominem is the manner in which one attacks an opponent's character rather than addresses the person's contentions). Don't be fooled by choice (C). Love is mentioned, but it's not the point. That leaves choices (A) and (E). There is no comparison in the sentence, so there can be no metaphor, thus eliminating choice (A). Choice (E) is the best answer.

11. **The correct answer is (A).** Once in a while you may get a seemingly easy question. This is one such question, and don't read too much into it. It is just what you think it is at first glance. Elizabeth wants to be remembered to her hearers' loved ones. A clue is in the next phrase when she commends "yours to my best care." The *yours* refers back to the loved ones again.

12. **The correct answer is (D).** Remember that tone and style are clues to purpose. If you answered question number 4 correctly, you know that the tone of the passage is persuasive. Choice (D) contains the word *convince*, which is part of the purpose of persuasion. Don't be distracted by the other choices. Choice (A) does not reflect the tone accurately; Elizabeth's expression of affection is secondary to her main point. Choice (B) is a misreading of Elizabeth's character, based on her speech. Choice (C) is one piece of support for her thesis. Choice (E) asks you to make an assumption without any basis in the passage and can be eliminated.

13. **The correct answer is (D).** Choices (A), (B), and (C) are not stated or implied in this paragraph. In fact, choice (B) is the opposite of what Elizabeth is saying. Choice (E) does not represent a comparison, leaving choice (D) as the answer.

14. **The correct answer is (B).** This is a straightforward vocabulary question. Choices (A), (D), and (E) are distracters. You may remember that the chimera was a mythical monster, but in the context of the selection, the connotation is on the word *mythical*. Imaginary then, choice (B), is a better answer than choice (C). A bit later on the author reinforces this idea by talking about the "false pretenses" that go with dueling.

**Test-Taking Strategy**

*Read each question stem and highlight important words. Restate the question to yourself to be sure that you know what you are being asked to look for.*

15. **The correct answer is (E).** Choices (A), (B), and (C) are easily ruled out, because the writer is not simply describing, explaining, or telling a story. Choice (D) can be eliminated because an argument implies a premise/conclusion relationship, which is not the case here. The writer seeks to persuade the reader to think as he does, therefore, choice (E) is the correct answer.

16. **The correct answer is (D).** The writer states in the first paragraph that "it is worth our consideration to examine into this chimerical groundless humor [dueling], and to lay every other thought aside, until we have stripped it of all its false pretenses . . ." This statement indicates that choices (B), (C), and (E) are incorrect. The author says nothing about alternatives or changes in dueling, and the tone of the piece is not amusing. The process of elimination then leaves choices (A) and (D). While the article may indeed educate the reader, choice (A), the stated purpose is to discredit the practice of dueling, choice (D).

17. **The correct answer is (C).** This is one of those questions in which each of the answer choices seems a little bit true. Go back to the passage. The writer makes repeated use of the word *honor*, which should give you a clue. In addition, choice (B) would be correct only if the writer were speaking metaphorically about a debt of honor, which he isn't. Choice (E) is incorrect because the last sentence in paragraph 4 indicates that the real purpose of the duel is to allow some foolhardy coxcomb to avoid having to admit he was wrong. That leaves choices (A), (C), and (D). While both choices (A) and (D) are true statements about duels, they do not answer the question, leaving choice (C) as the correct answer.

18. **The correct answer is (C).** A "brave man" is a gentleman, and a "hand below that of a common hangman" means a person of a lower social class than a hangman. Item I is not stated or implied in the passage, which rules out choices (A) and (D). Item II is true, but it does not relate to the statement from the passage, eliminating choices (B), (D) and (E). Only point III relates to the statement, so choice (C), item III only, is correct.

19. **The correct answer is (A).** In the third paragraph, the writer gives us an anecdote of "a country gentleman" to strengthen his position. Choice (B), satire, is a literary work that uses sarcasm and ridicule to expose vices and follies; this work is too serious in tone to be satire. There is little imagery, choice (C), in the third paragraph. In an allegory, characters and events represent abstract qualities, which is not true of the country gentleman. A parable, choice (E), is a short tale that teaches a moral. The purpose of the tale of the country gentleman is not to teach a moral but to illustrate the author's point.

20. **The correct answer is (B).** This is a recall question, meaning that the answer is stated directly in the text. In the second paragraph, the writer states "that all men fight against their will." Choice (A) can be eliminated because the question asks only about what the writer believes. Choice (C) is incorrect because the author is offering an alternative—not to duel. The author skewers choice (D) in his essay, and choice (E) is not stated in the text.

21. **The correct answer is (A).** In line 6, the author implies that he is writing an article, so he must be writing for a newspaper or magazine. (This piece is by Richard Steele of *Tatler* and *Spectator* fame.) Therefore, this is a professional piece with formal diction, quickly and easily eliminating choices (B), (C), (D), and (E).

22. **The correct answer is (A).** Looking for consistency among answers will help you rule out choice (C), because we already eliminated satire in question 19, and although the writer uses humor, the piece is not particularly witty. The piece is serious but not introspective, that is, told from the deep feelings of the author, choice (B). Neither is the piece impassioned or ardent, choice (D). While the author is obviously educated, the piece is not filled with allusions or factual references, thus eliminating choice (E). The piece is written to be persuasive using a reasonable tone, choice (A).

23. **The correct answer is (E).** In checking points I, II, and III against the first paragraph, you can see that all three are true about the rhetorical function of the first paragraph. Only answer choice (E) has all three items.

**Review Strategy**

*See Chapter 3 for a quick review of grammar.*

24. **The correct answer is (B).** This *not/except* question tests your knowledge of English grammar. The phrase "from a young lady" is an adjectival phrase, so choice (A) is true about the sentence and an incorrect answer to the question. "Into so fatal a folly" is an adverbial phrase, making choice (C) true and incorrect. Both are examples of prepositional phrases, so choice (D) is true and incorrect. "Written in the most passionate terms" is a participial phrase, so choice (E) is incorrect. A gerund is a word ending in *-ing*, and there is none in the sentence, so choice (B) is not true and the right answer.

25. **The correct answer is (B).** Recalling the figures of speech, you might remember that a simile, choice (A), requires the words *like* or *as*. Choice (C), personification, is the giving of human qualities to a nonhuman thing. An analogy, choice (D), is a comparison to a directly parallel case. Choice (E), an overstatement, is an exaggeration. Choice (B), a metaphor, is the only one that fits. A metaphor is a comparison of two things, often related, and does not employ *like* or *as*.

26. **The correct answer is (E).** Each item, I, II, and III, is true. None of them can be eliminated; therefore, choice (E), which contains all three items, is the correct answer.

**Study Strategy**

*Review educating guessing in Chapter 1.*

27. **The correct answer is (D).** You can determine the answer for this question using the process of elimination. The feeling created in this passage is lively and informative. You can eliminate choices (A) and (B) because there is nothing pedantic or folksy about the article. While the language is more elaborate than that commonly used today, there is no pretentiousness, so choice (C) can be ruled out. The passage may seem nostalgic from the viewpoint of a twenty-first century reader, but it would not have been to the writer's contemporaries, so choice (E) is also incorrect.

28. **The correct answer is (A).** The article tells about football. The writer does use descriptive language to support his thesis, but that does not make the major mode of the selection description, choice (D). There is little or no storytelling, nor effort to sway the audience, eliminating choices (B), (C), and (E). You might have felt the writer did attempt to influence readers, but that is a secondary purpose, not the mode of discourse.

29. **The correct answer is (D).** The reference is to the earliest home of football-style sports. The writer states in lines 4–5 that the earliest prototypes were developed in England. Choices (A), (B), and (C) make no sense in the context of the selection. Australia, choice (E), is a distracter.

**Review Strategy**

*To review literary and rhetorical terms, see Chapter 4.*

30. **The correct answer is (A).** This question tests your knowledge of rhetoric. The sentence has three clauses using the same subject, linking verb, and predicate adjective structure. In the final clause, there are three phrases beginning with the word *more*. All of these indicate parallel structure. This sentence is straightforward, without alliteration, irony, or allusion, choices (B), (C), and (E). Because of his enthusiasm and fervor, the writer could never be accused of using understatement, choice (D).

31. **The correct answer is (A).** This question is rather easy if you read the passage thoughtfully. The author does not mention that academics disapprove of the game nor does he advocate stricter rules, eliminating choices (B) and (D). Since he points out the differences between rugby and football, choice (C) is incorrect. While he might be in favor of more teams from Southern colleges, he does not indicate this, making choice (E) invalid.

32. **The correct answer is (B).** This question requires the same type of comprehension as the first two questions about the selection. The passage is in no way ironic, distant, or academic, so choices (A), (C), and (D) are incorrect. Choice (E) is too strong for the tone of the article.

**Test-Taking Strategy**

*In choosing the answer for a main idea question, don't confuse the main idea with the supporting details. Look for the broadest response.*

33. **The correct answer is (C).** The writer makes several points in the final paragraph: football is more exciting than many other sports, choice (A); fans create an atmosphere of excitement, choice (B); and war and football are similar, choice (E). However, these are supporting details. His thesis in the paragraph is that football, like war, teaches self-discipline and self-control. Choice (D), that the excitement counts for little, is a transitional element used to introduce the author's thesis.

34. **The correct answer is (D).** The main verb is *count*. Ask yourself what "counts for little." The answer is excitement and cheers, item I, and blowing, ebb and flow, item III. The subject cannot be within a prepositional phrase, so item II cannot be correct, and any alternatives that include item II, choices (B) and (E), must be eliminated. Thus, the correct answer must include both item I and III, choice (D).

35. **The correct answer is (D).** A good method for answering this type of question involves elimination. Cross out any alternative that you know is wrong. Then find the choice that includes all the alternatives that you think are correct. In this passage, there is no wide-ranging analysis, so choices (B) and (E) are incorrect. That leaves choices (A) and (C) as true responses. The choice that includes both is choice (D), two of these.

36. **The correct answer is (D).** This question is straightforward. If you read the selection carefully, you know the author's intention was to inform his audience about football. He did share his feelings about the game, choice (E), but that was not his primary purpose. Choices (A), (B), and (C) are distracters.

37. **The correct answer is (D).** The writer plainly states the ideas in choices (A), (B), and (E), so those responses can be ruled out. Although he does not state it, given his enthusiasm for the sport, the author most probably would agree with choice (C). Since he feels football is more exciting than rowing, choice (D) is the logical answer.

38. **The correct answer is (B).** Most of the writer's readers were Americans, so point I is illogical. To most of the writer's contemporaries, football was the English game of rugby, so item II is true. The title accurately reflects the content, so item III is incorrect. The only answer choice that includes only point II is choice (B).

39. **The correct answer is (E).** Coherence results from effective organization of support. The final paragraph contrasts the championship game with other sports and then compares it to wartime experiences. Time does not enter into the content, eliminating choice (A). Neither do distance or development, so choices (B) and (D) can be crossed off. The author does save his most important point for the end, choice (C), but that point is created by comparison.

**40.** **The correct answer is (B).** While choices (A) and (E) are mentioned in the selection, they only support the main idea—that slavery is intolerable—they do not restate it. While white children are mentioned in the passage, Douglass does not describe experiences with them, so choice (C) is incorrect. Choice (D) is wrong because there is no mention of the Constitution.

**41.** **The correct answer is (D).** The question is easily answered by working through the choices and eliminating the wrong ones. There is nothing amusing, ironic, or academic in this passage; thus, choices (A), (B), and (C) are eliminated. While the writer has every right to be angry, he does not express that emotion in this passage, eliminating choice (E). Certainly, the passage is both powerful and sincere, choice (D).

**42.** **The correct answer is (A).** If you know who Frederick Douglass was, you will know that his autobiographies are considered classic examples of the slave narrative genre. If you do not know who he is, then you will have to work your way through the choices. A picaresque novel, choice (B), is a fictional account of the adventures of a vagabond or rogue, which does not fit the life described here. Thus choice (B) is incorrect. Since Douglass wrote this, evidenced by the use of the first-person pronouns, it cannot be a biography, choice (C), nor can it be a textbook. The same logic eliminates choice (E), since a secondary source is a work written about another person or another time.

**43.** **The correct answer is (C).** If you correctly answered the question about tone, this one should have been easy. The style is plain, easy to understand, and eloquent in its simplicity. There are no tortured sentences, choices (A) and (D), or Shakespearean phrases, choice (E). While the writer does use some figurative language, the effect is not poetic, choice (B).

**44.** **The correct answer is (B).** This is another good question on which to use the process of elimination. At first glance, choice (A) seems as if it might have some validity; however, there is little mention of spiritual aspects in the passage. Likewise, choice (D) has possibilities, but the writer does not talk about dangers to owners, only the debilitating effects on those enslaved. Choice (C) is wrong because Douglass does not discuss the Constitution or the Bill of Rights. The issues in choice (E) do not appear in the selection.

**Test-Taking Strategy**

*Always go back and check the passage; don't rely on what you think it says.*

**45.** **The correct answer is (C).** This is a comprehension question. Douglass states that the book created in him a discontent with his status as a slave. You might feel that choice (D) is correct, but be aware that the writer already knew that he was a slave. The question asks about something that happened after Douglass bought the book, so choice (A) is incorrect since it states how much he paid for the book. Neither choice (B) nor choice (E) are mentioned in the selection.

**46.** **The correct answer is (D).** There are no literary allusions in the passage. An allusion is a passing reference to people, places, or events that readers will recognize. The writer does refer obliquely to the Declaration of Independence once, but that hardly qualifies as many allusions, and it is not a literary but a political allusion in any case. If you got question 43 right, you will know that Douglass's descriptions are straightforward, choice (A). Because choice (B) is an accurate description of the selection, so then is choice (E). The passage is also factual in nature, recounting what Douglass did and felt, choice (C).

**47.** **The correct answer is (D).** Here, the writer is using figurative language to emphasize the horror of slavery. He likens slavery to a dragon's lair. To answer this question, you need to figure out to what the "this knowledge" refers. It would be unlikely that Douglass was referring to a person with this phrase, eliminating choice (A). The closest reference is to the contents of the volume he was reading, but not the volume itself, *Columbian Orator*, choice (C). The contents relate to the value of liberty to illustrate the ills of slavery, choice (D). Choice (E) is too broad, and choice (B) is not relevant to the context.

**Review Strategy**

*Review literary and rhetorical terms on pages 173–179.*

**48.** **The correct answer is (B).** Structure refers to the design or arrangement of parts in a work of literature. Metaphors are figures of speech that compare two unlike things, so choice (A) does not apply. Choice (C), exaggeration, is overstatement, usually for the purpose of creating humor or horror, neither of which is the case in this passage. While the selection is eloquent, choice (D), eloquence is not a recognized structure. Cacophony, choice (E), is a sound device, not a structure.

**49.** **The correct answer is (E).** A gerund is a verb form ending in *-ing* that functions as a noun. *Thinking*, in this sentence, functions as a predicate nominative, or *noun*. A participle, choice (A), may also end in *-ing* (or *-ed*) but functions as an adjective, not a noun. A verb, choice (B), is the predicate in a sentence, the action word. An infinitive, choice (C), is almost always made up of *to* plus a verb. An adverbial phrase, choice (D), modifies a verb or adjective. None of these apply to the word *thinking*.

**50.** **The correct answer is (A).** This question tests your comprehension. The lines you are asked about record Douglass's recognition that slavery is intolerable. The writer can no longer be happy in his state of bondage. Choice (B) does not relate to anything in the selection. The words *gleesome* and *mirth* are used in the selection, but there is no mention of escape, choice (C). Choices (D) and (E) would require a metaphysical interpretation that you are not asked to make.

**51.** **The correct answer is (C).** *Redolent* does mean sweet-smelling, choice (B), as well as evocative, choice (C), but in context, choice (C) is the correct answer. Choice (A) might seem to fit with the speeches, but nature is not filled with liberty. Choices (D) and (E) are distracters.

**52.** **The correct answer is (B).** If you got question 42 right, this answer was easy. As a slave narrative, the mode of discourse is choice (B), narrative. Because slavery is described from the point of view of a personal story, the selection is more than exposition, choice (A), and description, choice (D). Although Douglass may wish to persuade the reader of the dehumanizing effects of slavery, his tone is neither argumentative nor persuasive.

# Suggestions for Essay Question 1

The following are points that you might have chosen to include in your essay on *Civil Disobedience*. Consider them as you complete your self-evaluation. Revise your essay using points from the list to strengthen it.

## Form
• Excerpt from an essay

## Mode
• Persuasion

## Subject
• Government
• The type of government Thoreau considers the best
• What's wrong with the government of his day

## Author
• Henry David Thoreau, Transcendentalist

## Theme
• Government should do as little as possible.

## Tone
• Sincere
• Persuasive
• Light and humorous

## Diction/Syntax/Style
• Sophisticated diction
• Complex sentence structure
• Use of first person plural pronoun: "us against them" relationship
• Humor through use of images such as wooden gun, punishment of obstructive legislators
• Order of importance organization

## Literary Devices
• Metaphor of wooden gun for the government
• Comparison of commerce and trade to rubber, able to bounce over obstructions that the government puts in their path
• Simile for government legislators

# SUGGESTIONS FOR ESSAY QUESTION 2

The following are points that you might have chosen to include in your essay on Elizabeth Keckley's memoir about the death of President Abraham Lincoln. Consider them as you complete your self-evaluation. Revise your essay using points from the list to strengthen it.

## Form
- Excerpt from an autobiography

## Mode
- Narrative

## Subject
- The death of President Abraham Lincoln

## Speaker
- Elizabeth Keckley, a former slave

## Audience
- Readers of her autobiography

## Point of View
- First person

## Tone
- Serious
- Subdued
- Concerned

## Setting
- Washington, D. C.
- The White House
- mid-1800's

## Diction/Syntax/Style
- Formal diction
- Educated vocabulary
- Varied sentence structure

## Literary Devices
- Descriptive writing
- Metaphor: Lincoln, "the Moses of my people"

## Purpose
- Her experience of the death of Lincoln
- Her comforting of Mrs. Lincoln after the death of her husband

## Important Point
- Of all the people available to her, Mrs. Lincoln wanted Mrs. Keckley, a black woman who had been a slave (an unusual friendship, given the times).

# SUGGESTIONS FOR ESSAY QUESTION 3

The following are points that you might have chosen to include in your essay on Woodrow Wilson's *Appeal for Neutrality*. Consider them as you complete your self-evaluation. Revise your essay using points from the list to strengthen it.

## Form
- Speech
- A formal proclamation of neutrality

## Mode
- Argument

## Tone
- Persuasive
- Paternal

## Speaker
- President Woodrow Wilson

## Subject
- Maintain U.S. neutrality in World War I

## Theme
- Neutrality
- Unity
- America first
- Division fatal to peace

## Diction/Structure/Style
- Formal diction
- Educated vocabulary
- Varied sentence structure
- Easily understood by all citizens

## Purpose
- Formal declaration of U.S. neutrality
- Appeal to citizens for impartiality in spirit as well as in actions
- Appeal for unity

**Note:** The discussion of your own attitude toward U.S. involvement in world conflicts should reflect a thoughtful review of the pros and cons of Wilson's argument in light of current world politics and the United States' role.

# SELF-EVALUATION RUBRIC FOR THE ADVANCED PLACEMENT ESSAYS

| | 8–9 | 6–7 | 5 | 3–4 | 1–2 | 0 |
|---|---|---|---|---|---|---|
| **Overall Impression** | Demonstrates excellent control of the literature and outstanding writing competence; thorough and effective; incisive | Demonstrates good control of the literature and good writing competence; less thorough and incisive than the highest papers | Reveals simplistic thinking and/or immature writing; adequate skills | Incomplete thinking; fails to respond adequately to part or parts of the question; may paraphrase rather than analyze | Unacceptably brief; fails to respond to the question; little clarity | Lacking skill and competence |
| **Understanding of the Text** | Excellent understanding of the text; exhibits perception and clarity; original or unique approach; includes apt and specific references | Good understanding of the text; exhibits perception and clarity; includes specific references | Superficial understanding of the text; elements of literature vague, mechanical, overgeneralized | Misreadings and lack of persuasive evidence from the text; meager and unconvincing treatment of literary elements | Serious misreadings and little supporting evidence from the text; erroneous treatment of literary elements | A response with no more than a reference to the literature; blank response, or one completely off the topic |
| **Organization and Development** | Meticulously organized and thoroughly developed; coherent and unified | Well organized and developed; coherent and unified | Reasonably organized and developed; mostly coherent and unified | Somewhat organized and developed; some incoherence and lack of unity | Little or no organization and development; incoherent and void of unity | No apparent organization or development; incoherent |
| **Use of Sentences** | Effectively varied and engaging; virtually error free | Varied and interesting; a few errors | Adequately varied; some errors | Somewhat varied and marginally interesting; one or more major errors | Little or no variation; dull and uninteresting; some major errors | Numerous major errors |
| **Word Choice** | Interesting and effective; virtually error free | Generally interesting and effective; a few errors | Occasionally interesting and effective; several errors | Somewhat dull and ordinary; some errors in diction | Mostly dull and conventional; numerous errors | Numerous major errors; extremely immature |
| **Grammar and Usage** | Virtually error free | Occasional minor errors | Several minor errors | Some major errors | Severely flawed; frequent major errors | Extremely flawed |

*Peterson's AP Success:*
*English Language & Composition*

Using the rubric on the previous page, rate yourself in each of the categories below for each essay on the test. Enter on the lines below the number from the rubric that most accurately reflects your performance in each category. Then calculate the average of the six numbers to determine your final score. It is difficult to score yourself objectively, so you may wish to ask a respected friend or teacher to assess your writing for a more accurate reflection of its strengths and weaknesses. On the AP test itself, a reader will rate your essay on a scale of 1 to 9, with 9 being the highest.

Rate each category from 9 (high) to 0 (low).

## QUESTION 1

**SELF-EVALUATION**

Overall Impression  _____
Understanding of the Text  _____
Organization and Development  _____
Use of Sentences  _____
Word Choice (Diction)  _____
Grammar and Usage  _____

TOTAL  _____
  Divide by 6 for final score  _____

**OBJECTIVE EVALUATION**

Overall Impression  _____
Understanding of the Text  _____
Organization and Development  _____
Use of Sentences  _____
Word Choice (Diction)  _____
Grammar and Usage  _____

TOTAL  _____
  Divide by 6 for final score  _____

## QUESTION 2

**SELF-EVALUATION**

Overall Impression  _____
Understanding of the Text  _____
Organization and Development  _____
Use of Sentences  _____
Word Choice (Diction)  _____
Grammar and Usage  _____

TOTAL  _____
  Divide by 6 for final score  _____

**OBJECTIVE EVALUATION**

Overall Impression  _____
Understanding of the Text  _____
Organization and Development  _____
Use of Sentences  _____
Word Choice (Diction)  _____
Grammar and Usage  _____

TOTAL  _____
  Divide by 6 for final score  _____

## QUESTION 3

**SELF-EVALUATION**

Overall Impression  _____
Understanding of the Text  _____
Organization and Development  _____
Use of Sentences  _____
Word Choice (Diction)  _____
Grammar and Usage  _____

TOTAL  _____
  Divide by 6 for final score  _____

**OBJECTIVE EVALUATION**

Overall Impression  _____
Understanding of the Text  _____
Organization and Development  _____
Use of Sentences  _____
Word Choice (Diction)  _____
Grammar and Usage  _____

TOTAL  _____
  Divide by 6 for final score  _____

# Practice Test 3

## AP ENGLISH LANGUAGE AND COMPOSITION

On the front page of your test booklet, you will find some information about the test. Because you have studied this book, none of it should be new to you, and much of it is similar to other standardized tests you have taken.

The page will tell you that the following exam will take 3 hours—1 hour for the multiple-choice section and 2 hours for the three essays—and that there are two booklets for this exam, one for the multiple-choice section and one for the essays.

The page will also say that SECTION I

- is 1 hour.

- has 50 questions (or some number from 50 to 60).

- counts for 45 percent of your total grade.

Then you will find a sentence in capital letters telling you not to open your exam booklet until the monitor tells you to open it.

Other instructions will tell you to be careful to fill in only ovals 1 through 50 (or whatever the number is) in Section I on your separate answer sheet. Fill in each oval completely. If you erase an answer, erase it completely. You will not receive any credit for work done in the test booklet, but you may use it for making notes.

You will also find a paragraph about the guessing penalty—deduction of one-quarter point for every wrong answer—as well as words of advice about guessing if you know something about the question and can eliminate several of the answers.

The final paragraph will remind you to work effectively and to pace yourself. You are told that not everyone will be able to answer all the questions. The page does suggest that you skip questions that are difficult and come back to them if you have time—just what we have been telling you.

# SECTION 1          TIME—60 MINUTES

> **Directions:** This section consists of selections of literature and questions on their content, style, and form. After you have read each passage, select the response that best answers the question and mark the corresponding space on the answer sheet.

**Questions 1 through 12** refer to this selection written by Thomas Paine, the colonial writer and radical.

Line   These are the times that try men's souls. The summer soldier and the sunshine patriot will in this crisis, shrink from the service of his country; but he that stands it NOW deserves the love and thanks of man and woman. Tyranny, like hell, is not easily conquered; yet we
5   have this consolation with us, that the harder the conflict, the more glorious the triumph. What we obtain too cheap, we esteem too lightly, 'tis dearness only that gives everything its value. Heaven knows how to put a proper price upon its goods; and it would be strange indeed, if so celestial an article as FREEDOM should not be
10   highly rated. Britain, with an army to enforce her tyranny, has declared that she has a right (not only to TAX) but "to BIND *us in* ALL CASES WHATSOEVER," and if being *bound* in that manner, is not slavery, then is there not such a thing as slavery upon earth. Even the expression is impious, for so unlimited a power can belong only to
15   God. . . .

    I have as little superstition in me as any man living, but my secret opinion has ever been, and still is, that God Almighty will not give up a people to military destruction, or leave them unsupportedly to perish, who have so earnestly and so repeatedly sought to avoid
20   the calamities of war, by every decent method which wisdom could invent. Neither have I so much of the infidel in me, as to suppose that he has relinquished the government of the world and given us up to the care of devils; and as I do not, I cannot see on what grounds the king of Britain can look up to heaven for help against us:
25   a common murderer, a highwayman, or a housebreaker, has as good a pretense as he. . . .

    I once felt all that kind of anger, which man ought to feel, against the mean principles that are held by the Tories: a noted one, who kept a tavern at Amboy, was standing at his door, with as pretty
30   a child in hand, about eight or nine years old, as I ever saw, and after speaking his mind as freely he thought was prudent, finished with the unfatherly expression, "Well! give *me peace* in *my* day." Not a man

lives on the continent but fully believes that a separation must some
time or other finally take place, and a generous parent should have
35   said, *"If there must be trouble let it be in my day that my child may
have peace"*; and the single reflection, well applied, is sufficient to
awaken every man to duty. Not a place upon earth might be so
happy as America. Her situation is remote from all the wrangling
world, and she has nothing to do but trade with them. A man can
40   distinguish himself between temper and principle, and I am as
confident, as I am that God governs the world, that America will
never be happy till she gets clear of foreign dominion. Wars, without
ceasing, will break out till that period arrives, and the continent must
in the end be conqueror; for though the flame of liberty may some-
45   times cease to shine, the coal can never expire. . . .

I turn with the warm ardor of a friend to those who have nobly
stood and are yet determined to stand the matter out: I call not upon
a few, but upon all; not on this state or that state, but on *every* state;
up and help us; lay your shoulders to the wheel; better have too
50   much force than too little, when so great an object is at stake. Let it
be told to the future world, that in the depth of winter, when
nothing but hope and virtue could survive, that the city and the
country, alarmed at one common danger, came forth to meet and to
repulse it. Say not that thousands are gone, turn out your tens of
55   thousands; throw not the burden of the day upon Providence, but
*"show your faith by your works,"* that God may bless you. It matters
not where you live, or what rank of life you hold, the evil or the
blessing will reach you all. The far and the near, the home counties
and the back, the rich and the poor, will suffer or rejoice alike. The
60   heart that feels not now, is dead: the blood of his children will curse
his cowardice, who shrinks back at a time when a little might have
saved the whole and made *them* happy. (I love the man that can
smile at trouble; that can gather strength from distress, and grow
brave by reflection.) 'Tis the business of little minds to shrink; but he
65   whose heart is firm, and whose conscience approves his conduct,
will pursue his principles unto death. My own line of reasoning is to
myself as straight and clear as a ray of light. Not all the treasures of
the world, so far as I believe, could have induced me to support an
offensive war, for I think it murder; but if a thief breaks into my
70   house, burns and destroys my property, and kills or threatens to kill
me, or those that are in it, and to *"bind me in all cases whatsoever,"*
to his absolute will, am I to suffer it? What signifies it to me, whether
he who does it is a king or a common man; my countryman, or not
my countryman; whether it be done by an individual villain or an
75   army of them? If we reason to the root of things we shall find no
difference; neither can any just cause be assigned why we should
punish in the one case and pardon in the other.

1. In the following clause, what is the best meaning for the word "mean"?

> I once felt all that kind of anger, which a man ought to feel, against the mean principles that are held by the Tories . . .

(A) Inferior
(B) Small-minded
(C) Selfish
(D) Miserly
(E) Bad-tempered

2. In the sentence beginning "My own line of reasoning" (lines 66–67), which figure of speech does the author employ?

(A) Image
(B) Analogy
(C) Simile
(D) Metaphor
(E) Figurative language

3. Which of the following best describes the mode of discourse used in this passage?

(A) Description
(B) Argument
(C) Narration
(D) Persuasion
(E) Exposition

4. Which of the following best describes the overall tone of this passage?

(A) Reasonable
(B) Angry
(C) Moralistic
(D) Bitter
(E) Passionate

5. Which of the following best describes the rhetorical device most in evidence in this essay?

(A) Aphorism
(B) Allegory
(C) Analogy
(D) Allusion
(E) Alliteration

6. The author develops all of the following points EXCEPT

(A) America's liberty is at stake
(B) America must go to war
(C) America's cause is just
(D) America must declare its independence
(E) America must fight all tyranny

7. To what does Paine compare Britain's actions toward its colonies?

(A) Tyranny and hell
(B) Murder and death
(C) Slavery and thievery
(D) Cowardice and villainy
(E) Calamity and calumny

8. In the sentence beginning "I turn with the warm ardor" (line 46), what is the best meaning for the word "ardor"?

(A) Glow
(B) Passion
(C) Interest
(D) Odor
(E) Energy

9. Given the passage as a whole, which of the following best characterizes Paine's opinions about war?

(A) There will always be war.
(B) God will not allow the just to perish.
(C) War is permitted against tyranny.
(D) Just wars and unjust wars are different.
(E) All war is the same as murder.

10. How does the writer view America's role in the world without Britain?

   I. A melting pot
  II. An independent trader
 III. A happy place

(A) I only
(B) II only
(C) III only
(D) I and II
(E) II and III

11. In the first paragraph, what does Paine mean when he refers to "the summer soldier" and "the sunshine patriot"?

    (A) Those who are brave only in times of peace
    (B) Soldiers who run from battle
    (C) People who fade when the going gets tough
    (D) People who do not stand against Britain's tyranny
    (E) Americans who align themselves with the Tories

12. What is the rhetorical function of the first sentence of the essay?

    (A) To demand the reader's attention
    (B) To identify with the writer's audience
    (C) To express the writer's own frustration
    (D) To present the subject of the essay
    (E) To set a religious tone

**Questions 13 through 25** refer to the passage below from a Southern woman's diary written during the Civil War.

Line  April 12, 1861. Anderson will not capitulate.

Yesterday was the merriest, maddest dinner we have had yet. Men were more audaciously wise and witty. We had an unspoken foreboding it was to be our last pleasant meeting. Mr. Miles dined
5   with us today. Mrs. Henry King rushed in: "The news, I come for the latest news—all of the men of the King family are on the island"—of which fact she seemed proud.

While she was here, our peace negotiator—or envoy—came in. That is, Mr. Chesnut returned—his interview with Colonel Anderson
10   had been deeply interesting—but was not inclined to be communicative, wanted his dinner. Felt for Anderson. Had telegraphed to President Davis for instructions.

What answer to give Anderson, etc., etc. He has gone back to Fort Sumter with additional instructions.
15   When they were about to leave the wharf, A. H. Boykin sprang into the boat, in great excitement; thought himself ill-used. A likelihood of fighting—and he to be left behind!

I do not pretend to go to sleep. How can I? If Anderson does not accept terms—at four—the orders are—he shall be fired upon.
20   I count four St. Michael chimes. I begin to hope. At half-past four, the heavy booming of a cannon.

I sprang out of bed. And on my knees—prostrate—I prayed as I never prayed before.

There was a sound of stir all over the house—pattering of feet in
25   the corridor—all seemed hurrying one way. I put on my double gown and a shawl and went, too. It was to the housetop.

The shells were bursting. In the dark I heard a man say "waste of ammunition."

I knew my husband was rowing about in a boat somewhere in
30   that dark bay. And that the shells were roofing it over—bursting toward the fort. If Anderson was obstinate—he was to order the forts on our side to open fire. Certainly fire had begun. The regular roar of the cannon—there it was. And who could tell what each volley accomplished of death and destruction.
35   The women were wild, there on the housetop. Prayers from the women and imprecations from the men, and then a shell would light up the scene. Tonight, they say, the forces are to attempt to land.

The *Harriet Lane* had her wheelhouse smashed and put back to sea.
40   We watched up there—everybody wondered. Fort Sumter did not fire a shot.

13. In the sentence beginning "Prayers from the women," (line 35) what is the best meaning for the word "imprecations"?

    (A) Shouts
    (B) Curses
    (C) Prayers
    (D) Cries
    (E) Entreaties

14. Which of the following best describes the overall tone of the passage?

    (A) Objective
    (B) Solemn
    (C) Factual
    (D) Formal
    (E) Informal

15. Which of the following best describes the purpose of Mrs. Chesnut's journal entry?

    (A) To record her personal travails
    (B) To record her family history
    (C) To record events of the day
    (D) To record her private thoughts
    (E) To record her husband's deeds

16. Which of the following best describes the mode of discourse of this passage?

    (A) Description
    (B) Narrative
    (C) Exposition
    (D) Persuasion
    (E) Argument

17. According to this entry, how does Mrs. Chesnut view her husband's role in these events?

    (A) As a brave man
    (B) As a brave colonel
    (C) As a peace envoy
    (D) As a good husband
    (E) As a loyal confederate soldier

18. According to Mrs. Chesnut, what is Mr. Chesnut's attitude toward Colonel Anderson?

    (A) Respectful
    (B) Admiring
    (C) Compassionate
    (D) Conciliatory
    (E) Benevolent

19. Which of the following rhetorical devices does the writer use to communicate her visual and auditory experiences in the early morning hours of April 13?

    (A) Imagery
    (B) Figurative language
    (C) Metaphor
    (D) Repetition
    (E) Anecdote

20. In the following sentence, what can be inferred from the phrase "but was not inclined to be communicative"?

    > That is, Mr. Chesnut returned—his interview with Colonel Anderson had been deeply interesting—but was not inclined to be communicative, wanted his dinner.

    (A) He was a quiet man.
    (B) He was a hungry man.
    (C) His visit could not be shared.
    (D) His visit was unsuccessful.
    (E) He was tired and needed to rest.

21. Which of the following best describes the mood shifts that occur in the passage?

    (A) Angry/wild/thoughtful
    (B) Detached/wild/concerned
    (C) Solemn/excited/concerned
    (D) Solemn/excited/resigned
    (E) Detached/excited/caring

22. The shifts in mood in the first three paragraphs have the effect of which of the following?

    I. Communicating the flow of daily events
    II. Shifting the focus from the home to the war
    III. Reflecting the vicissitudes of emotion at home

    (A) I only
    (B) II only
    (C) III only
    (D) I and II
    (E) II and III

23. Which of the following is found frequently in this passage but would not be found in a newspaper account of the same events?

    (A) Simple sentences
    (B) Complex sentences
    (C) Sentence fragments
    (D) Exclamatory sentences
    (E) Interrogative sentences

24. The main purpose of "At half-past four, the heavy booming of a cannon" (lines 20–21) is to make clear that

    (A) Anderson would not surrender
    (B) the Civil War had begun
    (C) Fort Sumter was under siege
    (D) the South had fired first
    (E) hope for peace was gone

25. Given the passage as a whole, what can be inferred from the writer's use of "Mr. Chesnut" in reference to her husband?

    I. Respect
    II. Social custom
    III. Emotional distance

    (A) I only
    (B) II only
    (C) III only
    (D) I and II
    (E) II and III

**Questions 26 through 36** refer to the passage below, a speech by Chief Joseph of the Nez Perce. Read the passage carefully and then choose the answers to the questions.

Line   Tell General Howard I know his heart. What he told me before, I have in my heart. I am tired of fighting. Our chiefs are killed. Looking Glass is dead. Toohoolhoolzote is dead. The old men are all dead. It is the young men who say yes and no. He who led on the young men is
5   dead. It is cold and we have no blankets. The little children are freezing to death. My people, some of them, have run away to the hills and have no blankets, no food; no one knows where they are—perhaps freezing to death. I want to have time to look for my children and see how many I can find. Maybe I shall find them
10   among the dead. Hear me, my chiefs, I am tired; my heart is sick and sad. From where the sun now stands I will fight no more forever.

26. Which of the following best describes the overall tone of the passage?

  (A) Angry
  (B) Resigned
  (C) Bitter
  (D) Despairing
  (E) Somber

27. The tone of the passage is revealed through which of the following?

  (A) Sentence structure
  (B) Emotional vocabulary
  (C) Direct statement about the speaker's feelings
  (D) Diction and syntax
  (E) Facial expressions

28. What is the purpose of Chief Joseph's speech?

  I. To emphasize the plight of his people
  II. To notify federal troops of his surrender
  III. To tell his people to lay down their arms

  (A) I only
  (B) II only
  (C) III only
  (D) I and II
  (E) II and III

29. Which of the following best describes the mode of Chief Joseph's speech?

  (A) Narrative
  (B) Exposition
  (C) Argument
  (D) Persuasion
  (E) Description

30. How does the speaker's use of short, simple sentences contribute to the impact of his speech?

    I. It adds emphasis to the main point.
    II. It adds a strong emotional appeal.
    III. It allows the facts to speak for themselves.

(A) I only
(B) II only
(C) III only
(D) I and II
(E) I and III

31. Which of the following best describes Chief Joseph's relationship with his people?

(A) He is their beloved chief.
(B) He wants to feed the children.
(C) He will give his life for them.
(D) He mourns the dead deeply.
(E) He is dedicated to their welfare.

32. Which of the following is contained in the sentence "I am tired of fighting" (line 2)?

(A) Predicate nominative
(B) Predicate adjective
(C) Gerund phrase used as a subject
(D) Gerund phrase used as a direct object
(E) Noun phrase used as a direct object

33. All of the following are reasons why Chief Joseph will "fight no more forever" EXCEPT

(A) he is tired of fighting.
(B) the old men are all dead.
(C) his people are cold and hungry.
(D) he knows that the government will feed his people.
(E) he wants to look for his children.

34. Which of the following best describes the pattern of organization used by Chief Joseph when he lists individuals and groups of people who are dead and dying?

(A) Classification
(B) Example
(C) Enumeration
(D) Analysis
(E) Synthesis

35. By including the details "The chiefs are killed," "The old men are all dead," and "The little children are freezing to death," Chief Joseph is communicating that

    I. His life is over.
    II. His people's past and their future are dead.
    III. He is without hope for the future.

(A) I only
(B) II only
(C) III only
(D) I and II
(E) I, II, and III

36. Which of the following best describes the emotion evoked in the reader by the rhetoric of Chief Joseph?

(A) Pity
(B) Sorrow
(C) Empathy
(D) Sympathy
(E) Despair

**Questions 37 through 51** refer to the following letter from Samuel Johnson to Lord Chesterfield. After the publication of *Samuel Johnson's Dictionary*, Lord Chesterfield wrote two articles that praised the book. Earlier, Chesterfield had ignored two requests from Johnson for financial assistance for producing the dictionary. Read the passage carefully and then choose the answers to the questions.

Letter to Lord Chesterfield

Line To the Right Honorable
The Earl of Chesterfield

February 7, 1755

My Lord:

5    I have been lately informed by the proprietor of the *World* that two papers in which my *Dictionary* is recommended to the public were written by your Lordship. To be so distinguished is an honor which, being very little accustomed to favors from the great, I know not well how to receive, or in what terms to acknowledge.

10    When upon some slight encouragement I first visited your Lordship, I was overpowered like the rest of mankind by the enchantment of your address* and could not forbear to wish that I might boast myself "*Le vainqueur du vainqueur de la terre*"**; that I might obtain that regard for which I saw the world contending, but I found

15    my attendance so little encouraged that neither pride nor modesty would suffer me to continue it. When I had once addressed your Lordship in public, I had exhausted all the art of pleasing which a retired and uncourtly scholar can possess. I had done all that I could; and no man is well pleased to have his all neglected, be it ever so

20    little.

    Seven years, my Lord, have now passed since I waited in your outward rooms or was repulsed from your door, during which time I have been pushing on my work through difficulties of which it is useless to complain and have brought it at last to the verge of

25    publication without one act of assistance, one word of encouragement, or one smile of favor. Such treatment I did not expect, for I never had a patron before.

    The shepherd in Virgil grew at last acquainted with love and found him a native of the rocks (Virgil's shepherd complains that love

30    must have been born among jagged rocks). Is not a patron, my Lord, one who looks with unconcern on a man struggling for life in the water and when he has reached ground, encumbers him with help? The notice which you have been pleased to take of my labors, had it

---

* conversation
** the conqueror of the earth

35 been early, had been kind; but it has been delayed till I am indifferent and cannot enjoy it, till I am solitary and cannot impart it, till I am known and do not want it.

I hope it is no very cynical asperity not to confess obligation where no benefit has been received, or to be unwilling that the public should consider me as owing that to a patron which Provi-
40 dence has enabled me to do for myself.

Having carried on my work thus far with so little obligation to any favorer of learning, I shall not be disappointed though I should conclude it, if less be possible, with less; for I have been long wakened from that dream of hope, in which I once boasted myself
45 with so much exultation, my Lord.

Your Lordship's most humble,
Most obedient servant,
Samuel Johnson

**37.** What was the purpose of this letter?

(A) To ask for a financial settlement now that the dictionary was completed
(B) To thank Chesterfield for his two glowing reviews
(C) To express Johnson's disapproval of Chesterfield's misleading praise for his work
(D) To inquire if Chesterfield might fund a second edition
(E) To castigate the earl in front of all of England

**38.** What tone is expressed in this letter?

(A) Subtly stated anger and resentment
(B) Grateful thanks
(C) Condescending superiority
(D) Obsequious fawning
(E) Vicious coldness

**39.** In the first sentence of the second paragraph, Johnson writes

When upon some slight encourage-ment I first visited your Lordship, I was overpowered like the rest of mankind by the enchantment of your address, and could not forbear to wish that I might boast my self '*Le vainqueur du vainqueur de la terre*'; that I might obtain that regard for which I saw the world contending. . . . (lines 13–14).

What stylistic device does he employ?

(A) Allusion
(B) Exemplum
(C) Parallelism
(D) Figurative language
(E) Overstatement

**40.** In the fifth paragraph, Johnson implies that Lord Chesterfield may have conveyed misinformation in one of his articles. What might Chesterfield have suggested?

(A) The earl may have hinted that he had encouraged and supported Johnson throughout his years working on the dictionary.

(B) Chesterfield might have suggested that he inspired Johnson to begin the dictionary.

(C) The earl might have implied that he provided Johnson with a house, servants, food, drink, and all other necessities of life.

(D) Chesterfield might have implied that he himself contributed to the dictionary.

(E) The earl might have implied that Johnson could not have completed the work without Chesterfield's help and monetary assistance.

**41.** Which of the following is an example of allusion?

(A) "Is not a patron, my Lord, one who looks with unconcern on a man struggling for life in the water and when he has reached ground, encumbers him with help?"

(B) "I have been long wakened from that dream of hope, in which I once boasted myself with so much exultation, my Lord."

(C) "I have been lately informed by the proprietor of the *World* that two papers in which my *Dictionary* is recommended to the public were written by your Lordship."

(D) "The shepherd in Virgil grew at last acquainted with love, and found him a native of the rocks."

(E) "Your Lordship's most humble, Most obedient servant, Samuel Johnson"

**42.** Samuel Johnson would have you believe which of the following about himself?

(A) He is a sycophant.

(B) He is indebted to Lord Chesterfield.

(C) He no longer needs Lord Chesterfield's help.

(D) He never sought assistance from a patron.

(E) Lord Chesterfield is a man of unquestioning largess.

**43.** Samuel Johnson's expression "the enchantment of your address" (lines 11–12) is

(A) witty
(B) argumentative
(C) metaphorical
(D) symbolic
(E) sarcastic

**44.** With which of the following statements would Samuel Johnson agree?

(A) No one likes one's work to be ignored.

(B) One should forget the little people.

(C) Samuel Johnson had done everything he could to get the earl's attention.

(D) Samuel Johnson had never done anything great before his dictionary.

(E) No one can be happy doing only little things.

**45.** The closing of the letter can best be interpreted as

(A) obsequious
(B) facetious
(C) punctilious
(D) traditional
(E) obligatory

46. What stylistic device can be found in the sentence, "Seven years, my Lord, have now passed since I waited in your outward rooms or was repulsed from your door, during which time I have been pushing on my work through difficulties of which it is useless to complain and have brought it at last to the verge of publication without one act of assistance, one word of encouragement, or one smile of favor" (lines 21–26)?

    (A) Parallelism
    (B) Overstatement
    (C) Allusion
    (D) Imagery
    (E) Quotation

47. All of the following are accurate descriptions of of Johnson's diction EXCEPT

    (A) clear
    (B) correct
    (C) effective
    (D) simple
    (E) too formal for today's tastes

48. What is the feeling that Samuel Johnson conveys in the phrase "till I am known and do not want it" (lines 35–36)?

    (A) People know who I am, and I don't need anyone's money.
    (B) I don't feel that you are a supporter of me.
    (C) Now that I am well known, I don't need your assistance.
    (D) He doesn't want anyone to help him publish his dictionary.
    (E) There are very few people who will spend time helping others.

49. The word "favorer" in line 42 refers to

    (A) student
    (B) teacher
    (C) audience
    (D) patron
    (E) adulator

50. Which of the following assessments does not accurately characterize the overall impression created by the selection?

    (A) Punctilious in courtesy
    (B) Faultless in manners
    (C) Ironic
    (D) Indignant
    (E) Forthright

51. What mode of discourse characterizes this selection?

    (A) Argument
    (B) Persuasion
    (C) Description
    (D) Narrative
    (E) Exposition

 **END OF SECTION I**

| SECTION II | TIME—2 HOURS |
|---|---|

**Question 1**
Suggested time—40 minutes.

> **Directions:** Read the passage below carefully. Write a well-developed essay that gives a detailed rhetorical analysis of the passage. Discuss how Abraham Lincoln uses language to achieve his purposes in his first Inaugural Address. Be sure to include elements such as diction, mode of discourse, selection of detail, and structure.

Inaugural Address, March 4, 1861

Line    In your hands, my dissatisfied fellow countrymen, and not in mine, is the momentous issue of civil war. The government will not assail you. You can have no conflict without being yourselves the aggressors. You have no oath registered in heaven to destroy the government,
5       while I shall have the most solemn one to "preserve, protect, and defend" it.

        I am loath to close. We are not enemies, but friends. We must not be enemies. Though passion may have strained, it must not break, our bonds of affection. The mystic cords of memory, stretch-
10      ing from every battlefield and patriot grave to every living heart and hearthstone all over this broad land, will yet swell the chorus of the Union when again touched, as surely they will be, by the better angels of our nature.

**Question 2**

Suggested time—40 minutes.

> **Directions:** Read the passage below carefully. It was written by Frances Kemble describing her trip as a young girl on the second railroad ever built. Write a well-organized essay in which you present a detailed rhetorical and stylistic analysis of the passage. Explain how the author uses language to achieve a certain effect on the reader. Be sure to consider rhetorical and stylistic devices such as imagery, tone, diction, mode of discourse, narrative structure, and selection of detail.

Line  My father knew several of the gentlemen most deeply interested in
the undertaking [the railway], and Stephenson having proposed a trial
trip as far as the fifteen mile viaduct, they, with infinite kindness
invited him and permitted me to accompany them, allowing me,
5  moreover, the place which I felt to be one of supreme honour, by
the side of Stephenson. . . . He was a rather stern-faced man, with
dark and deeply marked countenance. . . .

We were introduced to the little engine which was to drag us
along the rails. . . . This snorting little animal, which I felt rather
10  inclined to pat, was then harnessed to our carriage, and Mr. Stephenson having taken me on the bench of the engine with him, we
started at about ten miles an hour. The steam-horse being ill-adapted
to going up and down hill, the road was kept at a certain level, and
appeared sometimes to sink below the surface of the earth, and
15  sometimes to rise above it. Almost at starting it was cut through the
solid rock, which formed a wall on either side of it, about sixty feet
high. You can't imagine how strange it seemed to be journeying on
thus, without any visible cause of progress other than the magical
machine, with its flying white breath and rhythmical, unvaried pace.
20  . . . We were to go only fifteen miles, that distance being sufficient to
show the speed of the engine. . . . After proceeding through this
rocky defile, we presently found ourselves raised upon embankments
ten or twelve feet high; we then came to a moss, or swamp, of
considerable extent, on which no human foot could tread without
25  sinking, and yet it bore the road which bore us. . . .

We had now come fifteen miles, and stopped where the road
traversed a wide and deep valley. Stephenson made me alight and led
me down to the bottom of this ravine, over which, in order to keep
his road level, he has thrown a magnificent viaduct of nine arches,
30  the middle one of which is seventy feet high, through which we saw
the whole of this beautiful valley. . . . We then rejoined the rest of
the party, and the engine having received its supply of water, the

35

carriage was placed behind it, for it cannot turn, and was set off at its utmost speed, thirty-five miles an hour, swifter than a bird flies (or they tried the experiment with a snipe). You cannot conceive what that sensation of cutting the air was; the motion is as smooth as possible, too.

## Question 3
Suggested time—40 minutes

> **Directions:** To paraphrase Elie Weisel, "More dangerous than anger and hatred is indifference. Indifference is not a beginning, it is an end—and it is always the friend to the enemy."
>
> Do you believe that Weisel's views are valid? In an essay, support or oppose Weisel's position, using evidence drawn from your studies, reading, personal experiences, or observations.

 **END OF SECTION II**

# ANSWERS AND EXPLANATIONS

## Quick-Score Answers

| | | | | |
|---|---|---|---|---|
| 1. C | 12. B | 23. C | 33. D | 43. E |
| 2. C | 13. B | 24. E | 34. C | 44. A |
| 3. B | 14. E | 25. D | 35. B | 45. D |
| 4. E | 15. C | 26. D | 36. D | 46. A |
| 5. A | 16. B | 27. C | 37. C | 47. D |
| 6. E | 17. C | 28. D | 38. A | 48. C |
| 7. C | 18. C | 29. B | 39. E | 49. D |
| 8. B | 19. A | 30. E | 40. A | 50. E |
| 9. D | 20. D | 31. E | 41. D | 51. E |
| 10. E | 21. C | 32. B | 42. C | |
| 11. D | 22. C | | | |

## PRACTICE TEST 3

### Test-Taking Strategy

*For vocabulary questions, substitute each answer choice in the sentence. Look also at the sentences around the sentence in question for the context.*

### Review Strategy

*Review literary and rhetorical terms on pages 173–179.*

1. **The correct answer is (C).** This question is a bit tricky, in that all of the choices might reasonably fit. Given that, you have to determine the context to help you decide on the best answer. Paine finishes the sentence by relating an anecdote in which he uses the phrase "a more generous parent" to emphasize that the man in Amboy seems to care only for peace in *his* time rather than in his daughter's time. In the context, choice (C) is the best answer.

2. **The correct answer is (C).** Did you recognize the simile in this sentence? When you see a comparison and the words *as* or *like*, it is probably a simile. A ray of light is an image, choice (A), but because of the word *as*, it is too general an answer and incorrect. This is true also of choice (E), figurative language. A simile is a type of figurative language, and in this case, the specific answer is better than the general answer. An analogy, choice (B), is a comparison of two similar but different things; only one item is being compared in the sentence, so choice (B) can be eliminated. A metaphor, choice (D), refers to one thing as another; this is not true in this sentence, so choice (D) can be eliminated.

**3. The correct answer is (B).** To determine the mode of a passage, examine the purpose, the tone, and how the writer uses language to achieve his or her goals. In this case, choices (A), (C), and (E) can be easily ruled out, because the writer is not simply describing, telling a story, or explaining something. That leaves choices (B) and (D). What is the difference between argument and persuasion? Look at the structure of the essay. See clearly how the writer leads you from a premise through reasoned support to a conclusion. These are the characteristics of an argument, choice (B).

**4. The correct answer is (E).** This question is a bit difficult in that each of the answers is a little bit true. To identify tone, look at the writer's language and purpose. The writer may indeed by turns be reasonable, choice (A); angry, choice (B); moralistic, choice (C); and bitter, choice (D), but overall he is making a passionate argument for his beliefs, therefore, choice (E) is the best answer.

**5. The correct answer is (A).** Do you know your figures of speech? If you do, you can see that Paine salts the essay liberally with aphorisms, choice (A); short, witty statements of clever observation or general truths. If you're making an educated guess, you can rule out alliteration, choice (E), because there are no repeated initial consonant sounds in the selection. Likewise, there are no allegories present, choice (B); long, extended narrative stories. Next, you can cross off choice (C), because an analogy is a comparison of two similar but different things. Then, rule out choice (D), because an allusion is an indirect reference to something familiar to the reader. That leaves choice (A), aphorism (for example, "the harder the conflict, the more glorious the triumph").

**Test-Taking Strategy**

*Highlight key words in the question stem and then restate the question to yourself to be sure you understand what you are being asked to look for.*

**6. The correct answer is (E).** You are being asked to find the answer that does not fit—the statement that is not one of Paine's points. Choice (A) is developed in the first paragraph. Choices (B) and (C) are developed in the fourth paragraph, and choice (D) in the third paragraph. Only choice (E) is not discussed in the selection and, therefore, is the correct answer.

**7. The correct answer is (C).** Go back to the passage and scan it. Don't be tempted to pick an answer just because the word appears in a sentence in a selection. Choice (A), tyranny and hell, is tempting on a cursory reading, but the key word in the question is *compare*. The author does not compare Britain's actions to hell but says only that tyranny is like hell. Paine does compare "being bound in that manner" to slavery (lines 11–13) and reiterates the idea by saying "bind me in all cases whatso-ever" (line 71) after making an implied comparison that taxation is thievery. Choices (B), (D), and (E) are distractors. None of them relates to the selection. Did you also note that the answer choices have two parts? For an answer to be right, both parts must be correct.

8. **The correct answer is (B).** It's fairly easy to work your way through these choices to the correct one. Choices (D) and (E) do not make sense. Neither choices (A) nor (C), glow or interest, are strong enough, leaving choice (B), passion, which is what Paine feels toward those who have "nobly stood."

9. **The correct answer is (D).** Choice (A) is not a topic of the piece. Choice (B) is stated in the selection, but it is not a main point of Paine's writing here. The question asks how to best characterize Paine's opinions about war. Choice (C) is implied but still is not Paine's main thesis. Choice (E) is simply incorrect in the context of the passage—Paine states only that an "offen-sive" war is murder. Choice (D), the thought developed at the end of the final paragraph, is the best choice.

### Test-Taking Strategy

*In a tiered or multi-step question, first decide which point(s) answer the question. Then look for the answer choice that includes that point(s).*

10. **The correct answer is (E).** Point I is not in evidence in the passage, but both points II and III are. Only choice (E) contains both points.

11. **The correct answer is (D).** Paine's words could apply to choices (A), (B), (C), and (D). There is nothing in the context of these lines that implies that Paine is referring to those colonists who support Great Britain, so choice (E) is incorrect. Choice (A) can be eliminated because there is no mention at this point in the selection of either peace or war, only of differences in political philosophy. Cross off choice (B), again because there is no mention of war. Choice (C) is the broadest view of Paine's words and the meaning that has been given to these well-known phrases since Paine's time, but in the context of the passage itself, incorrect. Choice (D) relates directly to the topic of the piece.

### Review Strategy

*Remember that the word men's is a rhetorical conven-tion of Paine's time and refers to men and women.*

12. **The correct answer is (B).** Eliminate choice (A) immediately—the tone of the sentence is not demanding. Choice (C) relates only to the author, whereas the sentence refers to many people. While the opening sentence begins to establish the topic of the piece, it does not present the subject of the essay, thus eliminat-ing choice (D). Choice (E) is a distracter. Choice (B) is the best answer. Paine uses the sentence to draw in his audience by letting them know that he shares their feelings.

**Test-Taking Strategy**

*In vocabulary questions, always substitute each answer choice in the sentence.*

13. **The correct answer is (B).** In this sentence, all of the choices fit. If you don't know the actual definition of the word, then you must infer the meaning of the word from the context. Men would probably not be making entreaties, so cross off choice (E). Choices (A) and (D) are very similar in meaning, so that might be a clue that neither is correct. Consider the balance between what the women are doing—praying—and what the men might be doing. That would eliminate (C), prayers, and leave curses; so choice (B) is a good bet, and the correct answer.

14. **The correct answer is (E).** Choices (A) and (B) can be eliminated immediately. The piece was written in the heat of excitement and activity, which tends to obscure objectivity, choice (A). The word choice of the writer and the use of sentence fragments and nonstandard punctuation makes the tone anything but solemn, choice (B). While the events related may be factual, that is not the most accurate description, given that choice (E) is informal. That is the better choice to describe this journal entry. Choice (D) is the opposite of the piece and therefore, incorrect.

**Test-Taking Strategy**

*When you are asked to look for the purpose or the main idea of a piece, always look for the broadest, most inclusive answer.*

15. **The correct answer is (C).** The journal may include choices (A), (B), (D), and (E), but the *purpose* of the journal, which can be inferred from the nature of the entries, is to record the events of the day.

16. **The correct answer is (B).** While the writer describes certain scenes and much activity, the mode is not description, choice (A). Mary Chesnut is explaining events, but as a story unfolding, so this is not choice (C), exposition. There is nothing persuasive or argumentative about the piece, ruling out choices (D) and (E). The writer is simply relating events and personal experiences, choice (B).

17. **The correct answer is (C).** This is a recall question, meaning that the answer is stated directly in the text. In the third paragraph, Mrs. Chesnut refers to her husband as "our peace negotiator—or envoy . . ."

18. **The correct answer is (C).** Choice (E) can be eliminated quickly because one would probably not feel kindly towards one's enemy. There is no evidence of a feeling of conciliation on Chesnut's part, eliminating choice (D). While one might infer that Chesnut felt respect, choice (A), and even admiration, choice (B), for the commander of Fort Sumter under such difficult circumstances, there is no evidence to support either. But when you go back to the selection, you will find the sentence "Felt for Anderson" (line 11). That makes choice (C), compassionate, the best answer.

19. **The correct answer is (A).** Choice (B), figurative language, contains figures of speech, such as metaphors and similes. The writer uses neither, thus eliminating choice (B) and choice (C), metaphor. There is no repetition of words or phrases or sounds, making choice (D) incorrect. The whole selection is a story, so choice (E), anecdote, is incorrect. Mrs. Chesnut uses images such as "heavy booming of a cannon," "shells . . . over-bursting," "regular roar of cannon," and "a shell would light up the scene" to paint a picture of the scene.

20. **The correct answer is (D).** Choices (A), (B), (C), and (D) may all be a little bit true, but what can be inferred from the context is that his mission was unsuccessful. Had he been successful in his efforts to negotiate peace, Mr. Chesnut would have come in shouting and celebrating. Choice (E) is a distracter. The passage says he wanted his dinner; it says nothing about his being tired and needing a rest.

21. **The correct answer is (C).** Evaluate the mood of each paragraph, and then eliminate the incorrect choices based on the mood of the first third of the piece. The first third does not reflect anger or detachment, so choices (A), (B), and (E) can be eliminated. The mood of the second third can be called wild or exciting, leaving choices (C) and (D) still under consideration. The mood of the final third is concerned, not resigned, to making choice (C) the correct one.

22. **The correct answer is (C).** Point I is not valid because, although daily events are communicated in these three paragraphs, the words communicate this, not the mood or change in mood. Point II is not correct because the focus is from war to home to war. Only point III accurately describes the effect of the shift in moods and only choice (C) contains point III alone.

**23. The correct answer is (C).** This passage is from a journal, written in an informal style, and is filled with sentence fragments. A newspaper article could contain choices (A), (B), (D), and (E), but would probably not contain sentence fragments, since articles are usually written in a more formal style.

**24. The correct answer is (E).** Choices (A), (B), (C), (D), and (E) are all true statements, but choice (E) is the best answer. We have no way of knowing from the context that Mrs. Chesnut is sure that the Civil War has begun, so choice (B) is not a good response in this context. The sentence "I begin to hope" that precedes the quoted statement lends credence to choice (E) as the best response—her hope has been dashed.

**25. The correct answer is (D).** From her choice of words, it is evident in the passage that Mrs. Chesnut respects her husband (I). From your own knowledge and from your reading, you should have recognized that this form of address was indeed a social custom in the nineteenth century (II). There is no evidence in the selection of emotional distance between husband and wife, thus eliminating point III as an option. Working through the answer choices, you can eliminate all but choice (D), which contains both points I and II.

**26. The correct answer is (D).** Chief Joseph may feel angry, choice (A); resigned choice (B); and bitter choice (C); but his choice of words and details conveys his utter hopelessness and that of all Native Americans, choice (D). While the occasion is solemn, choice (E), despair is a better description of Chief Joseph's words.

**27. The correct answer is (C).** Choices (A), (B), and (D) might be true in other selections, but in this selection, the speaker makes direct statements about his feelings, choice (C). Choice (E) is a distracter; there is no reference to Chief Joseph's expression.

**28. The correct answer is (D).** The plight of the Nez Perce is stated eloquently in Chief Joseph's speech, so point I may be his purpose. The speech is one of surrender, so point II seems valid as well. Point III is not stated or implied in the speech. Looking at points I and II again, consider that the obvious purpose is point II, to notify federal troops of his surrender, but, point I is the greater purpose. Choice (D) contains both points I and II.

**29. The correct answer is (B).** To find the answer, ask yourself: What is Chief Joseph doing? He is explaining the reasons for his surrender. He is neither simply telling a story, choice (A); nor is he arguing, choice (C); persuading, choice (D); or describing, choice (E). Choice (B), exposition, is the right answer.

30. **The correct answer is (E).** Be careful here. This passage does have a strong emotional appeal, but it is because of the *content* of the passage, not its *structure*, eliminating point II. Both points I and III are true about the speaker's use of short, simple sentences, making choice (E) the correct answer.

31. **The correct answer is (E).** This question is a bit tricky in that choices (B), (C), (D), and (E) are true statements, but you must select the answer that best describes Chief Joseph's relationship with his people, based on the passage as a whole. Pay attention to the details in the passage. Chief Joseph's concern with food, blankets, and shelter falls under the category of concern for his people's welfare, choice (E). Choice (B) is a detail that supports choice (E). Choice (A) is a distracter because we know how he feels about his people, but we don't know how they feel about him.

32. **The correct answer is (B).** This question tests your knowledge of English grammar. *Tired* is a predicate adjective after the linking verb *to be* and modifys the subject *I,* thus making choice (A) incorrect and choice (B) correct. Don't be fooled by the answer choices containing a gerund, choices (C) and (D). Choice (E) is illogical.

33. **The correct answer is (D).** This is a simple recall question. The key word here is *except.* The statements in choices (A), (B), (C), and (E) are all stated in the text. Choice (D) is not and, therefore, is the correct answer.

34. **The correct answer is (C).** As you saw in question 29, this is expository writing, which means that you can identify a pattern of organization. The key word in this question is *list,* which can also mean enumerate. You could use the process of elimination to help you make an educated guess. Chief Joseph isn't assigning people to categories, so choice (A), classification, can be eliminated. He is not using the sentences as examples of anything, so choice (B) can also be eliminated. Chief Joseph is stating facts without dissecting them, choice (D), or creating any new meaning from them, choice (E). That leaves enumeration, choice (C), as the pattern of organization.

35. **The correct answer is (B).** Point I is not true; Chief Joseph does not say his life is over, nor does he imply it. Point III is tempting, but it is not inclusive or broad enough, nor is it explicitly stated. The old men symbolize the nation's past, and

the children symbolize its future, making point II the best answer. Only choice (B) contains point II alone.

36. **The correct answer is (D).** Choice (E) is a distracter. Despair is what the speaker is feeling. You, the reader, may feel a bit of each of the choices (A), (B), (C), and (D), but you are asked to give the best description of the emotion that is evoked by the passage as a whole. Choice (A), pity, means feeling sorrow for someone else's suffering, so choices (A) and (B), sorrow, are similar in meaning and discount both choices. Choice (C) means the ability to feel another persons emotion's or feelings. Considering each word and its nuances, choice (D), feeling compassion for another's suffering, is the best answer.

**Test-Taking Strategy**

*Be wary of answer choices that have absolutes like all or always in them.*

37. **The correct answer is (C).** Choices (A), (B), and (D) do not correctly recognize the subject of Johnson's letter. Choice (E) has identified the correct tone of the writing, but a letter is for an audience of one, not all of England.

38. **The correct answer is (A).** Johnson's disapproval of Lord Chesterfield is clear in this passage; therefore, choices (B) and (D) are incorrect. Of the remaining possibilities, you need to identify the best response. Choice (A), subtle anger and resentment, is the best reflection of the tone of the letter. Johnson may be cool to the earl, but there are no vicious remarks in the letter, choice (E), nor is he condescending, choice (C).

**Review Strategy**

*See Chapter 4 for a quick review of literary and rhetorical terms.*

39. **The correct answer is (E).** An overstatement is an intentional exaggeration, choice (E). Allusion is an indirect reference to historical or fictional characters, places, or events that a writer assumes you will recognize, choice (A). An exemplum is a brief tale or anecdote used to illustrate a moral lesson, choice (B). Parallelism shows that words, phrases, or other structures are comparable in content and importance by placing them side by side and making them similar in form, choice (C). Figurative language is an expression intended to be interpreted imaginatively, choice (D).

**Test-Taking Strategy**

*When all the answer choices seem to be correct, see if one may be the main idea or theme and the others, supporting details.*

40. **The correct answer is (A).** This is a difficult question because all the answers are true to a certain degree. Because you are being asked to make an assumption based on the tone and content of the letter, the best approach is to choose the most general answer. Choice (A) is the most general and conveys what Johnson had hoped to receive from Chesterfield when he went to call on him. Since you cannot read what Chesterfield wrote, you cannot know if the details in choices (B) or (C) or the implications in choices (D) and (E) are correct.

**41. The correct answer is (D).** Allusion is an indirect reference to historical or fictional characters, places, or events that a writer assumes you will recognize. In choice (D), Virgil's shepherd is an allusion to a classical Roman work. None of the other quotations have such a reference.

**42. The correct answer is (C).** The best approach to answering this question is through the process of elimination. Johnson is neither a sycophant, or he would not have written the letter, choice (A), nor is he indebted to Lord Chesterfield, or he would have no reason to write this letter, choice (B). He did seek assistance from the earl, who refused to become Johnson's patron, so choice (D) is incorrect. Lord Chesterfield could not be called generous from Johnson's experience, choice (E). The remaining answer, that Johnson no longer needs the earl's help, is the correct response.

**43. The correct answer is (E).** Johnson does not find anything to be witty about in his experience with Lord Chesterfield, choice (A). Sarcastic, choice (E), is the better of the two terms to explain a courteous word with an underlying pejorative intent. A metaphor states that something is something else, and a symbol represents an idea or a concept, choices (C) and (D), neither of which apply, nor does argumentative, choice (B).

**44. The correct answer is (A).** In the last sentence of the second paragraph Johnson says, "I had done all that I could; and no man is well pleased to have his all neglected, be it ever so little." In other words, no one likes to have what he or she has done, no matter how small, ignored. Choice (B) may be true, but it is not the major argument of the letter, while choice (E) has nothing to do with the selection. You cannot know from the selection whether choice (D) is true or not. Johnson says that he has done all he was going to do, but this does not mean that there were other things he might have done. What about choice (C)? Johnson might agree with that too.

**45. The correct answer is (D).** Obsequious, choice (A), means fawning or an overly anxious willingness to serve. This contradicts the point of the letter. Facetious, choice (B), means joking, and there is nothing lighthearted about this letter. Punctilious, choice (C), means very careful about observing ceremony and tradition, and according to choice (E), the closing is obligatory, which would tend to cancel out choice (C). The question asks for the best interpretation, and while the wording of the closing may be obligatory and Johnson is punctilious in using it, he is using it as one last jab of irony, choice (D).

46. **The correct answer is (A).** Parallelism is a technique of showing that words, phrases, or other structures are comparable in content and importance by placing them side by side and making them similar in form. The many conjunctions and prepositions in this passage are a clue that the lines have parallel structure. Overstatement, choice (B), is an exaggeration but to a lesser degree than hyperbole. Allusion, choice (C), is a reference to a famous person or to another work. Imagery, choice (D), refers to figures of speech in general, and Johnson is saying what he said, not quoting it, choice (E).

47. **The correct answer is (D).** The process of elimination guides you to the correct answer for this question. Johnson's writing is clear, correct, and effective, and his diction is difficult for readers today; choices (A), (B), (C), and (E). However, you cannot call this letter simple.

48. **The correct answer is (C).** In the context of the last sentence of the fourth paragraph, Johnson is chastising Lord Chesterfield for making his comments about Johnson's work so late that they did not help Johnson. Therefore, the best response is choice (C). Choice (A) is too specific in that it refers to money when Johnson had been looking for support in addition to money. Choice (B) is too simplistic. Choices (D) and (E) do not reflect the context of the phrase.

49. **The correct answer is (D).** In the context of the letter, the only answer that can be correct is choice (D). Johnson is saying that he has worked all this time without any help. He has made no reference in the letter to students, choice (A); teachers, choice (B); or an audience, choice (C). Choice (E) is a distracter because a patron is an admirer of the person assisted, but an adulator is one who admires another to excess.

**Test-Taking Strategy**

*For* not/except *questions, ask yourself if the answer choice is true in the context of the question. If it is, cross it off and go on to the next answer.*

50. **The correct answer is (E).** Although you should not have chosen *punctilious*, choice (A) in question 46 as the best answer, it does characterize Johnson's letter, and, therefore, should not be chosen here either. The letter does observe the formalities of the period, choice (B), and in its use of irony, choice (C), it shows Johnson's indignation. However, because he uses irony, it is not completely forthright, choice (E).

51. **The correct answer is (E).** Johnson has not laid out an argument with a premise, support, and a conclusion, so choice (A) can be eliminated. Johnson is not trying to persuade the earl to become his patron; Johnson says it is too late for that, making choice (B) incorrect. Although Johnson tells about events and places them in order, he is not describing anything or telling a story choices (C) and (D). He is explaining why he does not want Lord Chesterfield's praise, choice (E), in an effort to shame him.

# SUGGESTIONS FOR ESSAY QUESTION 1

The following are points that you might have chosen to include in your essay on Lincoln's first Inaugural Address. Consider them as you complete your self-evaluation. Revise your essay using points from the list to strengthen it.

## Form or Mode
- Inaugural Address, March 4, 1861
- Persuasion

## Theme
- Whether there will be war is up to the South

## Point of view
- First person

## Audience
- "Dissatisfied fellow countrymen," that is, Southerners

## Tone
- Reasonable, conciliatory
- Almost pleading but also firm

## Diction/Syntax/Style
- Formal
- Comprehensible to the average American
- Metaphors
- Imagery
- Invoking of shared memories of the Revolutionary War
- Simple sentences

# SUGGESTIONS FOR ESSAY QUESTION 2

The following are points that you might have chosen to include in your essay analyzing Frances Kimble's account of her trip on one of the first railroads. Consider them as you complete your self-evaluation. Revise your essay using points from the list to strengthen it.

## Form or Mode
- Excerpt from an autobiography
- Description

## Subject
- A ride on the world's second railroad

## Setting
- England in 1830

## Point of view
- First person

## Tone
- Conversational

## Diction/Syntax/Style
- Educated vocabulary
- Good use of visual imagery, vivid word pictures
- Varied sentence structure
- Informal

# SUGGESTIONS FOR ESSAAY QUESTION 3

This question asks for a persuasive essay arguing in support or opposition of Weisel's position. Your essay response to this type of question will be evaluated less by what you say and more by how you say it. The following aspects of argumentation should be present in your essay. Consider them as you complete your self-evaluation. Revise your essay using points from this list to strengthen it.

I. Stated premise or thesis

- Definition of issue

- Details on the nature of the issue

- Statement of differences between your definition and that of the opposition, or statement of support if you agree

- Analysis of the arguments

- Definitions based on

  - Denotation

  - Connotation

  - Example

  - Cause and effect

II. Reasoning and evidence

- Explanation of logic upon which your conclusion is based

- Supporting evidence

  - Comparison

  - Analogy

  - Authority

  - Quotation

  - Statistics

  - Experience

  - Observation

- Elimination of fallacies in reasoning and evidence

- Refutation of opposition's objections to the position proposed

- Solution or alternative

- Confirmation of validity of proposed position

*Peterson's AP Success:*
*English Language & Composition*

# SELF-EVALUATION RUBRIC FOR THE ADVANCED PLACEMENT ESSAYS

| | 8–9 | 6–7 | 5 | 3–4 | 1–2 | 0 |
|---|---|---|---|---|---|---|
| **Overall Impression** | Demonstrates excellent control of the literature and outstanding writing competence; thorough and effective; incisive | Demonstrates good control of the literature and good writing competence; less thorough and incisive than the highest papers | Reveals simplistic thinking and/or immature writing; adequate skills | Incomplete thinking; fails to respond adequately to part or parts of the question; may paraphrase rather than analyze | Unacceptably brief; fails to respond to the question; little clarity | Lacking skill and competence |
| **Understanding of the Text** | Excellent understanding of the text; exhibits perception and clarity; original or unique approach; includes apt and specific references | Good understanding of the text; exhibits perception and clarity; includes specific references | Superficial understanding of the text; elements of literature vague, mechanical, overgeneralized | Misreadings and lack of persuasive evidence from the text; meager and unconvincing treatment of literary elements | Serious misreadings and little supporting evidence from the text; erroneous treatment of literary elements | A response with no more than a reference to the literature; blank response, or one completely off the topic |
| **Organization and Development** | Meticulously organized and thoroughly developed; coherent and unified | Well organized and developed; coherent and unified | Reasonably organized and developed; mostly coherent and unified | Somewhat organized and developed; some incoherence and lack of unity | Little or no organization and development; incoherent and void of unity | No apparent organization or development; incoherent |
| **Use of Sentences** | Effectively varied and engaging; virtually error free | Varied and interesting; a few errors | Adequately varied; some errors | Somewhat varied and marginally interesting; one or more major errors | Little or no variation; dull and uninteresting; some major errors | Numerous major errors |
| **Word Choice** | Interesting and effective; virtually error free | Generally interesting and effective; a few errors | Occasionally interesting and effective; several errors | Somewhat dull and ordinary; some errors in diction | Mostly dull and conventional; numerous errors | Numerous major errors; extremely immature |
| **Grammar and Usage** | Virtually error free | Occasional minor errors | Several minor errors | Some major errors | Severely flawed; frequent major errors | Extremely flawed |

Using the rubric on the previous page, rate yourself in each of the categories below for each essay on the test. Enter on the lines below the number from the rubric that most accurately reflects your performance in each category. Then calculate the average of the six numbers to determine your final score. It is difficult to score yourself objectively, so you may wish to ask a respected friend or teacher to assess your writing for a more accurate reflection of its strengths and weaknesses. On the AP test itself, a reader will rate your essay on a scale of 1 to 9, with 9 being the highest.

Rate each category from 9 (high) to 0 (low).

## QUESTION 1

**SELF-EVALUATION**

Overall Impression _____
Understanding of the Text _____
Organization and Development _____
Use of Sentences _____
Word Choice (Diction) _____
Grammar and Usage _____

TOTAL _____
Divide by 6 for final score _____

**OBJECTIVE EVALUATION**

Overall Impression _____
Understanding of the Text _____
Organization and Development _____
Use of Sentences _____
Word Choice (Diction) _____
Grammar and Usage _____

TOTAL _____
Divide by 6 for final score _____

## QUESTION 2

**SELF-EVALUATION**

Overall Impression _____
Understanding of the Text _____
Organization and Development _____
Use of Sentences _____
Word Choice (Diction) _____
Grammar and Usage _____

TOTAL _____
Divide by 6 for final score _____

**OBJECTIVE EVALUATION**

Overall Impression _____
Understanding of the Text _____
Organization and Development _____
Use of Sentences _____
Word Choice (Diction) _____
Grammar and Usage _____

TOTAL _____
Divide by 6 for final score _____

## QUESTION 3

**SELF-EVALUATION**

Overall Impression _____
Understanding of the Text _____
Organization and Development _____
Use of Sentences _____
Word Choice (Diction) _____
Grammar and Usage _____

TOTAL _____
Divide by 6 for final score _____

**OBJECTIVE EVALUATION**

Overall Impression _____
Understanding of the Text _____
Organization and Development _____
Use of Sentences _____
Word Choice (Diction) _____
Grammar and Usage _____

TOTAL _____
Divide by 6 for final score _____

*Peterson's AP Success:*
*English Language & Composition*

# SAMPLE ANSWER SHEETS

**DIAGNOSTIC TEST**

| 1 | Ⓐ Ⓑ Ⓒ Ⓓ Ⓔ | 16 | Ⓐ Ⓑ Ⓒ Ⓓ Ⓔ | 31 | Ⓐ Ⓑ Ⓒ Ⓓ Ⓔ | 46 | Ⓐ Ⓑ Ⓒ Ⓓ Ⓔ |
|---|---|---|---|---|---|---|---|
| 2 | Ⓐ Ⓑ Ⓒ Ⓓ Ⓔ | 17 | Ⓐ Ⓑ Ⓒ Ⓓ Ⓔ | 32 | Ⓐ Ⓑ Ⓒ Ⓓ Ⓔ | 47 | Ⓐ Ⓑ Ⓒ Ⓓ Ⓔ |
| 3 | Ⓐ Ⓑ Ⓒ Ⓓ Ⓔ | 18 | Ⓐ Ⓑ Ⓒ Ⓓ Ⓔ | 33 | Ⓐ Ⓑ Ⓒ Ⓓ Ⓔ | 48 | Ⓐ Ⓑ Ⓒ Ⓓ Ⓔ |
| 4 | Ⓐ Ⓑ Ⓒ Ⓓ Ⓔ | 19 | Ⓐ Ⓑ Ⓒ Ⓓ Ⓔ | 34 | Ⓐ Ⓑ Ⓒ Ⓓ Ⓔ | 49 | Ⓐ Ⓑ Ⓒ Ⓓ Ⓔ |
| 5 | Ⓐ Ⓑ Ⓒ Ⓓ Ⓔ | 20 | Ⓐ Ⓑ Ⓒ Ⓓ Ⓔ | 35 | Ⓐ Ⓑ Ⓒ Ⓓ Ⓔ | 50 | Ⓐ Ⓑ Ⓒ Ⓓ Ⓔ |
| 6 | Ⓐ Ⓑ Ⓒ Ⓓ Ⓔ | 21 | Ⓐ Ⓑ Ⓒ Ⓓ Ⓔ | 36 | Ⓐ Ⓑ Ⓒ Ⓓ Ⓔ | 51 | Ⓐ Ⓑ Ⓒ Ⓓ Ⓔ |
| 7 | Ⓐ Ⓑ Ⓒ Ⓓ Ⓔ | 22 | Ⓐ Ⓑ Ⓒ Ⓓ Ⓔ | 37 | Ⓐ Ⓑ Ⓒ Ⓓ Ⓔ | 52 | Ⓐ Ⓑ Ⓒ Ⓓ Ⓔ |
| 8 | Ⓐ Ⓑ Ⓒ Ⓓ Ⓔ | 23 | Ⓐ Ⓑ Ⓒ Ⓓ Ⓔ | 38 | Ⓐ Ⓑ Ⓒ Ⓓ Ⓔ | 53 | Ⓐ Ⓑ Ⓒ Ⓓ Ⓔ |
| 9 | Ⓐ Ⓑ Ⓒ Ⓓ Ⓔ | 24 | Ⓐ Ⓑ Ⓒ Ⓓ Ⓔ | 39 | Ⓐ Ⓑ Ⓒ Ⓓ Ⓔ | 54 | Ⓐ Ⓑ Ⓒ Ⓓ Ⓔ |
| 10 | Ⓐ Ⓑ Ⓒ Ⓓ Ⓔ | 25 | Ⓐ Ⓑ Ⓒ Ⓓ Ⓔ | 40 | Ⓐ Ⓑ Ⓒ Ⓓ Ⓔ | 55 | Ⓐ Ⓑ Ⓒ Ⓓ Ⓔ |
| 11 | Ⓐ Ⓑ Ⓒ Ⓓ Ⓔ | 26 | Ⓐ Ⓑ Ⓒ Ⓓ Ⓔ | 41 | Ⓐ Ⓑ Ⓒ Ⓓ Ⓔ | 56 | Ⓐ Ⓑ Ⓒ Ⓓ Ⓔ |
| 12 | Ⓐ Ⓑ Ⓒ Ⓓ Ⓔ | 27 | Ⓐ Ⓑ Ⓒ Ⓓ Ⓔ | 42 | Ⓐ Ⓑ Ⓒ Ⓓ Ⓔ | 57 | Ⓐ Ⓑ Ⓒ Ⓓ Ⓔ |
| 13 | Ⓐ Ⓑ Ⓒ Ⓓ Ⓔ | 28 | Ⓐ Ⓑ Ⓒ Ⓓ Ⓔ | 43 | Ⓐ Ⓑ Ⓒ Ⓓ Ⓔ | 58 | Ⓐ Ⓑ Ⓒ Ⓓ Ⓔ |
| 14 | Ⓐ Ⓑ Ⓒ Ⓓ Ⓔ | 29 | Ⓐ Ⓑ Ⓒ Ⓓ Ⓔ | 44 | Ⓐ Ⓑ Ⓒ Ⓓ Ⓔ | 59 | Ⓐ Ⓑ Ⓒ Ⓓ Ⓔ |
| 15 | Ⓐ Ⓑ Ⓒ Ⓓ Ⓔ | 30 | Ⓐ Ⓑ Ⓒ Ⓓ Ⓔ | 45 | Ⓐ Ⓑ Ⓒ Ⓓ Ⓔ | 60 | Ⓐ Ⓑ Ⓒ Ⓓ Ⓔ |

**PRACTICE TEST 1**

| 1 | Ⓐ Ⓑ Ⓒ Ⓓ Ⓔ | 16 | Ⓐ Ⓑ Ⓒ Ⓓ Ⓔ | 31 | Ⓐ Ⓑ Ⓒ Ⓓ Ⓔ | 46 | Ⓐ Ⓑ Ⓒ Ⓓ Ⓔ |
|---|---|---|---|---|---|---|---|
| 2 | Ⓐ Ⓑ Ⓒ Ⓓ Ⓔ | 17 | Ⓐ Ⓑ Ⓒ Ⓓ Ⓔ | 32 | Ⓐ Ⓑ Ⓒ Ⓓ Ⓔ | 47 | Ⓐ Ⓑ Ⓒ Ⓓ Ⓔ |
| 3 | Ⓐ Ⓑ Ⓒ Ⓓ Ⓔ | 18 | Ⓐ Ⓑ Ⓒ Ⓓ Ⓔ | 33 | Ⓐ Ⓑ Ⓒ Ⓓ Ⓔ | 48 | Ⓐ Ⓑ Ⓒ Ⓓ Ⓔ |
| 4 | Ⓐ Ⓑ Ⓒ Ⓓ Ⓔ | 19 | Ⓐ Ⓑ Ⓒ Ⓓ Ⓔ | 34 | Ⓐ Ⓑ Ⓒ Ⓓ Ⓔ | 49 | Ⓐ Ⓑ Ⓒ Ⓓ Ⓔ |
| 5 | Ⓐ Ⓑ Ⓒ Ⓓ Ⓔ | 20 | Ⓐ Ⓑ Ⓒ Ⓓ Ⓔ | 35 | Ⓐ Ⓑ Ⓒ Ⓓ Ⓔ | 50 | Ⓐ Ⓑ Ⓒ Ⓓ Ⓔ |
| 6 | Ⓐ Ⓑ Ⓒ Ⓓ Ⓔ | 21 | Ⓐ Ⓑ Ⓒ Ⓓ Ⓔ | 36 | Ⓐ Ⓑ Ⓒ Ⓓ Ⓔ | 51 | Ⓐ Ⓑ Ⓒ Ⓓ Ⓔ |
| 7 | Ⓐ Ⓑ Ⓒ Ⓓ Ⓔ | 22 | Ⓐ Ⓑ Ⓒ Ⓓ Ⓔ | 37 | Ⓐ Ⓑ Ⓒ Ⓓ Ⓔ | 52 | Ⓐ Ⓑ Ⓒ Ⓓ Ⓔ |
| 8 | Ⓐ Ⓑ Ⓒ Ⓓ Ⓔ | 23 | Ⓐ Ⓑ Ⓒ Ⓓ Ⓔ | 38 | Ⓐ Ⓑ Ⓒ Ⓓ Ⓔ | 53 | Ⓐ Ⓑ Ⓒ Ⓓ Ⓔ |
| 9 | Ⓐ Ⓑ Ⓒ Ⓓ Ⓔ | 24 | Ⓐ Ⓑ Ⓒ Ⓓ Ⓔ | 39 | Ⓐ Ⓑ Ⓒ Ⓓ Ⓔ | 54 | Ⓐ Ⓑ Ⓒ Ⓓ Ⓔ |
| 10 | Ⓐ Ⓑ Ⓒ Ⓓ Ⓔ | 25 | Ⓐ Ⓑ Ⓒ Ⓓ Ⓔ | 40 | Ⓐ Ⓑ Ⓒ Ⓓ Ⓔ | 55 | Ⓐ Ⓑ Ⓒ Ⓓ Ⓔ |
| 11 | Ⓐ Ⓑ Ⓒ Ⓓ Ⓔ | 26 | Ⓐ Ⓑ Ⓒ Ⓓ Ⓔ | 41 | Ⓐ Ⓑ Ⓒ Ⓓ Ⓔ | 56 | Ⓐ Ⓑ Ⓒ Ⓓ Ⓔ |
| 12 | Ⓐ Ⓑ Ⓒ Ⓓ Ⓔ | 27 | Ⓐ Ⓑ Ⓒ Ⓓ Ⓔ | 42 | Ⓐ Ⓑ Ⓒ Ⓓ Ⓔ | 57 | Ⓐ Ⓑ Ⓒ Ⓓ Ⓔ |
| 13 | Ⓐ Ⓑ Ⓒ Ⓓ Ⓔ | 28 | Ⓐ Ⓑ Ⓒ Ⓓ Ⓔ | 43 | Ⓐ Ⓑ Ⓒ Ⓓ Ⓔ | 58 | Ⓐ Ⓑ Ⓒ Ⓓ Ⓔ |
| 14 | Ⓐ Ⓑ Ⓒ Ⓓ Ⓔ | 29 | Ⓐ Ⓑ Ⓒ Ⓓ Ⓔ | 44 | Ⓐ Ⓑ Ⓒ Ⓓ Ⓔ | 59 | Ⓐ Ⓑ Ⓒ Ⓓ Ⓔ |
| 15 | Ⓐ Ⓑ Ⓒ Ⓓ Ⓔ | 30 | Ⓐ Ⓑ Ⓒ Ⓓ Ⓔ | 45 | Ⓐ Ⓑ Ⓒ Ⓓ Ⓔ | 60 | Ⓐ Ⓑ Ⓒ Ⓓ Ⓔ |

**PRACTICE TEST 2**

| 1 Ⓐ Ⓑ Ⓒ Ⓓ Ⓔ | 16 Ⓐ Ⓑ Ⓒ Ⓓ Ⓔ | 31 Ⓐ Ⓑ Ⓒ Ⓓ Ⓔ | 46 Ⓐ Ⓑ Ⓒ Ⓓ Ⓔ |
|---|---|---|---|
| 2 Ⓐ Ⓑ Ⓒ Ⓓ Ⓔ | 17 Ⓐ Ⓑ Ⓒ Ⓓ Ⓔ | 32 Ⓐ Ⓑ Ⓒ Ⓓ Ⓔ | 47 Ⓐ Ⓑ Ⓒ Ⓓ Ⓔ |
| 3 Ⓐ Ⓑ Ⓒ Ⓓ Ⓔ | 18 Ⓐ Ⓑ Ⓒ Ⓓ Ⓔ | 33 Ⓐ Ⓑ Ⓒ Ⓓ Ⓔ | 48 Ⓐ Ⓑ Ⓒ Ⓓ Ⓔ |
| 4 Ⓐ Ⓑ Ⓒ Ⓓ Ⓔ | 19 Ⓐ Ⓑ Ⓒ Ⓓ Ⓔ | 34 Ⓐ Ⓑ Ⓒ Ⓓ Ⓔ | 49 Ⓐ Ⓑ Ⓒ Ⓓ Ⓔ |
| 5 Ⓐ Ⓑ Ⓒ Ⓓ Ⓔ | 20 Ⓐ Ⓑ Ⓒ Ⓓ Ⓔ | 35 Ⓐ Ⓑ Ⓒ Ⓓ Ⓔ | 50 Ⓐ Ⓑ Ⓒ Ⓓ Ⓔ |
| 6 Ⓐ Ⓑ Ⓒ Ⓓ Ⓔ | 21 Ⓐ Ⓑ Ⓒ Ⓓ Ⓔ | 36 Ⓐ Ⓑ Ⓒ Ⓓ Ⓔ | 51 Ⓐ Ⓑ Ⓒ Ⓓ Ⓔ |
| 7 Ⓐ Ⓑ Ⓒ Ⓓ Ⓔ | 22 Ⓐ Ⓑ Ⓒ Ⓓ Ⓔ | 37 Ⓐ Ⓑ Ⓒ Ⓓ Ⓔ | 52 Ⓐ Ⓑ Ⓒ Ⓓ Ⓔ |
| 8 Ⓐ Ⓑ Ⓒ Ⓓ Ⓔ | 23 Ⓐ Ⓑ Ⓒ Ⓓ Ⓔ | 38 Ⓐ Ⓑ Ⓒ Ⓓ Ⓔ | 53 Ⓐ Ⓑ Ⓒ Ⓓ Ⓔ |
| 9 Ⓐ Ⓑ Ⓒ Ⓓ Ⓔ | 24 Ⓐ Ⓑ Ⓒ Ⓓ Ⓔ | 39 Ⓐ Ⓑ Ⓒ Ⓓ Ⓔ | 54 Ⓐ Ⓑ Ⓒ Ⓓ Ⓔ |
| 10 Ⓐ Ⓑ Ⓒ Ⓓ Ⓔ | 25 Ⓐ Ⓑ Ⓒ Ⓓ Ⓔ | 40 Ⓐ Ⓑ Ⓒ Ⓓ Ⓔ | 55 Ⓐ Ⓑ Ⓒ Ⓓ Ⓔ |
| 11 Ⓐ Ⓑ Ⓒ Ⓓ Ⓔ | 26 Ⓐ Ⓑ Ⓒ Ⓓ Ⓔ | 41 Ⓐ Ⓑ Ⓒ Ⓓ Ⓔ | 56 Ⓐ Ⓑ Ⓒ Ⓓ Ⓔ |
| 12 Ⓐ Ⓑ Ⓒ Ⓓ Ⓔ | 27 Ⓐ Ⓑ Ⓒ Ⓓ Ⓔ | 42 Ⓐ Ⓑ Ⓒ Ⓓ Ⓔ | 57 Ⓐ Ⓑ Ⓒ Ⓓ Ⓔ |
| 13 Ⓐ Ⓑ Ⓒ Ⓓ Ⓔ | 28 Ⓐ Ⓑ Ⓒ Ⓓ Ⓔ | 43 Ⓐ Ⓑ Ⓒ Ⓓ Ⓔ | 58 Ⓐ Ⓑ Ⓒ Ⓓ Ⓔ |
| 14 Ⓐ Ⓑ Ⓒ Ⓓ Ⓔ | 29 Ⓐ Ⓑ Ⓒ Ⓓ Ⓔ | 44 Ⓐ Ⓑ Ⓒ Ⓓ Ⓔ | 59 Ⓐ Ⓑ Ⓒ Ⓓ Ⓔ |
| 15 Ⓐ Ⓑ Ⓒ Ⓓ Ⓔ | 30 Ⓐ Ⓑ Ⓒ Ⓓ Ⓔ | 45 Ⓐ Ⓑ Ⓒ Ⓓ Ⓔ | 60 Ⓐ Ⓑ Ⓒ Ⓓ Ⓔ |

**PRACTICE TEST 3**

| 1 Ⓐ Ⓑ Ⓒ Ⓓ Ⓔ | 16 Ⓐ Ⓑ Ⓒ Ⓓ Ⓔ | 31 Ⓐ Ⓑ Ⓒ Ⓓ Ⓔ | 46 Ⓐ Ⓑ Ⓒ Ⓓ Ⓔ |
|---|---|---|---|
| 2 Ⓐ Ⓑ Ⓒ Ⓓ Ⓔ | 17 Ⓐ Ⓑ Ⓒ Ⓓ Ⓔ | 32 Ⓐ Ⓑ Ⓒ Ⓓ Ⓔ | 47 Ⓐ Ⓑ Ⓒ Ⓓ Ⓔ |
| 3 Ⓐ Ⓑ Ⓒ Ⓓ Ⓔ | 18 Ⓐ Ⓑ Ⓒ Ⓓ Ⓔ | 33 Ⓐ Ⓑ Ⓒ Ⓓ Ⓔ | 48 Ⓐ Ⓑ Ⓒ Ⓓ Ⓔ |
| 4 Ⓐ Ⓑ Ⓒ Ⓓ Ⓔ | 19 Ⓐ Ⓑ Ⓒ Ⓓ Ⓔ | 34 Ⓐ Ⓑ Ⓒ Ⓓ Ⓔ | 49 Ⓐ Ⓑ Ⓒ Ⓓ Ⓔ |
| 5 Ⓐ Ⓑ Ⓒ Ⓓ Ⓔ | 20 Ⓐ Ⓑ Ⓒ Ⓓ Ⓔ | 35 Ⓐ Ⓑ Ⓒ Ⓓ Ⓔ | 50 Ⓐ Ⓑ Ⓒ Ⓓ Ⓔ |
| 6 Ⓐ Ⓑ Ⓒ Ⓓ Ⓔ | 21 Ⓐ Ⓑ Ⓒ Ⓓ Ⓔ | 36 Ⓐ Ⓑ Ⓒ Ⓓ Ⓔ | 51 Ⓐ Ⓑ Ⓒ Ⓓ Ⓔ |
| 7 Ⓐ Ⓑ Ⓒ Ⓓ Ⓔ | 22 Ⓐ Ⓑ Ⓒ Ⓓ Ⓔ | 37 Ⓐ Ⓑ Ⓒ Ⓓ Ⓔ | 52 Ⓐ Ⓑ Ⓒ Ⓓ Ⓔ |
| 8 Ⓐ Ⓑ Ⓒ Ⓓ Ⓔ | 23 Ⓐ Ⓑ Ⓒ Ⓓ Ⓔ | 38 Ⓐ Ⓑ Ⓒ Ⓓ Ⓔ | 53 Ⓐ Ⓑ Ⓒ Ⓓ Ⓔ |
| 9 Ⓐ Ⓑ Ⓒ Ⓓ Ⓔ | 24 Ⓐ Ⓑ Ⓒ Ⓓ Ⓔ | 39 Ⓐ Ⓑ Ⓒ Ⓓ Ⓔ | 54 Ⓐ Ⓑ Ⓒ Ⓓ Ⓔ |
| 10 Ⓐ Ⓑ Ⓒ Ⓓ Ⓔ | 25 Ⓐ Ⓑ Ⓒ Ⓓ Ⓔ | 40 Ⓐ Ⓑ Ⓒ Ⓓ Ⓔ | 55 Ⓐ Ⓑ Ⓒ Ⓓ Ⓔ |
| 11 Ⓐ Ⓑ Ⓒ Ⓓ Ⓔ | 26 Ⓐ Ⓑ Ⓒ Ⓓ Ⓔ | 41 Ⓐ Ⓑ Ⓒ Ⓓ Ⓔ | 56 Ⓐ Ⓑ Ⓒ Ⓓ Ⓔ |
| 12 Ⓐ Ⓑ Ⓒ Ⓓ Ⓔ | 27 Ⓐ Ⓑ Ⓒ Ⓓ Ⓔ | 42 Ⓐ Ⓑ Ⓒ Ⓓ Ⓔ | 57 Ⓐ Ⓑ Ⓒ Ⓓ Ⓔ |
| 13 Ⓐ Ⓑ Ⓒ Ⓓ Ⓔ | 28 Ⓐ Ⓑ Ⓒ Ⓓ Ⓔ | 43 Ⓐ Ⓑ Ⓒ Ⓓ Ⓔ | 58 Ⓐ Ⓑ Ⓒ Ⓓ Ⓔ |
| 14 Ⓐ Ⓑ Ⓒ Ⓓ Ⓔ | 29 Ⓐ Ⓑ Ⓒ Ⓓ Ⓔ | 44 Ⓐ Ⓑ Ⓒ Ⓓ Ⓔ | 59 Ⓐ Ⓑ Ⓒ Ⓓ Ⓔ |
| 15 Ⓐ Ⓑ Ⓒ Ⓓ Ⓔ | 30 Ⓐ Ⓑ Ⓒ Ⓓ Ⓔ | 45 Ⓐ Ⓑ Ⓒ Ⓓ Ⓔ | 60 Ⓐ Ⓑ Ⓒ Ⓓ Ⓔ |

*Peterson's AP Success:*
*English Language & Composition*